POLICING THE BIG APPLE

POLICING THE BIG APPLE

THE STORY OF THE NYPD

JULES STEWART

REAKTION BOOKS

For Rita Jakubowski

Published by Reaktion Books Ltd
Unit 32, Waterside
44–48 Wharf Road
London N1 7UX, UK
www.reaktionbooks.co.uk

First published 2021

Printed and bound in Great Britain by TJ Books Ltd, Padstow, Cornwall

A catalogue record for this book is available from the British Library

ISBN 978 1 78914 482 6

CONTENTS

Foreword
by Charles Campisi

This is the story of the NYPD: The very good, the very bad and the very ugly. Today's NYPD is perhaps the global epitome of law enforcement – an agency that is far greater than the sum of its parts. The NYPD always seems to be in the midst of controversy, but that's because it is always out in front and center. *Policing the Big Apple* tells the whole story, thoroughly researched, from the onset of the New World to the twenty-first century.

The history of policing in New York City begins before there even was a New York City. At its first Dutch settlement, the City of New Amsterdam was a small hamlet at the southern tip of today's Manhattan Island. With an ever-growing population, the area experienced the problems found all over the world when large groups of people live together, sometimes in harmony, but often in conflict. To promote safety, the early settlers appointed a Schout Fiscal, or sheriff, and as time went on policing, with all its issues and problems, grew. When the English took over the burgeoning metropolis that was to become New York City, policing as we know it today was up and running.

In 1845 the first formal police department in the New World was formed. Mired in controversy from its inception, the New York City Police Department was a politically infused system of patronage, corruption, and favoritism. The original eight hundred members were politically appointed and had to buy their way on to the force. Rank and good assignments, of course, were extra. Notwithstanding the early growing pains, the NYPD has led an extraordinary life in its 175-year history.

The annals of the NYPD are full of accounts of heroism and bravery unrivalled in the world of policing. The NYPD has taken on enormous challenges: from the defense of defenseless children at the "Colored Orphanage" fire in the mid-nineteenth century, to the arrest of innumerable felons, to the counter-espionage measures during the First and Second World Wars, to crime-fighting techniques that make New York City the safest big city in America and to the unprecedented U.S. search and rescue efforts undertaken after the terrorist attack on the World Trade Center, the NYPD has risen to every occasion. The NYPD can hold their collective heads up high and wave their banner proudly. But alongside all the accolades showered over the NYPD over the decades, we have to acknowledge the episodes of corruption, misconduct, and brutality.

In fact, corruption scandals have plagued the NYPD throughout its history. Their recurring nature often gives rise to the notion that corruption is an endemic and durable feature of police work. The literature and the experience of individual agencies often evince a cyclical pattern of corruption followed by reform and a period of apathy with the ultimate reemergence of scandal at a later time. This recurring nature of police corruption scandals often makes people, including Police Executives, believe that corruption is a natural part of police work and will never go away.

IF YOU WERE to plot the periods of scandal within law enforcement in New York City on a timeline, the casual observer would conclude that corruption in the NYPD is cyclical: appearing every twenty years or so, followed by a commission, recommendations, and temporary reform only to change characteristics and mutate into other forms. New York City, however, is not alone. There are similar corruption scandals throughout the United States and around the world, in National, State, and local agencies, in both large and small departments. The bad actions of a single police officer can, and many times do, eclipse the millions of positive, noteworthy daily public interactions of the overwhelming majority of dedicated, hard-working men and women in blue. The newspaper headlines are stolen by the bad cops, and the good cops are relegated to the back pages. But nobody said being a cop was going to be fair.

In 2020 "De-fund the Police" became a nationwide battle cry for the anti-police groups. The motto seemed to catch on and, especially in New York, was chanted at every demonstration. While police officers stood in defense of the protestors and kept the counter-demonstrators away, the chanters continued to berate their defenders. One protestor even remarked ironically that the police were the only reason why the protestors could assemble safely. Yet their slogan grew in crescendo as they marched. Furthermore, the mayor supported legislation to curtail the police from doing their job and vowed to cut $1 billion from the police budget. This action was echoed in major cities across the country resulting in rising crime and homicide rates. Unfortunately, the people who will suffer the most are the people who need the police the most, and the negative effect on the police officers themselves will be long lasting. Similar to the fiscal crisis of the mid-1970s, the public will suffer along with the police.

In 1975, due mainly to financial mismanagement, New York City went broke. In order to highlight the need for State and Federal bailout, then mayor Abraham Beame, who was the city's fiscal manager prior to becoming mayor, laid off thousands of essential workers, including more than 5,000 cops. Crime soared to all-time highs. The demoralized police were severely handicapped in providing basic services. Slowly the city rehired the laid-off cops, fire fighters, and other essential service workers, but the damage was done. It took almost a decade for the trauma to fade from memory, and only with the expanded hiring of thousands of new men and women unscathed by the layoffs did the city start to recover.

UNFORTUNATELY, the writing is already on the wall. Demoralized cops are condemned for doing their jobs and are withdrawing from engaging in tried-and-true police work. They are reverting to being report-takers, and not the protectors of the people. It will take a lot to turn this back around, but the future of New York and other cities may rest with the elected officials striking a balance between maintaining law and order and not playing politics with the lives of the people they claim to serve.

As you read *Policing the Big Apple*, you will encounter the very "finest" New York has to offer, and some of the worst, greediest politicians, elected officials, and cops you can imagine. The police may be the most visible, and are certainly responsible for their own actions, but the most sinister are not necessarily on patrol. They hide behind the walls of their offices, put in place by a system that governors, mayors, judges, and other elected officials didn't want to change, because they all profited. No one from the top-down had the incentive to change. As you read through the pages of this book you will see that the NYPD has put in place, and maintained, a robust system to combat and vigorously investigate corruption and misconduct. If you forget your history, you are doomed to repeat your mistakes over again. This book should serve as a reminder to remain vigilant.

Introduction

A glorious New York autumn morning sparkled before me as I gazed out the picture window of my room at The Wagner Hotel in Battery Park. I stood enthralled by the view of the Statue of Liberty and marvelled at the ceaseless toing and froing of water traffic in the broad spread of the harbour. Tugs with barges in tow, sailing yachts, low-riding cargo vessels, passenger liners and ferries, all manner of ships plying their way cross-harbour from the row of terminal rail and marine docks on the New Jersey Shore.

New York City's oldest settled neighbourhood has always been the gateway to the sea, as well as the point of entry for the people and goods that made Battery Park the city's hub of commercial activity and served to inspire 'mortal men fixed in ocean reveries'. As Herman Melville remarked on observing the blue expanse leading to where lurked the great white whale:

> There now is your insular city of the Manhattoes, belted round by wharves, as Indian isles by coral reefs – commerce surrounds it with her surf. Right and left, the streets take you waterward. Its extreme downtown is the battery, where that noble mole is washed by waves, and cooled by breezes, which a few hours previous were out of sight of land. Look at the crowds of water-gazers there.[1]

It was the morning of 11 September, the ominous 9/11 that marks the anniversary of the 2001 terrorist attacks that obliterated the Twin Towers and took the lives of more than 2,600 people. The commemorations being observed that day were encircled by a massive security cordon – after all, the 104-storey tower that in 2014 replaced the World Trade Center was only a twenty-minute Uptown stroll from my hotel and could not be discounted as a tempting jihadist target. The sky was buzzing with blue-and-white NYPD helicopters that wheeled over the southern tip of Manhattan, as if competing for airspace with the seagulls. Speeding police boats churned up the waters of the bay where the East and Hudson rivers meet. Patrol cars were parked along West Street, facing the harbour, while officers kept a lookout on the ferry slips, where tourists queued for the outing to the Statue of Liberty and Ellis Island.

Surveying this land, air and sea deployment of New York's Finest, it came to mind that here was not only a city in a state of perpetual reincarnation, but a four-hundred-year-old metropolis that has been underpinned by a number of enduring institutions. Pushcarts have vanished from the Lower East Side, replaced by what seems to be a limitless array of hipster coffee shops and designer boutiques. The crime haven of the Five Points in Lower Manhattan has been transformed into a neighbourhood of quiet tree-lined streets and playgrounds. The blighted South Bronx, a place previously synonymous with inner-city decay and criminality, has become 'SoBro' in estate agent parlance, where luxury flats are let for up to $3,500 a month. Restaurants, hotels and entertainment venues have disappeared only to be reinvented in stylish gentrification. Even an icon like the Carnegie Deli, featured in the opening scene of Woody Allen's 1984 film *Broadway Danny Rose*, went out of business to make way for the rising towers of Billionaires' Row. Urban transformation has swept across the Big Apple, so named in the 1920s after sportswriter John J. Fitz Gerald's catchphrase in his horse-racing column 'Around the Big Apple' in the *New York Morning Telegraph*: 'There's only one Big Apple. That's New York.'[2] The city has witnessed a relentless shift in landscape and a potpourri of cultures. Yet for more than a century an unbroken blue line, one might say its backbone, has run through the city's history: the New York Police Department.

* * *

THE NYPD IS celebrated in popular entertainment media – from cinema and radio to television and literature – more than any other police force in the world. The forerunner of fictional portrayals was Anna Katharine Green's 1878 novel *The Leavenworth Case*, whose central character is Detective Ebenezer Gryce of the New York Metropolitan Police Force. Gotham's law enforcement bodies, in one guise or another, have served as the framework for no fewer than two hundred films, television programmes, musical scores and video games. The earliest screen portrayal was Jules Dassin's 1948 film *The Naked City*, in which New York police officers set out to hunt down a young model's killer. The movie was filmed in the streets of Manhattan, set against backdrops familiar to all New Yorkers, like the Williamsburg Bridge and the Whitehall Building.

The police force has featured in numerous TV shows. *Car 54, Where Are You?* is a slapstick sitcom of the early 1960s, which has viewers laughing at two rather bumbling but loveable NYPD officers based at the fictional 53rd Precinct in the Bronx. *NYPD Blue* is a procedural television series that began airing in 1993. This hard-hitting drama is about the day-to-day lives of police having to take on New York's worst criminal elements. Another famed show is *Hill Street Blues*, a police drama series that aired on the NBC Television Network from 1981 to 1987. It chronicles the lives of the staff of a single police station located at fictional Hill Street. The city isn't specified, but the flavour is unmistakably New York.

In the 1960s the comic-book series *Your Friend, the Policeman* depicted the New York cop as ally and friend to juvenile readers. The NYPD was popularized in literature between 1956 and 2005 by the U.S. novelist Evan Hunter. Writing under the pseudonym Ed McBain, the *87th Precinct* series documents the daily work of the police detective squad in Isola, a large fictional metropolis based on New York. Isola is the name of the entire city and also its central district, which is modelled on Manhattan.

The NYPD stands as a vital ingredient in New York's genetic make-up, and it is a household name for millions of visitors from around the world. Only scarcely does a foreign tourist depart the Big Apple without a baseball cap, T-shirt, teddy bear, mug, keychain or other souvenir emblazoned with the NYPD logo. Marvel Comics has even launched a Spider-Man and NYPD line of casual clothing and souvenirs. Their pitch is that New York City has always been the spiritual home of the company's comic-book creations, and the reason why they placed one of its marquee stars in tandem with the NYPD.

Towering above all of Gotham's law enforcement protagonists stands Batman. The Dark Knight has been intrinsically linked to the NYPD since his first appearance in 1939, when New York was in the grip of a crime wave that saw more than two hundred murders committed in a single year, a record at that time. From the outset, the Batman stories focus on the hero's crime-busting relationship with the commissioners of the Gotham City Police Department, a euphemism for the NYPD. Commissioner Jim Gordon works hand-in-glove with Batman, despite the frequent ups and downs in their personal relationship. But it is a different case with Gordon's successor, Commissioner Michael Akins. After a falling out between Batman and the commissioner, Akins orders the Bat-Signal to be removed from the roof of Gotham Central (Grand Central Station). When Gordon is reconfirmed in the job, the Bat-Signal once more beams its commanding ray over the city streets. The next Batman film, scheduled for release in March 2022 with Robert Pattinson in the starring role, keeps aloft the epic of Gotham's idol fighting crime alongside the city's police force.[3]

This is the story of a corps of men and women, often illustrated in films and television dramas as tough, growly characters, at once unpitying with law breakers yet prepared to chase a child's runaway spaniel across a busy road. It is a schmaltzy image, to put it in the New York vernacular, one verging on the razzmatazz, a saga embracing more than four hundred years of history. It is a New York saga to the core. Musing on the display of blue uniforms below my hotel room window, I envisaged a history of the NYPD and felt my pulse quicken at the prospect of writing it. On my return to London, fired up with my project, friends would ask, 'What are you working on these days?' When I said I was writing a history of the NYPD, the initialism provoked eager nods and words of encouragement for a story that needed to be told.

1

The Green Light

‘The long history of the Bowery is one of crime, misadventure, debauchery, desperation, and death. Pickpockets and thieves hung out in every bar. People were drugged, robbed, and kidnapped. Muggers lurked in the shadows.’[1]

This alarming portrayal of the Bowery would have left Johann Lampo scratching his head in bewilderment. Lampo was arguably the most underemployed patrolman in New York City's history of policing, spending six years doing his rounds, during which time there is no record of him having made a single arrest. His remit was to settle minor disputes and alert colonists if fires broke out at night.

It is a tribute to the city's long history of cultural diversity that its first law enforcement officer was a French- and Dutch-speaking Belgian from England. Johann Lampo was born of Walloon parents in Canterbury in 1591. At the age of eighteen, he sailed to the New World to seek his fortune in the Dutch trading outpost of New Amsterdam. He was followed a year later by Peter Minuit, the colony's first governor, who purchased the island of Manhattan from the Lenape tribe for the equivalent of $24 in trinkets and beads. He struck the deal in the mistaken belief that the Native Americans held title to the land they inhabited, in the sense of Roman-Dutch Law. One of Minuit's responsibilities was to ensure the proper policing of the colony. He engaged Lampo as *schout-fiscal*, a rank roughly equivalent to sheriff, a lawman charged with keeping the peace.

Lampo had established his home on a farm, or 'bowerie', north of Canal Street. In the seventeenth century the neighbourhood today known as the Bowery was 'the liveliest spot of the settlement, the heart of the primitive metropolis, the society centre of wilderness.'[2] Lampo spent his working hours patrolling New Amsterdam's waterfront, later to be known as Battery Park after the artillery battery that was installed by the British. Lampo wended his way along the dirt pathways and twisting cobbled streets of Battery Park, one of which was a new highway leading north that would eventually bisect the island roughly through the middle. The Dutch called it *de Brede Weg*, or Broadway in English. He was empowered to administer punishment to, one might imagine, the few lawbreakers he encountered on his rounds. This ranged from the humiliation of being confined in the stocks to the more painful penalty of the whipping post. In 1632 Lampo sailed back to Amsterdam on the schooner *De Eendracht*, in the company of Minuit and a cargo of 5,000 beaver hides bound for the Dutch West India Company.

The *schout-fiscal* system was eventually replaced by the Rattle Watch, a squad of eight patrolmen and a captain charged with a sunset-to-dawn patrol in the increasingly hazardous streets of Battery Park. The team carried green glass lanterns to illuminate the poorly lit lanes. Before the invention of the whistle, they were also equipped with wooden rattles to alert citizens to impending danger, be it from criminals, fires or other threatening situations. Upon hearing this sound, the colonists would rally to defend themselves or form bucket brigades to put out fires. When the lawmen ended their rounds, they returned to the Watch House, the forerunner of the modern police station, and placed their lanterns on a hook by the front door to show they were on the job. The green light became synonymous with assistance for protection against criminal elements, and it is still placed outside the entrances of NYPD precincts to symbolize that the 'Watch' is present and vigilant.[3]

* * *

NEW AMSTERDAM expanded in size and prosperity, and with this growth came an influx of fur hunters, sailors on shore leave and runaway servants from New England or Virginia. To quench the thirst of these rough-and-tumble arrivals, the township experienced a proliferation of taverns, which frequently became the scene of scuffles and brawls in a hard-drinking community. As the settlement was a port of call for international merchant trade, it served as a sanctuary to a large transient population, from which trouble could often be expected.

Sailors on shore leave frequented low waterfront groggeries where flourished gambling and vice and drunken brawls occurred, sometimes ending in murder. Then, too, incoming ships brought hundreds [of] convicts transported fresh from English prisons to the colonies. These unfortunates, without immediate means of subsistence, would often steal or break into houses.[4]

The spiral in criminal activity was such that, in 1638, the municipality attempted to prevent vessels docking in the harbour from allowing their crews to spend the night in town.

The Dutch authorities responded to a surge in lawlessness by dispensing swift and unmerciful justice. In 1646 Jan Creoly, 'Negro slave of the Honourable Company', was convicted of sodomizing a ten-year-old boy. The defendant was condemned 'to be brought to the place of justice, to be strangled there to death and his body to be burned to ashes, as an example to others'. In 1654 Gerrit Trompetter was convicted of sexually assaulting Anna Tymens, a servant girl, and leaving her pregnant. Trompetter also threatened another woman at knifepoint when she refused to sleep with him. 'Therefore, the plaintiff concludes that the detainee should be whipped with rods at the customary place, also that all his wages and credited monthly allowances be confiscated for the benefit of the deflowered woman's child.' Around that same time, the Dutch *schout-fiscal* alerted the citizens of New Amsterdam that 'inhabitants are being attacked and robbed by villainous evil doers in this city and elsewhere in this province'. As part of his crusade against crime, he arrested Hans Breyer, 'who is notorious on suspicion of and has been convicted of various thefts, and who has sought to lure others from the path of honesty to thievery'. Breyer was turned over to the authorities 'to carry out a more thorough examination and subjected to torture in order to extract a confession from the obstinate delinquent by customary methods'. The court subsequently ruled that Breyer 'be punished with the rope until death follows'. Not all cases brought before the courts had so grisly an outcome. The soldier Andries Matthias was arrested for threatening his commanding officer with a knife. Before sentence could be passed, the prisoner managed to escape by leaping over a clapboard fence, while 'pointing his backside to the fiscal and lifting his leg and slapping it'.[5]

* * *

WHEN THE ENGLISH took New Amsterdam from the Dutch in 1664, they renamed it New York, a tribute to the Duke of York, the future King James II. Nine years later, the Dutch briefly regained possession of the colony, which they called New Orange after the ruling House of Orange-Nassau. The Dutch reoccupation lasted but one year, after which they permanently ceded the colony to England under the terms of the Treaty of Westminster, which brought to an end the Third Anglo-Dutch War. The arrival of the English brought a heightening of ethnic tension never previously experienced in the colony, despite it being home to speakers of eighteen languages. In 1679, for instance, a party of Dutchmen involved in a brawl with a group of English were heard shouting, 'Slay the English doggs! Slay the English doggs!'[6] It was a portent of the sort of racial conflict that was to become a regular feature of policing New York City, with the law enforcers themselves often cast in the unflattering limelight as perpetrators of abuse against minorities. The colony's English judicial authorities were forced to ensure proper behaviour by the supposed defenders of law and order. They levied fines well in excess of what had been imposed by the Dutch on officers found guilty of shirking sentinel duty or absence from the Watch, playing cards, swearing, drinking or fighting.

Under English rule, law enforcement was still carried out in much the same way as in the days of the Rattle Watch introduced by the Dutch. The colony's population was growing swiftly, and it became clear that the homespun model of law enforcement as practised in early colonial days was becoming unworkable. The combination of crushing poverty, massive immigration and desperate crowding turned parts of Manhattan into a hotbed of crime and vice. In the Five Points district, in what is now Manhattan's Lower East Side, there were reports of at least one murder a night, along with a proliferation of prostitution, drunkenness, pickpocketing and the occasional street riot.

In the early years of the eighteenth century, the haphazard system of the Night Watch was losing its effectiveness. Every adult male was required to undertake watch duty on a rotating basis, though none of them had undergone any semblance of police training. In 1731 the city raised what was planned as a permanent Citizens' Watch, in which all men living south of today's Canal Street had to serve or pay for a substitute. The alderman of each ward kept a list of those liable for service, and the constable took eight of them each night for watch duty. Women were theoretically eligible to participate, but there is no record of any ever having served. However, in 1734, one Deborah Careful complained to the press of being 'forced to pay as much as the richest man in Town for a substitute, tho' God knows I can hardly buy my bread. I was told

I must do it, 'til there was an Act of Assembly to remedy the evil'.[7] That same year, numerous complaints similar to that of Deborah Careful led to the abandonment of the Citizens' Watch and the creation of a more professional, salaried Constables' Watch.

Gotham on the Rise

By the mid-1700s New York was on its way to becoming an economic powerhouse. The city is located on the Atlantic seaboard, an ideal site for unloading goods shipped from Europe and the Caribbean, and it could now claim a population of 10,000 inhabitants. Of these, almost one in five was an African slave, most of whom worked as household servants or manual labourers. In 1741 tensions between the slaves and their masters reached a flashpoint. Slavery had been instituted by the Dutch, and their numbers increased sharply under the English, who recognized New York's need for a workforce to serve the booming economy. The first recorded slave revolt took place in 1712, when a small group of Africans set fire to a white farmer's barn. People with buckets of water who rushed to the scene were ambushed, and in the ensuing melee nine white people were killed. The rioters were rounded up by an enraged group of citizens. Of those brought before magistrates, eighteen were put to death.

Lower Manhattan fell into the grip of fright. The lawmakers reacted by enacting emergency legislation that restricted black burials to a swampy zone outside the city limits. As a further humiliation, funerals needed to be conducted before dark and could not be attended by more than a dozen mourners. It was feared that large crowds might easily be incited to riot. In this climate of mutual mistrust and animosity, it was only too foreseeable that, when in 1741 a blaze broke out at Fort George, now the home of the U.S. Custom House in Lower Manhattan, a furious public immediately pointed the finger at black arsonists. A rash of fires followed, and in less than a fortnight seven homes had been torched to the ground. In none of these instances was it proven that slaves were responsible. Nonetheless, a large number of black people were rounded up and put on trial for conspiracy. The day the guilty verdicts were handed down, seventeen of the accused were hanged and thirteen others burnt at the stake.

* * *

AT THE TIME New Amsterdam fell into English hands, the colony's only semblance of an organized law-and-order presence was the military. Army regulars, known as the Militia Watch, made the rounds of the port until 1700. After that date they were replaced by the Constables' Watch, a small patrol unit staffed by civilians. This team consisted of a high constable and twelve sub-constables, whose work is commemorated in the twelve stars that today figure on the NYPD Medal of Honour.[8] This turned into little more than a token effort to eradicate a spreading epidemic of attacks on property, burglaries and street muggings. John Holt, a New York printer, complained in 1762 that 'such various attempts to rob, and so many robberies actually committed, having of late been very frequent within the circuits of this city, both day and night, it has become hazardous for any person to walk in the latter'.[9]

During the American War of Independence, the New York authorities had little time to devote to such minutiae as raising a municipal police force. The British Army occupied the city in 1776, retaining dominion over it – and, most critically, its port – for the next thirteen years. This was crucial to their strategy of using the city's harbour as a base for expeditions against other targets in the rebellious colonies. George Washington, commander-in-chief of the Continental Army, was humiliated in several major battles in Manhattan, and the British managed to keep control of New York until they were driven out when the war ended in 1783.

Three years after New York and the other twelve American colonies gained their independence from Britain, the city stepped up what was still a largely informal regime of guarding the streets by reinstating the Night Watch. This comprised one captain and thirty patrolmen. Later, another twenty men were added to the force, as a consequence of the frequent robberies taking place in New York. It was a perfunctory gesture at policing a city whose population in 1786 had swollen to 25,000. The proportion of police and civilian law enforcement agents to civilians at the time was not much different to that of modern New York City: one officer for every 172 citizens in the late eighteenth century, compared with one for every 236 today. The difference, it hardly needs to be emphasized, lay in the paucity of training and equipment of the early units.

The arrival of the British redcoats in 1776 had ushered in an era of unruliness, compared with which the job of keeping the lid on common criminality might have been considered a minor administrative affair. The first British troops to enter New York embarked on a rampage, 'looting private houses and vandalising City Hall, where they smashed equipment belonging to King's College, mutilated paintings and destroyed books. On New Year's Eve 1777, after performing a play entitled *The Devil to Pay in the West Indies*, a party of drunken officers – one dressed up like Old Nick himself, complete with horns and tail – disrupted services at the John Street Methodist Church.'[10] Terrified civilians bore witness to an outbreak of incidences of theft, fraud, robbery and murder, committed by the army of occupation. Along with this disorderly band of soldiers, Loyalists from surrounding war zones escaped to what they imagined to be the safety of New York. Many of these refugees turned into an unruly lot. Having abandoned their homes and the social controls of established communities, they compounded the dilemma of social disorder.

New York was placed under martial law during the war. A commandant was selected by the army to take charge of civil municipal administration. Part and parcel of this restructuring was the creation of an embryonic police corps to enforce military regulations and support the Night Watch. However, this department proved helpless in handling the frequent outbreaks of violence between ordinary citizens and the poorly disciplined troops. Civilian cases against army personnel inundated the courts, but were rarely resolved in the plaintiff's favour. The courts functioned without juries, leaving justice in the hands of a magistrate who was almost invariably biased in favour of the military defendants.

Wartime New York was in desperate need of a professional police force: what it lacked was a template for building one. In January 1777, with war still raging between Loyalist and Patriot armies, a group of civilians took it upon themselves to create their own patrols to make up for the lack of protection from the military. One of their greatest fears was a repetition of the arsonist attack of September 1776, which destroyed about one-third of the inhabited city and triggered an outbreak of looting and pillaging. The devastated streets between Broadway and Whitehall became a no man's land, a place that in short order acquired a reputation for crime and vice that lasted almost to the end of the century. Hundreds of destitute refugees lived cheek by jowl in this area, called 'Canvas Town', a pestilent camp of makeshift tents that sprawled westward from the foot of Broad Street through the ruins left by the fire.

This group of eighty patrolmen was still thought of as inadequate. In May 1778, the commandant assigned three civilians to form a quasi-civil department of police whose duties were to suppress vice and licentiousness, support the poor, direct the night watch and regulate all matters which concerned the economy, peace and good order of the city.[11]

Lacking the full cooperation of the military, New York's embryonic civilian police department was doomed to be ineffective. Locals still complained about the hazards of walking the streets at night or mingling in a crowd during the day. For a time, some of the army served as a voluntary police force, with summary punishments for violations handed down by any one member of the City Council.

It is not without a twinge of irony that, following the evacuation of British war vessels in the autumn of 1783, New York citizens found themselves facing an even more acute problem of policing the now American city. Almost every member of the British enlightened class – legislators, lawgivers, civil administrators, artisans and entrepreneurs – had joined the exodus to Britain. This brought on a breakdown in the social structure that had held the city's people together for nearly 120 years. The temporary collapse of morality and social stability that is often the aftermath of armed conflict took its toll on the city's previous good order.

Peace also brought a wave of economic dislocation to the city. New York had prospered during the war as headquarters of the British Army. When the troops departed, the army's infrastructure was dismantled, but the press gangs employed by the navy and an assortment of ruffian hangers-on remained in the streets. This triggered an upsurge in hostility by the ordinary citizenry. People frustrated by depressed economic conditions formed mobs, which on many occasions took to the streets to confront these social undesirables.

* * *

IN 1784 James Duane became New York's first post-war mayor. Duane's appointment raised hopes of a return to peace and normal civil order. In a gesture of goodwill towards the city's disenfranchised population, Duane donated money to the poor that was earmarked for the customary entertainment following a mayor's inauguration. He was the city's top law administrator, 'who presided over the Common Council, the Mayor's Court, or Court of Common Pleas, which heard civil cases, and the Court of General Sessions for criminal cases'.[12] Duane also gained favour among the enlightened classes for his instrumental role in creating the New York Manumission Society in 1785, whose objective was to abolish slavery. At the time of his appointment, New York and New Jersey were the only northern states that still allowed the keeping of slaves, a practice that began to be eradicated in 1799, ten years after Duane left office.

Remarkably, for a city whose population soared from 33,000 at the time of Duane's resignation to 123,000 thirty years later, New York was beginning to enjoy a semblance of renewed civic harmony. A return to economic prosperity was a vital influence in the process, and this was driven, to an extent, by a resumption of overseas trade. In 1784 a fleet of merchant vessels sailed from the East River wharves, bound for the markets of China with their cargo of goods, from beaver furs to ginseng, a root plant highly prized by the Chinese for what they believed to be its medicinal powers. Then, in 1792, two dozen stockbrokers gathered under a Buttonwood tree in Wall Street to create the New York Stock Exchange, set up to serve the burgeoning U.S. securities market. New York was on its way to becoming the fledgling republic's economic dynamo.

* * *

IT IS ALMOST axiomatic that criminality in a society is inflamed by a lack of shared prosperity. Taking the story forward some two centuries, the violence and destitution that enveloped New York in the 1970s, when the city came within a whisker of declaring bankruptcy, led to the poorest neighbourhoods falling prey to continual looting, vandalism and worse. In 1973 New York reported 1,680 homicides. This fuelled a widely shared conviction that the city had tumbled into irreversible decline. By the end of that decade, signs of an economic upswing began to surface and, within twenty years, with the city's population roughly unchanged, the number of homicides had been cut by half. As the recovery progressed, a group of economists was able to declare that 'the turnaround can be classified as nothing short of phenomenal. The doom-and-gloom predictions of the city going belly-up that permeated the atmosphere of the mid-1970s have been replaced with predominantly positive views in almost every sector of the economy.'[13]

Just as in the New York of the 1980s, a return to economic well-being on its own did not account for the decline in lawbreaking, and so too in post-colonial times a firm hand was required to crack down on felonies. The Broken Windows approach to tackling crime, brought into being by Mayor Rudolph Giuliani and Police Commissioner William Bratton in the 1990s, has become a household name for beating felonies. The system attained a status akin to stardom, but not without drawing its fair share of criticism. In late eighteenth-century New York, in the absence of a professional police force, delinquent elements who engaged in opportunistic wrongdoings posed an almost unchallenged threat to the unwary and most vulnerable inhabitants of the city. Concurrent with the felonies committed by villains lurking in the shadows of the docks and alleyways of Lower Manhattan, a well-organized 'white-collar' culture of lawlessness also made its appearance. This organization camouflaged its misdeeds behind a facade of well-intentioned benevolence.

* * *

TAMANEND was a chieftain credited by the Delaware tribe with the feat of having carved Niagara Falls from the rocks. The New York political machine that took its name from this legendary Native American was perhaps not equal to so Herculean a task, but its power to exercise almost limitless hegemony over the city's administration and its agencies, including the police, is not to be sold short. The cabal that was to extend its rule of corruption and patronage across New York for more than two centuries was founded in 1789 as a Democrat political club. Its vernacular name was The Society of St Tammany, or Columbian Order, Inc. The organization's guiding spirit was an Irish American veteran of the War of Independence by the name of William Mooney. He became the society's first 'Boss', or 'Sachem', the name given to a North American Indian paramount. Mooney's idea for what he envisaged as an altruistic, beneficent association founded to support the common citizen came to him at the conclusion of a parade to celebrate the ratification of the U.S. Constitution. The Society was based in a large brownstone in East 14th Street, known to its members as the Wigwam and to the world at large as Tammany Hall.

Tweed Rules Supreme

The power and wealth accumulated by some of the Tammany bigwigs was of a truly colossal magnitude. Among the Tammany Hall elite, the nineteenth-century political baron and hulking thug William M. Tweed was an outstanding example of unbridled corruption and greed. At the height of his career, 'Boss Tweed' held directorships of a railway, a printing company and two banks. He also sat on the boards of three industrial firms and was the owner of a New York hotel, as well as being the major shareholder in several iron and gas companies. When his toady, the urbane Abraham Oakey Hall, won the mayoralty election in 1869, Tweed's control of New York City government became absolute. By the mid-1860s Tweed had risen to the top Tammany position and formed the 'Tweed Ring', a syndicate that openly bought votes, fed on judicial corruption and extracted millions from city contracts. The end of his reign came in 1877, when he was convicted for pocketing up to $45 million in taxpayer money. Tweed escaped jail and fled to Madrid, only to be tracked down in a joint operation by the New York and Spanish police. He was returned to the Ludlow Street Jail, where he died a year later.

Number One Cop

Into a city that was becoming increasingly difficult to police stepped steely eyed, wooden-staff-wielding Jacob Hays, precursor to the New York 'super cop'. Hays was born in 1772 into a Jewish family one generation removed from Dutch settlers. He was given the job of marshal at the age of 26 in 1789, coinciding with Tammany's debut on the New York political stage. In four short years his meteoric rise in policing propelled him into the post of New York's first high constable. This came about thanks in no small measure to connections with people in high places, specifically Aaron Burr, who served as U.S. vice president under Thomas Jefferson.

Hays epitomized the single-minded 'he got his man' detective. Following up on a jewellery robbery in 1834, armed only with his much-feared nightstick and his own shrewdness, he set out to find the culprits. Forty-eight hours later Hays had recovered the greater part of the property, which was buried in a field about 6 miles (10 km) from the city, and arrested two of the thieves, in whose possession he found the remainder of the property.

Hays became something of a celebrity in his own time: his name resonated in foreign circles and among those who knew him in New York. In 1842 Charles Dickens paid a visit to New York, where Hays took him on a tour of the slums of Five Points. Dickens described the area as a place drenched in 'poverty, wretchedness and vice'. When the novelist climbed to the attic of one of the 'leprous houses', he observed debauched, half-awakened creatures who crawled from their corners 'as if the judgment hour were at hand and every obscene grave giving up its dead'. Dickens mordantly observed that 'where dogs would howl to lie, women, men, and boys slink off to sleep, forcing the dislodged rats to move away in quest of better lodgings'. Dickens found Five Points the peer of London's St Giles and its Seven Dials, among the vilest rookeries of the British capital.[14]

Hays acquired a great number of admirers in the police department and not a few enemies in criminal circles over the course of nearly fifty years of pounding the pavement.

> Short, stocky and powerfully built, he prowled the streets attired in a black suit and stovepipe hat, with a white kerchief tied around his neck. His only weapon was a gold-tipped staff of office: he used it to break up riots by scooping the hats off the first group of combatants he reached. When they stopped to retrieve their bonnets, Hays would push them down until their bodies formed a neat pile.[15]

Hays can rightly be called New York City's first detective. He oversaw a small constabulary of 28 part-time watchmen, who joined the patrol after their day job and made their rounds until the wee hours of the morning. Hays's initial role as high constable dealt mainly with administrative chores involving court proceedings. Hays was never going to let bureaucracy constrain him: he took it upon himself to expand his duties to include keeper of the peace and criminal investigator. Part of his self-imposed eighteen-hour work shift entailed shadowing suspected and known criminals to their lairs, from which they would be dragged to justice, literally by the scruff of their necks. Small wonder that he was depicted by one newspaper as 'the terror of rascals of every grade'.[16]

The temptations to engage in corruption were around even in the early years of policing. The offices of constable and high constable were unsalaried positions. Small sums could be made by handing out writs and warrants, while a far more lucrative practice was to claim rewards on stolen and lost goods. It could be argued that, from a lawman's perspective, this corrupt routine only served to encourage theft. Hays recognized the moral dangers of allowing it to carry on unchecked and petitioned his City Hall superiors to introduce a regular wage package for officers. The request was granted, but not until 1812, and even then on a temporary basis until it was reinstated in 1825.

Hays can also be credited with setting up New York's first international police liaison. Counterfeiting was big business before 1862, when the U.S. established a national currency. Any forger worth his salt, in cahoots with a printer, could run off innumerable bogus notes nearly indistinguishable from those issued by private banks. The crime was considered serious enough to carry a penalty of life imprisonment for the unlucky few who were apprehended. In 1818 Hays's investigative talents and his contacts with Canadian law enforcers enabled him to break up a gang of forgers working in rural Ontario. Hays worked with the Canadian authorities to stage a raid on a clandestine printing plant and seize a hoard of notes running well into six figures.

New York's illustrious chief constable was in possession of something akin to a photographic memory of underworld characters, a kind of mental rogues' gallery. On one occasion, Hays exercised almost clairvoyant powers in identifying from a handful of clues a housebreaker who had made off with a well-known lawyer's expensive tailored suit. The culprit was apprehended, wearing the very suit he had stolen. On another case, Hays spent days canvassing the waterfront for a murderer. Following an instinct, he spotted his man, picked him up and took him to a local church for interrogation. The suspect denied the charge until Hays dramatically confronted him with the corpse, at which point he extracted a tearful confession, followed by a court conviction that saw the murderer marched off to the gallows.

Hays did not restrict his pursuit of lawbreakers to the lower strata of New York society. In the 1820s billionaire magnate Cornelius Vanderbilt was found to be running an illegal ferry service across the Hudson River, from New Jersey to New York, in defiance of the monopoly held by the Livingston family. They obtained an injunction against the intruder, and Hays was assigned to the case. The wily Vanderbilt relied on spies to warn him when Hays or his men were in the vicinity. According to Vanderbilt himself, "I was mad enough to defy the whole Livingston tribe, but when I saw that calm, smiling face with a twinkle saying *If you don't obey the court's law, and obey it damn soon, I'll make you, by God,* I concluded to surrender."[17]

Hays remained on active service until the early 1840s, though even after his retirement he retained the title of high constable until his death in 1850. One New York newspaper recalled that 'he was known to every man, woman and child as "Old Hays, the thief catcher".'[18] Hays left an abiding image of more than four decades of tireless, practical police work, almost all of it wearing out his boot leather on the beat. His presence stares down from an ink portrait hanging in an office on the thirteenth floor of NYPD headquarters at One Police Plaza in Lower Manhattan. In this rectangular, Brutalist-style building one can find Benjamin Singleton, Hays's grandson four times removed, crunching crime statistics and developing computer programs that identify criminal patterns in the city. One of Hays's descendants is also to be found in the media world, in the person of the late Arthur Hays Sulzberger, long-serving publisher of the *New York Times*.

* * *

WITH NEW YORK'S population having climbed past the 300,000 mark by the mid-nineteenth century, it was becoming increasingly evident that policing the city could no longer be a one-man task, especially when that man was in his sixties. Hays headed a small and woefully undermanned force, one that might have served to carry out the occasional arrest but was certainly not equipped or trained to take on widescale and much-needed anti-crime duties across the city. Anti-abolitionist riots broke out in 1834, and the following year more than five hundred buildings were destroyed in what became known as 'The Great Fire of New York'. All this mayhem took place against a backdrop of economic collapse. In 1837 New York banks began suspending payments in hard currency, triggering mass panic and the collapse of several institutions.

One of the most short-lived of New York's civil disturbances took place on a cold winter afternoon on 12 February 1837. Given the city's extremes of climate, it was an unusual time of year for demonstrators to take to the streets. On this occasion, poverty-stricken tenement dwellers were incited to attack warehouses in Lower Manhattan. They had been assured by a team of rabble-rousers that food was being hoarded on the premises by wealthy merchants. The significance of the Flour Riot, as it was dubbed by the penny press, went beyond a humble demand for food. It underscored a deepening chasm in the city between the prosperous merchant class and a fast-growing proletariat of Irish immigrants, many fresh off the boat. That day more than 5,000 people assembled in front of City Hall in response to signs posted about the city calling for 'Bread! Meat! Rent! Fuel! The voice of the people shall be heard and will prevail.' One after the next, hothead agitators clambered up the steps of the colonnaded facade to speak out against the price of flour.

The final speaker, of unknown identity, rallied the crowed to move on Eli Hart & Co., saying, 'Fellow citizens, Mr Eli Hart has now

53,000 barrels of flour in his store.' Upon hearing the roar of the mob, the clerks there began locking the place up, but in their haste one door was inadvertently left open, allowing the crowd to burst in, and before long they were rolling out flour-filled barrels and throwing out sacks of grain into the street below and carried away.[19]

Hart arrived in haste with a detachment of watchmen in tow. The police were instantly set upon and disarmed by the crowd. Mayor Cornelius Lawrence rushed from his City Hall office to urge the protestors to disperse. He was bombarded by a hail of stones and ice balls and forced to seek safety inside. Fortunately for him, a contingent of the New York Militia appeared on the scene and, before nightfall, the Flour Riot had been brought to an end. One of the ironies of the day was that, in one way, the event played into the hands of the merchant class that had been demanding a larger police force specifically to manage incidents of this sort. Within 24 hours, Lawrence passed a law increasing the number of New York City watchmen by 192 officers.

The initial effort to establish a professionally trained, citywide corps of law enforcement agents capable of responding to cataclysmic events, such as those the city had recently experienced, came about in 1843. In that year Mayor Robert H. Morris was invested with supreme police authority. He raised a body of 1,000 men, who were instructed to make the rounds south of a line extending from the Hudson to the East rivers, between 28th and 40th streets. The next year saw the abolition of the Night Watch, which by now was looking woefully out of date. For many New Yorkers it had become an almost laughable institution. These Buster Keaton-lookalike cops were equipped with 33-inch (84 cm) wooden batons to protect them from evildoers. As for 'making the rounds', they were mostly tucked away in narrow sentry boxes to shield them from the elements. Their uniform, such as it was, consisted of a hard and heavy leather-covered helmet, which gave rise to the nickname 'leatherheads'. The image of the snoring leatherhead in his box became the butt of jokes and pranks. Men out for a night on the town would top off the evening by arrogantly tipping over a sentry box, along with its inhabitant.

The Cops Get Organized

A new system brought in a chief of police to exercise supreme command in a city whose population had by now topped the 400,000 mark. The year 1845 saw the foundation of the Municipal Police, a 24-hour force of eight hundred officers, who were issued eight-pointed copper stars to wear on their chests. Almost since the inception of the New York police, it has been widely accepted as fact that the badge bearing the seal of the city denotes the origin of the word 'cop' for a police officer. There are, in fact, multiple versions of how this slang expression might have come about. One theory was that the buttons on the police uniform, when the force finally got round to wearing one, were of pressed copper, hence the origin of the somewhat pejorative term for a patrolman.[20] Curiously enough, the men of the newly formed Municipal Police rejected a proposal to wear uniforms, which they considered a symbol of servitude. It is most likely that the nickname is drawn from the verb 'to cop', meaning to apprehend a criminal. The expression was in use in Victorian Britain and found its way across the Atlantic with immigrants, a great number of them Irish, who joined the force. Be that as it may, under the Municipal Police Act of 1845 Mayor William Havemeyer set up what could be termed the city's first proper police force, in fact rather than merely in legislative theory. It was Havemeyer who is credited with having coined the phrase 'New York's Finest', which is still a term of endearment for the city's police force. The expression first appeared in a *New York Times* article on 17 November 1865, which reported on the annual parade of the Metropolitan Police from City Hall to Uptown Manhattan.

The department adopted a military-style hierarchy of rank and authority. The system was largely modelled on London's Metropolitan Police, which was then regarded as the foremost crime-fighting agency in the world. Although the New York police might have in many ways resembled their London counterpart, there were substantial differences between the two forces. London's political administrators stressed careful control of the use of police powers and kept patrolmen from having to perform unpopular duties like shutting down bars and taverns on a Sunday. In New York, authority over the police lay in the hands of locally elected officials – ultimately the mayor – who were more disposed to let the police take a tougher approach to the job than their London counterparts. The New York police were more inclined to use physical force and make arrests on the mere suspicion of an offence. Of course, a crucial difference was that London police did not carry firearms, a policy that in the main still holds true for the bobby on the beat. Nevertheless, the first step had now been taken towards the creation of the NYPD.

2

Turn of the Century Blue

The birth of the NYPD coincided with the heyday of neighbourhood policing, when officers on patrol were instructed to preserve the peace as well as 'check doors and windows at night, stop loiterers and suspicious people, prevent soliciting and make bureaucratic reports on dead animals, unlighted street lamps and other subjects'.[1] Their multifarious duties ranged from stopping runaway horses and shooting those with broken legs to, on one occasion, a patrolman affectionately known as Old John chasing down the thieves of a load of hams from a butcher's shop by sniffing in hallways for telltale ham and cabbage cooking on someone's stove.

This wide range of duties was at the heart of the New York Police Department, as it is known around the world today, which is often assumed to have come into being with the establishment of the Municipal Police. It is argued that the NYPD traces its historical roots to 1845 and the replacement of New York's existing constabulary with this department numbering about eight hundred officers. There were, however, major differences in structure between the Municipal Police, their successors the Metropolitan Police and today's NYPD. The tainting hand of Tammany had left its mark on the earlier forces, when it was taken for granted that the police were a compliant ally of political power and patronage. Among the Municipal Police's responsibilities was the supervision of elections, and because officers were Tammany appointees, they had a vested interest in the outcome of these polls. In other words, they were to a large extent a Tammany tool.

The 1901 reorganization of the department abolished the bipartisan board of commissioners. This was replaced with an agency under the

Socialist demonstrators being driven from Tomkins Square
by mounted police in 1874.

control of a single police commissioner, who was in turn chosen by the
mayor. An element in the NYPD's modernization process was a reduction in political patronage and improper, that is Tammany, influence on
the department. A civil service system was introduced, while procedures
were taken on board to impose stricter accountability on patrolmen and
officers alike. Sitting an exam became mandatory to determine eligibil-
ity for promotion, all under a more streamlined bureaucratic structure.

The creation of a body of professionally trained, full-time law
enforcement agents could not have come about at a more opportune
moment. Between 1820 and 1860, New York City's population had
grown more than sevenfold. City officials had previously considered the
problem of crime and disorder to be a manageable, albeit challenging,
undertaking. By the mid-1830s, however, they were worried about indiscriminate eruptions of violence. In the space of four decades, from 1834
to 1874, New York City was rocked by a number of full-scale riots that
left the streets running red with the blood of hundreds of victims, demonstrators and police. Life in the city could at times be likened to sitting
atop a powder keg. By mid-century immigrants were piling into New

York, not in their thousands, but in their millions. For the most part, these new arrivals sought to partake in the riches to be made in the country's fastest-growing metropolis. In the five years between 1847 and 1852 almost 1.4 million immigrants disembarked in the port of New York. Many continued their journey, mainly Germans and Scandinavians, to establish new communities in the vastness of the American West. On the other extreme, the most destitute of these newcomers never ventured far beyond the New York docks.

Gangs like the fearsome Daybreak Boys, who specialized in ransacking and scuttling ships in the wee hours, amounted in essence to a band of marauding pirates: vicious thugs prepared to cut a ship watchman's throat at the slightest provocation. Municipal Police Chief George Washington Matsell had calculated in 1850 that up to five hundred river brigands operated out of Manhattan's Fourth Ward on the Lower East Side. Matsell and other police officials had lobbied ceaselessly for a harbour force to protect shipping and the docks from criminal raids. Matsell's associate, the prominent diplomat and lawyer James W. Gerard, travelled to Britain in 1853 to carry out an exhaustive study of London's Metropolitan Police. On his return, he demanded that New York's waterways be given similar protection to that enjoyed in the shipping lanes of the River Thames and the London Docklands. The municipal authorities set up New York's first harbour police unit in 1858. It was a small and scarcely adequate force of a handful of men, whose remit was to patrol Lower Manhattan's offshore waterways. This was the forerunner of today's Harbour Unit, with its team of more than 150 officers on duty in the waters surrounding New York. The gangs that roamed the seamier districts of Manhattan are a memory of the past, but the police are still kept busy, rescuing distressed people in the water, assisting in boating-related accidents, monitoring for signs of terrorist activity on the waterfront and protecting the ferries that transport thousands of passengers daily.

Gerard's fact-finding mission also shed light on an alarming level of criminality that prevailed in mid-nineteenth century New York. He speaks of 'no outward rowdyism in London', where he felt 'more safe and secure than in walking the Bowery or even Broadway'. On the other hand, he invites New Yorkers to 'look at your morning paper and see what a black record of crime has been committed in your public streets the day and the night before, what stabbings, what knockings down, what assault by slung shots and otherwise, insults to women and other disgusting details of violence'.[2]

NYPD boat parking in the North Cove Marina at Battery Park in Manhattan.

Gerard lays the blame for New York's lawbreaking on defects in the policing system and the small number of officers on the beat. London's Metropolitan Police, he asserts, with 7,000–8,000 officers, exposes the inadequacy of New York's 1,040-strong force. Moreover, he points out, four-fifths of reported crime in London is non-violent, in exact opposition to New York. Gerard's treatise paints a bleak picture of a city rife with violent behaviour, which, in 1851 alone, registered 270 arrests for murder and offences committed with intent to kill, four times the average for the six previous years. The disproportion in misdemeanours for both cities is reflected in the number of arrests for all categories of felonies. These amounted to 70,827 overall for London in that same year, a considerable figure until one takes into account that New York, with a quarter of London's population, registered more than half of that number. Clearly, the NYPD had a job on its hands.

In the previous century, those who dreamt of a fusion of different nationalities, ethnicities and cultures in New York and the rest of the country had coined the phrase 'the great melting pot'. This was meant to reflect the coming together of peoples from every corner of the world, all of whom shared the American Dream. 'Stew pot' would be a more accurate metaphor. This certainly held true for the waves of immigrants who landed in New York in the mid-nineteenth century. The different 'ingredients' that settled in the city never 'melted' into one another, in the sense of sharing a living space with those of a different Old Country background. They lived in the same 'pot', which could be defined as the boundaries of the New York metropolis, but there was little in the way of social integration in these ghettoized communities.

From the earliest days of mass immigration, the climate among ethnic groups had been one of reciprocal avoidance, if not open hostility. This was most clear between the patricians of British or Dutch ancestry on the one hand, and the city's blue-collar working classes and people of colour on the other. Then came a dislike of the Irish by almost all the established immigrant groups. They resented these newcomers who appeared on the scene so suddenly and in such massive numbers. The 1845–9 potato famine touched off the greatest mass exodus of people in history, with 2.5 million people fleeing Ireland in a single decade. More than a million settled in New York, a maelstrom of newcomers that engendered a disruption of the city's social order unlike anything it had seen in the past. The Catholic religion they brought with them was viewed with distaste by followers of the dominant Protestantism in its various persuasions. Many Irish pulled no punches in declaring their abhorrence of New York's sizeable black population, which numbered almost 14,000, while simultaneously denouncing the abolitionist cause. Given this high-voltage scenario, it was always going to be a matter of time before breaking point was reached.

The impotency of what passed for a New York police force had first come to light on a blisteringly hot evening in July 1834. Violence had erupted at the Bowery Theatre in Lower Manhattan when a mob attacked the playhouse. The crowd had been galvanized into action by a rumour that a British actor had voiced anti-American remarks on stage. They marched on the home of Arthur Tappan, a prominent abolition-ist. Someone in the crowd declared that the hanging of an abolitionist would finish off the night's pleasure. The man they were after happened to be president of the American Anti-Slavery Society and founder of the *Journal of Commerce* newspaper. Fortunately, Tappan was not at home on the night the lynch mob turned up at his door. 'They forced their way into the house, hurled the furniture into the street and made a bonfire of it. In the next two days the mob wrecked New York's Episcopal African Church and pulled down and looted the houses of many Negroes and abolitionists,' writes U.S. historian James F. Richardson.[3] The rabble was never going to be brought under control by a detachment of the Night Watch, so the city authorities had no option but to call in several thou-sand troops to restore order.

Like the Bowery Theatre riot of 1834, one of the more bizarre spates of violence at that time also had a popular Manhattan theatre as its setting. The resources of the newly formed Municipal Police were severely put to the test in May 1849, when squads of officers, along with army units, were called in to quell a spate of rampaging that ended with twenty dead and more than a hundred wounded. It resembled nothing so much as a precursor to a modern rampage by football fans, only on this occasion the field of battle was the former luxurious Astor Place Theatre, where there now stands an off-Broadway venue and New York landmark in Greenwich Village. The bust-up originated in a feud between supporters of two rival Shakespearean thespians: the British stage star William Macready and the American actor Edwin Forrest, who were appearing in competing productions of *Macbeth*.

Macready's first night on stage on 7 May was greeted with a storm of abuse from pro-Forrest infiltrators in the audience. The British actor courageously attempted to carry on in defiance of the verbal abuse being hurled at him, along with a fusillade of pennies, rotten eggs and even chairs from the upper tiers. Matsell, who was New York's first police chief, was present in the theatre, at the head of a contingent of officers, but found himself in the pitched battle that erupted. The curtain came down, and with deep resignation Macready accepted this as the end of his New York engagement. The next day, a number of influential citizens, among them the novelist Washington Irving, encouraged Macready to stage another performance on 10 May.

On that night the Astor Place Opera House, as the Astor Place Theatre was then known, was once more playing host to Macready when, without warning, the theatre was stormed by a horde of Forrest loyalists. The attacking mob was motivated by sentiments that ran far deeper than the simple dislike of an actor. The underlying cause was the seething contempt of the city's poor and downtrodden for the affluent upper classes, who had never hidden their sympathies for all things British. This was not the first time the Macready–Forrest antagonism had surfaced: the British actor's previous u.s. tour had suffered from competing bookings from Forrest, while across the Atlantic Macready's followers insured that Forrest was properly snubbed on his English tour.

An outburst of hissing and booing once more erupted in the hall on the night of Macready's second performance. A mob of up to 15,000 people was milling about outside, many of whom abruptly took to hurling stones at the theatre's windows. The police were frantic, trying to arrest as many troublemakers as they could lay their hands on. It was literally a life and death struggle as the cops were driven back by a shower of paving stones. The situation skidded irretrievably out of control just at the moment companies of mounted infantry galloped up, brandishing their bayonets. Pandemonium broke out in the streets around the theatre, as troopers were dragged off their mounts and the outnumbered police were routed by the frenzied rioters. The tumult was by now at fever pitch, when from somewhere in the group of massed police the order was given to open fire. The first broadside brought down a handful of rioters. This was followed almost immediately by an even more furious onslaught by the crowds and another death-dealing volley of bullets.

A contemporary eye-witness account offers a melancholy depiction of the aftermath of these tragic events:

> The scene which followed the firing of the military beggars all description. The wounded, the dying and the dead, lay scattered in every direction. There were groans of agony, cries for help and oaths of vengeance. Some of the dead and wounded were laid out upon the billiard tables of Vauxhall Saloon. A large crowd gathered around and speeches were made by excited orators.[4]

Irish on the Defensive

Disturbances sparked by ethnic or religious conflict were not confined to the streets of Manhattan. In early April 1844 the xenophobic, anti-Catholic and anti-immigration Native American Party made its appearance in Brooklyn, aiming to provoke conflicts with Irish immigrants who were scorned as outsiders and, moreover, professed a hated religion.[5] At a rally in Fulton Street militants harangued the crowd with abusive and violent diatribes against the Irish, a number of whom were in attendance and armed with bludgeons. Just as the rally was breaking up, one of the speakers encouraged people to go home and added, 'If the Irish attempt to interfere we'll eat them without pepper or salt!' Several persons thought it would be a good idea to demolish the Catholic church in Court Street, a move that sent some fifty Irishmen rushing to protect the chapel. Within minutes, the two groups found themselves engaged in a free-for-all, with the Natives threatening to gut the church. Gunshots rang out, but there were no reports of casualties. The police, once again heavily outnumbered and ill-equipped, got off lightly on this occasion.

A much uglier confrontation took place on 12 July 1871. A clash between Irish Protestant and Catholic militants resulted in the death of some sixty people, making what became known as the Orange Riot one of the deadliest street battles in New York's stormy history. Trouble began building at the start of the annual parade by Irish Protestants, known as the Orangemen. The event was held every year to celebrate the victory of the Protestant King William of Orange over the Catholic monarch James II at the Battle of the Boyne in Ireland in 1690. In fact, the disturbances that year were in essence a matter of unfinished business. The Metropolitan Police had on past occasions managed the annual Orangemen parades with no major incidents reported. However, the previous march in 1870 had left five dead, at least a hundred with wounds of varying severity, and a thirst for revenge on the part of the marchers.

That afternoon in 1871 a large force of police, backed by a contingent of national guardsmen, positioned themselves near the starting point of the march at Orange Lodge Headquarters on 29th Street. As the procession made its way up Eighth Avenue, Irish Catholic onlookers from what was then the crime-infested neighbourhood of Hell's Kitchen began taunting the marchers. It soon rose to a point at which the situation was fated to escalate into a major outbreak of violence. The mounting tension was aggravated by the arrival of armed militia to back up the beleaguered police, who found themselves under attack from both factions. A shot rang out, though it was never ascertained which camp it came from. There were conflicting versions: one maintained that it was fired from a nearby window of a building on the corner, while another had it that a soldier had accidentally discharged his rifle. No order was given to respond to the mob's provocations with firearms, but nevertheless someone in the police line panicked and opened fire, at which point the forces began shooting indiscriminately into the crowd. Thirty-seven people were killed on the spot and nearly two hundred lay wounded in the streets.

'Yesterday was a day never to be forgotten in the history of New York,' is how the *New York Times* summed up the tragic march. 'From early morning until late at night, the excitement everywhere was intense and at times the reign of terror was complete. No civilized city, in a time of supposed profound peace, ever presented a stranger aspect than did New York at the dawn and during the morning hours of yesterday.'[6]

Riots Galore

New York's outbreaks of violence, from the mid-1800s to the end of the century, seemed as inconsequential as a passing summer thunderstorm when compared with the wave of criminality that consumed the city a century later, a time when New York was wavering on social and financial collapse. The nineteenth-century riots had the police chasing social and political protesters from pillar to post in a largely vain effort to suppress ethnically or religiously motived attacks. It was Irish on black people, or the mainly immigrant working classes having a go at affluent members of the Establishment, Catholics on Protestants, and even Jews – a people not usually associated with street violence – in one tumultuous incident that took place in 1901 in the Orthodox area of Manhattan's Lower East Side. On that occasion, a scuffle erupted when a funeral procession carrying the coffin of a popular rabbi came under fire by a barrage of bricks. The assailants were factory workers taking delight in mocking the cortège of bearded mourners in their traditional black hats and overcoats. The police had detailed fifty patrolmen to supply security along the route. When they failed to act, for reasons that were never clarified – though it would not be wide of the mark to assume there was little sympathy for Jews among a largely Irish force – the enraged pallbearers and followers broke away to storm the factory building. The row that ensued required the dispatch of two hundred police reservists to the scene. The fact that the police reinforcements sided with the factory workers, and used their batons to beat back the Jews, would substantiate the antisemitic hypothesis.

In this swirling stew pot of mutually hostile ethnicities, religions and political persuasions, little incitement was needed for people to take their grievances to the streets. Two incidents that took place in 1857 made this one of the most turbulent years in New York City's history. The Dead Rabbits Riot could be considered a dress rehearsal for a prolonged and poisonous ritual that has since stretched police resources to their maximum.[7] In the gang jargon of that period, a 'rabbit' was a laddish tag for a lout. Taking it up a notch, a 'dead rabbit' was a thug with hefty muscles. The Dead Rabbits Riot was a crime spree of looting and turf warfare by two of the city's roughest gangs, the Dead Rabbits of the Five Points and the Bowery Boys. The Bowery Boys took their name from a once respectable neighbourhood that by mid-century had become a slum overrun with brothels, pawn shops and flop houses.

No sooner had the Metropolitan Police come into existence in 1857 than a succession of department commissioners were obliged to cope with massive street battles between these two gangs, along with a number of other bands of ruffians. The riot that took place the year the new force was founded was an upshot of the deep, prevailing hatred between the enemy mobs. It also resonated with political undertones involving the police. The previous year, Democratic Mayor Fernando Wood, a Tammany Hall 'Grand Sachem', knew he could always rely on the complicity of the Municipal Police, who moreover were shockingly obliged to contribute to his campaign fund. Wood had already demoted a number of captains who had shown themselves unfriendly to his candidacy, and he levied on each policeman a portion of his salary for his mayoral campaign chest: captains $15 to $25 each, and a lesser amount for patrolmen. Anyone who refused to pay was placed on the Mayor's List, which meant he risked being dismissed for the most trivial offence. Wood was doing his best to transform the public force into an organization he could smoothly slip into his pocket. He had even persuaded his commissioners to allow him to sack officers who in his view were not performing their duties properly. Wood's ploy was to hire police of known Democratic Party persuasion to replace these officers. The police thus effectively became the mayor's political cronies. Wood also enlisted immigrant gangs, like the Irish American Dead Rabbits, to ensure him an election victory and a second term as mayor. His henchmen would routinely dispatch this gaggle of thugs to break up rallies by opposition candidates.

Election campaign sleaze and embezzlement were the hallmarks of Wood's years in office. New York State Republican Governor John King took action to pull the rug out from under his political opponent and Tammany backers with a bill that replaced the Municipals with the Metropolitan Police force. This new corps was placed under the jurisdiction of the five boroughs that were soon to be amalgamated into present-day New York City. The new police department was controlled by five commissioners, to be selected by the state governor. Wood flatly refused to hand over police jurisdiction to King. Instead, he moved into the Matsell camp. In the mêlée that broke out for control of the police, Matsell was forced to resign when the state-appointed commission assumed administrative control of the department. He was replaced by the well-known reformer Frederick Augustus Tallmadge.

Two days of gang warfare between the Dead Rabbits and the Bowery Boys framed the background to this political squabble between rival police forces. Every attempt by the beleaguered police to put down the riots on those sweltering July days backfired: both mobs joined forces to stage a concerted attack on the officers. As the encounter heated up, some of the thousand or so Dead Rabbits and Bowery Boys taking part in the clashes upped the stakes, from fists and bricks to firearms. Once again, the militia was called in to shore up the outnumbered patrolmen. Taking advantage of the disorganized state of the police, the fighting spiralled into general looting and wreckage of property at the hands of gangsters and other criminals from every part of the city. Hundreds of people exploited the chaos to loot the Bowery and its adjacent neighbourhoods, in what was the worst outbreak of civic disorder since the Astor Place Riot of 1849. It was also the worst rash of gang violence before the New York Draft Riots that lay ahead, which were described by Major General Charles W. Sandford as 'a riot of the most serious character . . . more serious in its consequence than any before known in our city.'[8] After 48 hours of mayhem between the gangs, order was at last restored on 5 July by Sandford's New York State Militia, backed up by whatever support detachments the city police were able to muster.

It was at this point that one of New York's most prestigious police officers, coincidentally named George Washington Walling, stepped into the fray. Walling later served as police superintendent, a reward he earned for his heroic leadership in restoring order during New York's Draft Riots of 1863, which saw the city hit by two days of what resembled open field combat over conscription in the Civil War. In the midst of the conflict between the Union and Confederate states, Congress passed a law stating that men between the ages of 20 and 45 were eligible for conscription into the Union Army, with the exemption of the affluent who could afford to buy their way out of military service.

What started as a protest against the Draft Law quickly turned into a full-scale race riot in which white, mostly Irish, dissenters began attacking black people throughout the city. Many Irish refused to fight for the abolition of slavery and spoke out with resentment at having to risk their lives for a people they disliked and who, they stated, competed for their jobs. During four days of violence, the mob attacked, tortured and killed a large number of black people, including one man who was lynched. The ferocity of the street violence was such that President Abraham Lincoln was forced to divert five regiments of the Union Army from the battlefield of Gettysburg to restore order.

The crowds, particularly the women, beat policemen and soldiers, the agents of upper-class and federal power. After Colonel Henry O'Brien of the Eleventh New York Volunteers used a howitzer to clear Second Avenue and killed a woman bystander and a child, the crowds (when they found him the next day) smashed his face to a pulp, then stripped, tortured and shot him in the head and hung his broken body from a lamppost.[9]

Of all the horrific events that took place during the riots, without doubt the most reprehensible was the arson attack on the Colored Orphan Asylum, which was located on Fifth Avenue between 42nd and 43rd Street. The asylum was managed by the Association for the Benefit of Colored Orphans and, at any given time, housed between six hundred and eight hundred children. On 13 July an infuriated mob of five hundred rioters broke into the house and set it alight. While the staff and children were making their escape, New York police, most of whom were Irish, valiantly saved all the remaining children. At the same time, a crew of firefighters simultaneously fought the flames and the horde. When it was over, more than a hundred people lay dead, though there were unconfirmed reports of the death toll reaching significantly higher numbers. What is certain is that, in terms of loss of human life, it was the most destructive outbreak of urban civil unrest in New York's history.[10]

Walling made his reputation as a tough and honest law officer, who worked tirelessly to free the force from its connections with corrupt Tammany politics. He was asked by the newly formed Metropolitan Police to arrest Mayor Wood on charges of corruption and inciting a riot. Walling volunteered to make the arrest unescorted and went to City Hall to see Wood. The Mayor flatly refused to submit to arrest and had Walling dragged out of City Hall by a squad of Municipal Police officers.

After being ejected from the mayor's office, Walling returned to the office of the City Hall judge. The magistrate issued an arrest warrant, and there, in the presence of Sheriff Jacob Westervelt, they put their heads together to consider the legal options available for bringing to book Mayor Wood. As they pondered the matter, a crowd of disgruntled Metropolitan officers were taking matters into their own hands. The cops were understandably less than delighted to learn of the mayor's refusal to comply with the order to abolish the Municipal Police. They did not hesitate to take their anger to the streets, which touched off what became the most surreal of all New York riots.

A throng of angry Metropolitan officers in uniform marched on Wood's office, demanding the mayor's head for his complicity in supporting the Municipals. The moment they reached the steps of City Hall, the group was met by hundreds of waiting Municipals, batons at the ready. Sticking his head behind Wood's door, Commissioner Matsell reported excitedly and a trifle overhastily that the Metropolitans had been beaten back:

> Unwilling to push their luck too far, Walling and his party withdrew from City Hall. But just as they did, the Seventh Regiment of the National Guard came marching down Broadway with drums and bugles blaring, en route to a ship that would take the troops to Boston for a patriotic celebration. Halting the procession, the Metropolitan Police commissioners called on National Guard commander, Major General Sandford, the same soldier who had cleared the streets of gang rioters, for assistance. He ordered the regiment to fix bayonets and deploy for action.[11]

Walling's second attempt to place Wood under arrest met with success. This time the respected police officer marched into the mayor's office accompanied by the imposing military figure of Sandford. One look out the window at the cordon of troops surrounding the building sufficed to persuade Wood that it was game over. The mayor gave himself up and was led away under armed escort. Reporting on the events of the day, the *New York Times* declared it was

> the firmness and energy of Major General Sandford that prevented the Mayor from plunging into a short but desperate career of still more reckless crimes, the consequences of which it is fearful to contemplate. As it is, the offences for which he has already been either arrested or prosecuted form but a small portion of those for which it is to be hoped that he will be brought to punishment.[12]

Alas, a few hours later the Tammany scion was back at his desk, following an appearance before a magistrate crony and Tammany Machine apparatchik who summarily dismissed the charges against him.

The tentacles of the all-powerful Tammany extended to every nook of New York officialdom, and even gained notoriety in literary fiction and cinema. In Leslie Charteris's 1935 detective novel *The Saint in New*

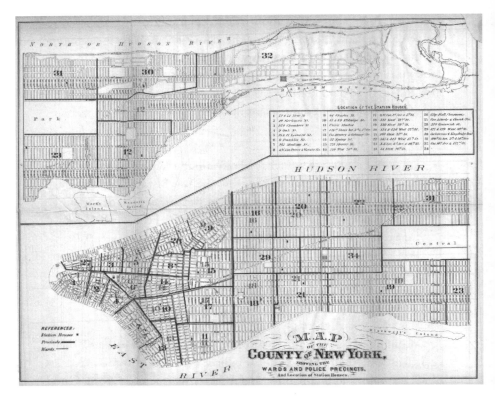

Vintage map of the New York City police precincts, 1871.

York, set in the early twentieth century when Tammany ruled the city's political roost, Inspector Henry Fernack explains the sinister machinations of Tammany to Simon Templar ('The Saint'):

> 'Up, up at the top of this city,' he said slowly, 'there's a political organisation called Tammany Hall. They're the boys who fill all the public offices, and before you were born, they'd made electioneering into such an exact science that they just don't even think about it anymore. They turn out their voters like an army parade, their hired hoodlums guard the polls, and their employees count the votes.'

The book became a hit 1938 film of the same title, starring Louis Hayward as Simon Templar.[13]

Wood's release had the effect of injecting even greater fighting spirit into the opposing police forces. The conflict was played out in the remaining weeks of summer, when New York found itself plunged into a scenario resembling that of a Wild West town. The city now had two police departments, the Metropolitan and Municipal forces, each claiming legitimacy, while in the absence of any semblance of effective law enforcement the streets of New York fell prey to criminals of every description. There was, in fact, little if any sign of police control in the weeks that followed Wood's farcical arrest. The Metropolitans and Municipals engaged in an ongoing skirmish for possession of police stations and office buildings. There were even instances when a suspected felon would find himself the victim of a tug of war, with one officer trying to place him under arrest and another fighting to release him. The outcome of this ludicrous rumpus was finally settled in the courts, which ruled once and for all to disband the Municipals.

Tammany Shenanigans

Wood's departure from office in 1862 did not bring down the curtain on a deep-rooted conspiracy of corruption by Tammany Hall and the police. This snaky tale of graft, kickbacks and fraud between the Tammany bosses and police officialdom continued to poison city life for a century thereafter. Meanwhile, in 1894, New York was hit by a bombshell development: the formation of the Lexow Committee and its exposure of a flourishing culture of graft within the police force. The city's first major police scandal involved organized prostitution, counterfeiting, extortion and voter fraud, sprinkled with a liberal measure of brutality. This deluge of criminality at the hands of the people entrusted to pursue the city's criminals was brought to light by a crusading clergyman, Reverend Dr Charles Parkhurst.

> The tall, slender, be-whiskered minister launched a vitriolic attack on Mayor Hugh John Grant, who had taken office in 1889, and his Tammany cohorts. They were, Parkhurst thundered at a Sunday sermon in 1892, nothing more than a pack of 'polluted harpies that, under the pretence of governing this city, are feeding day and night on its quivering vitals. They are a lying, perjured, rum-soaked and libidinous lot.'[14]

This was a period in which immigration and the growth of manufacturing intensified ethnic tensions. Recent arrivals from Europe and the Caribbean fell prey to swindlers and were fingered as the source of widespread lawlessness, public drunkenness and more serious crimes. Assaults on black people were common coin and led to violent racial riots. Prostitution and gambling flourished in this anarchic atmosphere, while New York's red-light Tenderloin district became a national symbol for urban depravity.

Grant, the youngest mayor in the city's history, taking office at the age of 31, defied Parkhurst to substantiate his charges. The minister was hauled into court, a humiliating experience since Parkhurst admitted he was unable to offer proof of the accusations against the police. He then embarked on a fact-finding crusade into New York's underworld, accompanied by private detective Charles Gardner. Disguised as ruffians, they both paid a nocturnal visit to a dance hall, lodging house, whisky saloon and opium den. Parkhurst left somewhat shaken from these houses of horrors to deliver an impassioned sermon recounting what he had experienced. The Presbyterian minister then organized the multi-faith City Vigilance League, which launched a citywide grassroots surveillance team. Parkhurst was two years into his campaign when one of his parishioners, the former senator Thomas Collier Platt, who was boss of the New York State Republican Party, decided to go on the attack against his Tammany enemies. Platt pushed through the appointment of a joint investigative committee headed by his ally, State Senator Clarence Lexow. The threat of a full-blown judicial review into corruption prompted Tammany strongman Richard 'Boss' Croker to flee to Europe, while a number of saloon owners decamped to other cities in the United States or to Canada.

When New Yorkers picked up their morning paper to read the committee's final report, they found themselves gazing in disbelief at what amounted to a catalogue of immorality and vice. The pay-offs were euphemistically listed under the police department's 'annual budget'. In addition to the government's official appropriation of $5.1 million for the police, the department was able to rake in brothel contributions amounting to $8.1 million. The committee heard testimony that police officers took bribes of $300 to $500 for opening a brothel and collected monthly fees of $50 to $100 from the operators. Saloon owners' contributions amounted to $1.8 million a year and gambling-house receipts totalled $165,000. This was in addition to collections from merchants, street-corner peddlers and others to the tune of $50,000, not to overlook a hefty $60,000 in fees squeezed out of new members of the force. This brought the grand total of annual graft money to more than $15 million.

Eyewitness accounts can exercise a powerful influence on the outcome of judicial proceedings, and the Lexow Committee was no exception. At one point during the hearings, a brothel owner said that when she tried to shut down the business and retire, her police 'protectors' demanded that she keep it going. They were determined to continue collecting their fees, which in most cases ranged from $25 to $50 a month. To refuse, she added, would have brought a painful reprisal. There was a standard $500 charge for allowing a bordello to reopen after a raid, usually when a new captain took over a precinct. The police graft machine operated across a diverse range of businesses throughout the city. Even steamship company managers spoke of monthly payments to patrolmen for keeping a sharp eye on the piers. But the most damning evidence of all, collected by Chief Counsel John Goff, came from within the police force itself.

One of the principal whistle-blowers to appear before the inquiry was Captain Max Schmittberger, a German American police officer who gave evidence on corruption in the force in exchange for a promise of leniency. He presented the committee with a catalogue of underhanded dealings involving himself and his former boss, the thuggish Broadway squad officer Alexander 'Clubber' Williams, also known as 'Czar of the Tenderloin'. Schmittberger was let off the hook, and in 1912, his reputation restored, he served a brief spell as police commissioner. Williams was called to the stand, where he unleashed a sufficiently aggressive and arrogant display of vitriol that effectively discredited his claims of innocence. His feeble attempt to explain how he had come by the money to purchase a seventeen-room house and a yacht on a policeman's salary verged on the risible: 'I bought real estate in Japan and it has increased in value.' Next to step into the dock was Timothy J. Creeden, who admitted having shelled out $15,000 of borrowed money to pay a police official to approve his promotion to the rank of captain. And on it went.

By the end of 1894, the Lexow Committee had amassed more than 10,500 pages of testimony, of which no less than 9,500 were related to corruption in the department. The evidence presented exposed police cooperation in electoral ballot fraud, which, if successful, earned the officer involved a promotion. But that was a mere drop in the overflowing bucket of sleaze. Brothels were taxed from $35 to $50 a month. With the connivance of a number of rotten police and politicians, the city played host to more than a thousand numbers racket establishments. From each of these places, the officer involved collected $15 a month. Saloon proprietors paid

$20 a month for police 'protection'. In some neighbourhoods, shopkeepers forked out as much as $60 for the privilege of allowing policemen to carry their goods from one side of the street to the other. The racket of payments handed over for joining the force and obtaining promotions netted the police $7 million a year, though the committee stressed this was in all likelihood a modest estimate.

Public disgust at this display of entrenched vice in the police force was expressed by the *New York Times*, which pointed the finger at the department's highest echelons in an editorial. 'It cannot be expected that the public will be credulous enough to believe that the Commissioners have tolerated these profitable abuses without having any share in them.'[15] This outrage brought about what became known as the Committee of Seventy. This was an alliance of prominent citizens who put together a nonpartisan ticket aimed at ousting the Tammany mob in the 1894 mayoral election. The strategy worked and the Machine suffered an epic setback that November. The reformist William Lafayette Strong won a landslide victory in the New York race, a win achieved in no small measure thanks to the Lexow Committee's shocking revelations. The successful outcome of this inquiry was twofold: the issuance of a grand jury presentment against the Metropolitan Police, and Tammany's electoral hammering.

Enter the Rough Rider

William Lafayette Strong, like the crusading Fiorello La Guardia, the sworn enemy of the Mafia who came along half a century later, was elected to office in 1895 on a Fusion Party ticket. This coalition was made up of Republicans and anti-Tammany Democrats. One of Strong's first acts on moving into City Hall was to appoint former U.S. Civil Service Commissioner Theodore Roosevelt as president of the four-man Board of Police Commissioners. Located in a large stone building at 300 Mulberry Street in the heart of the city's squalid tenement area, the police headquarters housed the members of the Board of Police Commissioners, inspectors and captains who commanded the rank and file of the force along with the Detective Bureau. At that time, the New York police maintained 36 police stations with a force of about 3,600 patrolmen, roundsmen and officers.

Many people's abiding image of Theodore Roosevelt is that of a sabre-waving Rough Rider leading a cavalry charge up San Juan Hill in the 1898 Spanish–American War. Perhaps an even more daunting task for the future U.S. president had been his fight to end corruption while serving as New York City police commissioner, a post he was given three years previous to his illustrious military exploit. Roosevelt by no measure conformed to the popular stereotype of a tough, growly New York police official. He was a scion of the New York upper classes, who dressed and spoke as befitted a man of privileged upbringing. 'He favoured a pair of eyeglasses with a gold chain over his ears, a cutaway coat with tails that almost reached the top of his shoes, a gold-topped cane and a silk hat. He used expressions such as *dee-lighted*, that struck the city police as bizarre, causing them to ask one another, "Who's the dude?"'[16]

New York Police Commissioner – and later U.S. president – Theodore Roosevelt, at his desk in 1895.

A month after taking office in 1895, Roosevelt took his first step towards professionalizing the police by requiring every man on the force to learn how to swim. This came after the case of one Policeman Michael Nolan, who had leapt into the Harlem River to rescue a boy who had fallen into the water. Nolan was rewarded with a medal, but shortly afterwards one of his colleagues, who had dived into the Hudson, failed to save a woman committing suicide because he was unable to swim. By the next year, the police were for the first time routinely equipped with firearms, when Roosevelt authorised the purchase of the .32 calibre Colt New Police Revolver.

Roosevelt was in every respect a hands-on commissioner, most conspicuously when it came to instilling discipline in the force. It was a common sight to find him, along with his friend the social reformer and journalist Jacob Riis, keeping a watch on New York streets at night. They would meet between midnight and 2 a.m. on the steps of the Union League Club on 37th Street, off Fifth Avenue, and amble about on the lookout for patrolmen, many of whom tended to spend their shifts drinking beer in the darkened recesses of saloons off the main avenues. On one occasion, Roosevelt discovered that only one out of ten patrolmen was pounding the beat – others were spotted chatting on street corners, while one was slumped fast asleep on a butter tub in the middle of the pavement. When roused by this bothersome outsider and told to go about his duty, the officer groggily waved him off. He was one of several officers ordered to report to police headquarters the day after Roosevelt's late-night tour.

The commissioner had no tolerance for officers who flouted their duties. In remarks addressed to 22 newly promoted roundsmen in November 1895,[17] Roosevelt thundered:

> The board thinks well of you, but we shall hold you to a rigid account-ability for what you do. In one precinct we reduced all the Roundsmen because they were not attending to their duties. We shall judge you by the discipline of the men under you. I am disappointed with the way the men patrol. They don't patrol. They lounge, loiter and talk with each other. I don't want a multitude of small, frivolous com-plaints. We want you to see that the men do their duty.[18]

Roosevelt can be applauded for his rigorous effort to shake up some of the corrupt institutions deeply embedded within the police. A note-worthy and lasting action taken shortly before he left office was to beef up the force with 1,600 new patrolmen, who were recruited on a merit system that prioritized physical and mental ability. Until that time, jobs were handed out to those who could demonstrate the appropriate political allegiances. In spite of his most strenuous efforts, Roosevelt's years as police commissioner cannot be deemed a resounding success. One of the thorniest issues about his reformist zeal is that it came into conflict with large segments of the population. The most controversial campaign was Roosevelt's failed attempt to put a stop to Sunday drinking in saloons, a practice that thrived in blatant defiance of the law. The commissioner's puritanical crusade involving blue-collar workers ended in a head-on collision, above all with the city's large community of German immigrants. The problem was that, with most people working a six-day week, Sunday was the only time they had for relaxed socializing with a few beers.

By the end of 1896 Roosevelt had begun to direct his ambitions to attaining national office. He sensed that his calamitous anti-drinking campaign was the tipping point of his career at Mulberry Street police headquarters. His instinct proved correct: city elections that year saw Mayor Strong's Republican-led coalition turned out of office by New York voters, who were angry over the attempt to deprive them of their weekend pleasures. In the 1897 mayoral election, Tammany once more grabbed the reins of power in City Hall with Democratic candidate Robert A. Van Wyck.

A City Is Born

A defining moment in New York's history came on 1 January 1898 when Manhattan and the four outlying boroughs of Queens, the Bronx, Staten Island and Brooklyn were consolidated into the City of Greater New York. At the previous night's New Year's Eve celebrations, with temperatures hovering below the freezing mark, the first mayor of New York City, Robert A. Van Wyck, bundled in his camel hair overcoat to brave the bitter cold atop a podium, led the official proceedings to mark the event. Thousands of people flocked into Manhattan that night in defiance of a driving snowstorm to participate in the festivities and thrill to the thunder of a hundred-gun salute in Central Park. On that first day of 1898, a new metropolis had come into being, one of 3 million inhabitants, a city larger than Paris and not far behind the sprawl of London. Gotham had taken a bold and pivotal step into the twentieth century.

New York City police patrol wagon, 35th Precinct, 1887.

A team of City Hall officials, along with the city's lawgivers, had spent more than a year preparing for this day. The outcome of their labours was the Greater New York Charter, enacted in 1897. In magnitude, this was a document worthy of Tolstoy's *War and Peace*. Its 1,250 pages embraced every conceivable facet of city activity, from fixing boundaries and the functioning of the municipal courts to setting the rules for street cleaning and sewer maintenance, not to overlook improbable topics like levying taxes on foreign insurance companies. By far the most extensive section of this ponderous tome, occupying 63 pages, was devoted to the organization and functions of the newly created New York City Police Department, whose acronym became NYPD.

At the stroke of a pen, the consolidation of Greater New York into a single political and administrative entity with one law enforcement agency placed a range of more than 300 square miles (780 sq. km) under the NYPD umbrella. Until that time, the various communities beyond the waters of Manhattan were policed by a patchwork of semi-independent forces. Brooklyn had its patrolmen, doormen (security guards, in today's parlance), bridge-keepers, medical teams and superintendents of telegraph operators. Within the City of Brooklyn itself (the third largest metropolis in the U.S. at the time), Coney Island maintained its own detachment of law enforcers, so too Staten Island, Long Island City and other districts of the outlying boroughs.

These officers were transferred to the NYPD, an organization set up along almost military lines, similar to the structure adopted by the Municipal Police more than half a century earlier. The governing body of the department was the Police Board, on which, as in the past, sat four persons supervising a hierarchy formed by a chief of police, four deputy chiefs of police, two inspectors of police and a range of officers. Each had responsibility for units of fifty patrolmen, starting with one captain, four sergeants, an equal number of roundsmen, two doormen and an unspecified number of detective sergeants, not to overlook a corps of forty police surgeons.

The early years of the new century brought substantial changes in the police department's modus operandi, especially for the cop on street patrol. The policeman's working day was modified from a system of two patrols and four sections to a six-section system, while doing away with the platoon designation. What this achieved was to set a daily tour of duty to twelve hours, of which eight were spent on patrol and four in reserve. The six sections were divided into two on patrol, one in reserve and three off duty.

The six-section system wiped out the hardships patrol officers were obliged to endure under the two-patrol regime. It also did away with some of the abuses committed by the police themselves, such as going home for meals and leaving their streets unattended. Cops now needed to eat near the precinct and spend no longer than thirty minutes at the local cafeteria. NYPD Commissioner General Francis V. Greene demanded legislation to permit the urgent expansion of the force. His reason was to boost the numbers of the night patrol force in order to take advantage of the new telephone signal system installed for police use.

These were testing days for the fledgling NYPD. A recently enacted bill known as Raines Law increased the cost of liquor licences, raised the drinking age from sixteen to eighteen and prohibited the sale of alcoholic beverages on Sundays, except in hotels. It was foreseeable that scores of 'Raines Law hotels', often located directly above saloons, would start to flourish across the city. A year after the law came into force, 1,500 were in operation in New York. Thus saloons became hotels with bedrooms, which in turn fomented prostitution. New Yorkers were much given to raucous living at the turn of the century. This was, after all, the preeminent American city, built on the back of the great waves of European immigration and the consolidation of the five boroughs, and bolstered by the development of the city's infrastructure and the incredible construction boom that took place over the next thirty years. This great and rapid development was the precursor to the furore of the Roaring Twenties.

New Yorkers were not inclined to have their lust for drink and pleasure curtailed by puritanical lawmakers. The police were often to bear the brunt of this libidinous celebration of the new urban powerhouse. One night a few months after the consolidation of the five boroughs in 1898, Patrolman Francis Quinn found himself confronted by a 1,000-strong mob in Broadway. The enraged crowd was protesting the arrest of Aloysius Van Slyck, a drunk who had climbed onto a hansom cab to deliver a speech against alcohol restrictions. Quinn swung his nightstick at the mob, but on they came, until he pulled out his revolver. Three officers on adjoining posts rushed to his rescue, scattering the crowd right and left with their sticks. Van Slyck was dragged to the 30th Street Precinct, where he was locked up on a charge of disorderly conduct.

The NYPD could boast of some remarkable officers in the ranks in the early days. On 30 May 1903, Inspector William McLaughlin at the Adams Street Brooklyn headquarters could scarcely believe his eyes when he opened the previous night's booking ledger. Eleven arrests in less than 24 hours, all made by one policeman, Patrolman Francis Carberry, who had been sent out on his first patrol as a plainclothesman. Strolling about in what is now the stylish Brooklyn Heights, Carberry pulled in an Italian organ grinder whose two sons were soliciting pennies from

William Stephen 'Big Bill' Devery was the police department's last super-intendent, and the first to hold the title of Chief of Police in 1898.

passers-by. The man and his children were booked for begging. He then returned to his assigned area and promptly arrested a couple who were 'misbehaving' in the open. He later came across three 'beer-filled' young men entertaining a crowd with songs and dances. They too were marched off to the station house. Finally, Carberry brought in three more men found drinking in public, bringing his catch to eleven, a record for a police officer in a single night.[19]

With the election of Van Wyck in 1897, the Tammany Machine had regained control of City Hall. Under the leadership of Richard Croker, before his flight to Europe, the Machine once again reigned supreme until the election of Mayor Seth Low in 1902. Tammany had essentially gobbled up the Democratic Party, turned the local ward heelers' clubs into gangs and the gangs into clubs, so that organizations like the Limburger Roarers or the Bowery Indians served as a front for criminals as well as a social welfare agency, pursuing the management of vice in a business-like fashion.

Tammany bosses acted swiftly to put one of their stalwarts into office as chief of police. William Stephen 'Big Bill' Devery, a puppet of Boss Croker, began his career as a Bowery bartender. That was until 1878, when he bribed a Tammany politician to allow him to join the police force. Not only was Devery corrupt to the core, he cheerfully accepted the role of crooked cop and once crowed, 'If there's any graftin' to be done, I'll do it. Leave it to me.' His lust for graft rose to outrageous levels, even by Tammany standards. Along with two Machine cohorts, Devery formed a syndicate that was netting the trio more than $3 million a year from a multitude of illegal gambling rackets, ranging from pool halls to full-scale casinos. In a display of breathtaking arrogance, when in March 1900 Devery was summoned to appear before a grand jury investigating charges of corruption, he replied to every question put to him with a stark, 'I won't talk.'

In 1902 the reformist politician Seth Low stepped into the mayor's office, and as one of his first acts, he sacked the chief of police. Devery expressed few regrets over his dismissal, for by now he had amassed enough dirty money to purchase a West End Avenue mansion and open a property business in Queens.

* * *

THE NYPD BEGAN life as an organization wholly different in structure and scope to its predecessors. The composition of the new force gradually started to reflect the growing ethnic diversity of New York City itself. A decade after its constitution, the department put its first black patrolman on the beat. Samuel Battle was an immigrant from North Carolina whose early years hardly presaged a career in law enforcement: he was caught stealing money from a safe as a teenager. Even his own family predicted he would spend his life behind bars. Determined to prove them wrong, he moved to New York, where he studied for the NYPD civil service exam and was sworn in as an officer in 1911. Battle, all 6 feet, 3 inches and 280 pounds of him, became an icon of his day. He was assigned to a district of Harlem, where he worked with delinquent youths and set up summer camps and sports activities. Many years later in his career, in 1943, the shooting of a black suspect by a white police officer triggered a race riot that lasted two days and resulted in six deaths, some five hundred injuries and a similar number of rioters and looters placed under arrest. Battle was well known to Mayor Fiorello La Guardia, who called him in to restore calm. That feat alone earned him celebrity status in the force. The corner of West 135th Street and Lenox Avenue is now named the Samuel J. Battle Plaza in his honour.[20]

* * *

THE FRAMERS OF the new police regulations had taken into account the vast increase in size of New York's waterways that came with the city's consolidation. This needed to be kept under surveillance and afforded protection following the merger. Overnight the police found themselves placed in charge of 146 square miles (380 sq. km) of navigable sea and 576 square miles (1,490 sq. km) of waterfront surrounding New York City. Thievery at the piers had been an almost everyday occurrence from as far back as the mid-nineteenth century.

Police regulations specifically singled out the waterways as an issue requiring special attention. New York was at the time the country's busiest port, with vessels steaming in daily from all parts of the world, laden with cargo and unwitting passengers who became a tempting morsel for even the most casual dock thief. It now fell under the NYPD's remit to impart and enforce 'proper rules and regulations for the safety of passengers . . . in the navigable waters embraced within the public limits'. An offensive was launched mainly against the thugs of Corlears Hook, a Lower East Side slum and the site of the city's first tenements, located between the Manhattan and Brooklyn bridges. Ingloriously, Corlears Hook was the neighbourhood with New York's greatest number of

Tammany Hall octopus, depicting the many tentacles of the Democratic Party's control of New York City government.

prostitutes, which gave rise to the expression 'hooker'. This reflects how difficult living conditions in New York's poorer areas could be: many of these sex workers were engaged in dual occupations, employed as fur seamstresses, book folders, umbrella sewers, tailoresses and milliners by day, and street walkers in their after-work hours.

The charter laid down strict rules of conduct, pertaining to officials and patrolmen alike, for carrying out their duties 'at all times of day and night, to preserve the public peace, prevent crime, suppress riots, mobs and insurrections, disperse unlawful or dangerous assemblages, protect the rights of persons and property, preserve order at elections and at all public meetings . . . arrest street mendicants and beggars and observe and inspect all houses of ill-fame and gambling houses'. On pain of dismissal it was forbidden to accept gratuities and make contributions to, or join, any political organization. The document even took into account Roosevelt's bête noire concerning drinking while on duty, stating in no uncertain terms: 'Intoxication is sufficient ground for the removal of a police officer, whatever may be its extent.' However, these provisos were somewhat mollified by a curious loophole: 'The taking of liquor in a sudden emergency and with a reasonable expectation that it will sustain failing ability, is justifiable. In such a case a police officer commits no breach of discipline and no conduct unbecoming an officer.'[21]

In spite of the list of stringent regulations that set standards for proper police behaviour, not least of which was the threat of dismissal for transgressors, documentary evidence reveals that massive pay-offs to the police from assorted quarters were still a way of life at the turn of the century. Perhaps 'way of survival' might be a more fitting epithet, at least for those patrolmen with large Irish and German families to feed. It was standard procedure in the early twentieth century for a captain to collect $40 from a patrolman to approve a request for enrolment in his precinct. This was a useful source of income to defray the $200 bribes these same captains were obliged to hand over to the local Tammany bosses each year to keep their relationship sweet. Salaries in the NYPD at the outset ranged from $1,500 a year for a roundsman to $6,000 for a chief of police. Patrolmen were hired on a starting salary of $800, roughly equivalent to $23,000 today. The wage for entry-level police is currently $40,500, a salary still pitifully below the $57,800 median individual income in New York City.

Low-level corruption was embedded throughout the force. This might take the form of free meals, discounted services, gratuities at Christmas from local merchants and other instances of petty misconduct. Instances of truly eye-catching delinquency, such as those exposed by the Lexow Committee, were comparatively few in number and well concealed from the public eye. Police involvement in unlawful activities can only be partially explained as a response to difficult living conditions. A century ago, as now, financial difficulties were a standard feature of other low-paid professions such as teaching and nursing. The difference was that the cop in the street worked in close proximity to criminals and their illegal activities. These felons were only too happy to dole out bribes to law enforcers prepared to look the other way and allow them to get on with their criminal activities. On the patrolman level, this amounted to small-time gangsterism. Moving up in the ranks, far larger sums routinely exchanged hands between precinct captains and Tammany politicians. From the early years of the twentieth century onwards, the scourge of corruption was to worsen beyond anyone's imagination. This came with the advent of Prohibition and the rise of New York's organized Mafia, who saw the stakes of graft and violence ratcheted up to truly epic proportions.

3

The Slippery Slope

The new century started on a particularly grim note for NYPD investigators, most prominent among them Detective Sergeant Giuseppe Petrosino, known to all as 'Joseph', who in 1908 was named head of the recently created Italian Squad. The unit was put together five years after the formation of the department's Bomb Squad. It was set up by Petrosino himself, later promoted to lieutenant, to deal with dynamite bombs used by the Mafia to intimidate immigrant Italian merchants and residents. The police had a desperate need for Italian speakers in a city with more than half a million Italians, an immigrant group that accounted for a full sixth of New York's population. Petrosino, all 5 feet 3 inches of him, was a cop held in high regard. He had earned the esteem of even so demanding a taskmaster as Theodore Roosevelt. Petrosino was also fluent in several dialects. This enabled him to take in hand offences in every cultural segment of the Italian community. He was assigned to the Lower East Side, the home turf and breeding ground for New York criminality.

One problem for the department was that most police officers were of Irish, German and, to a smaller extent, Jewish extraction. This played conveniently into the hands of the Italian-dominated Mafia that had by now taken almost complete control of the city's underworld. Italian immigrant mobsters would plan and discuss their criminal activities in the cafés that dotted Little Italy's Mulberry Street and its environs. They crafted their strategies with impunity, in Sicilian and Neapolitan dialects, knowing the cops were unable to understand them.

One of the Mafia's inaugural actions in becoming an airtight and vicious syndicate centred on the so-called Murder Stable in East Harlem, a neighbourhood that was home to many Italian immigrant families in the early 1900s. The stable was a row of makeshift wooden shacks between East 107th and 108th streets that served as a dumping ground for victims of Mafia executions. The targets were mostly racketeers who had unwisely attempted to muscle in on Mafia territory. In 1901 Petrosino uncovered this ill-famed stable, which contained at least sixty bullet-ridden bodies. He raised the alarm at the NYPD by also revealing that more than 1,000 gangsters from Sicily and Naples had now made New York their base of operations. Petrosino was acutely aware of the dangers posed by the mass influx of Italian immigrants, among whom were many accustomed to living beyond the law. In 1905 he warned that, unless more effective measures were taken, the police would find themselves powerless to take on the army of some 5,000 *camorristi* (crime syndicate members) who had moved into the tenements of lower New York. A news report of the time stated, 'So systematized has the campaign of brigandage become, that members of the band are employed in many of the small Italian banks scattered around the East Side, to monitor the deposits of the small merchants. As the law stands at present, we are helpless to a great extent against these desperadoes.'[1]

The Mafia rang in the New Year by leading the NYPD a merry chase on one particularly ghastly homicide, the 1903 barrel murder of Benedetto Madonia, a droopy-eyed, hook-nosed member of a Sicilian counterfeiting ring who had fallen foul of the mob. The police had been staking out a Lower East Side butcher's shop to gather evidence against three Sicilians who topped their list of suspects. These were Ignazio 'Lupo the Wolf' Saietta, Tomasso 'The Ox' Petto, and Saietta's cousin and Mafia supremo Giuseppe Morello. On the evening of 12 April, a mysterious new face turned up at the shop in Stanton Street in the Bowery. When the suspect, dubbed 'the newcomer' by the police surveillance team, emerged alone from the shop, officers followed him to a patisserie in Elizabeth Street, a Mafia hangout owned by Pietro Inzerillo. He was subsequently tailed to a small bistro belonging to Morello. A stake-out was called that night when it became apparent the suspect intended to remain until the late hours inside the restaurant.

Early in the morning of 13 April, police received a call from a horror-stricken housewife in Little Italy. The woman had come across a barrel lying in the street – not an infrequent sight in a neighbourhood of back-to-back shops that every morning received deliveries of produce. Empty barrels were often left outside for collection by goods suppliers. The one in question contained a melange of sawdust and sugar, along with a scattering of cigar ends – and a corpse, its throat slashed from ear to ear. The victim had taken seventeen stab wounds, his genitals had been severed and stuffed into his mouth and his tongue had been sliced in two, a special practice reserved for squealers who had violated the Mafia's code of *omertà*, manly silence. New York's debut barrel murder was to underscore the complexities often involved in obtaining a police conviction of Mafia villains.

The news of this grim discovery instilled dread in the local citizenry. It was feared that a ruthless syndicate was preparing to unleash a violent crime wave throughout the city. This was compounded by a lack of faith in a police force scorned by many as lacking the skills and, above all, the experience to take effective action against the criminals. Newspapers like the *New York Times* fanned the flames of fear with almost daily coverage of the barrel murder and its aftermath, pointing the finger squarely at Sicilian mobsters. Three days after the mutilated corpse was discovered, the paper ran a front-page story on the arrest of a handful of suspects:

> Eight Sicilians, said to be members of the Italian Mafia and one of the most dangerous bands of counterfeiters that ever operated in this country, were arrested on the Bowery last evening, and the United States Secret Service agents and the local police are certain that they were responsible for the murder of the man whose body was found in a barrel in East Eleventh Street, near Avenue D, early Tuesday morning.[2]

This was followed over the next few days by headlines that clearly revealed the authorities' inability to track down the murderers, despite the fact that, by now, Police Inspector George W. McClusky had rounded up another five suspects. 'Barrel Murder Unsolved' declared the *New York Times* on 19 April. It was reported that at least fifty people had viewed the victim's remains, but none had been able to make a positive identification. 'While Inspector McClusky does not doubt that the murderers are among the men he has in his custody, he confesses that the failure to identify the body has sadly hampered him in his work and that as a result, he might be forced to let most of them go.'

McClusky himself lamented that the investigation was being conducted in a back-to-front fashion. 'If we knew the identity of the man, we

Detective Lt. Joseph Petrosino (left), with two colleagues, escorting a Mafia hitman into custody (second from left).

could go ahead and work on a motive for the crime, and thus obtain some tangible information.'[3] Police found the search for local witnesses an unforgiving task. At the mere mention of some suspects' names, in particular that of the Sicilian Mafia boss Giuseppi 'Clutch Hand' Morello, many Little Italy residents would cross themselves in fear, and others frequently appealed to parish priests for spiritual protection.[4] The *New York Times's* story the next day was captioned in laconic terms: 'Barrel Murder Deepens'. The days rolled on, with the police still unable to establish the victim's identity, much less that of his killers. Then, on 21 April, the *New York Times* was able to report: 'Barrel Murder Plot and Victim Known'.

Joseph Petrosino, the NYPD detective with the closest ties to New York's Sicilian community, was assigned to the case. Petrosino picked up hints from local informants that if an unnamed convict in Sing Sing Prison were to be approached, he might be able to establish the identity of the barrel victim. Petrosino found out that the prisoner in question was Giuseppi De Primo, a towering figure who was behind bars on a four-year term for counterfeiting U.S. currency. Petrosino travelled 30 miles (50 km) north of Manhattan to the maximum-security prison on the banks of the Hudson, where he and De Primo spent a few minutes chatting about the hardships of life in New York for Italian immigrants, and other mundane subjects. The detective then dramatically whipped out a photograph of the dead man. De Primo's huge body trembled. The convict identified the corpse as his brother-in-law, Benedetto Madonia.

The police were now convinced they had enough circumstantial evidence to arrest and obtain a conviction of Saietta, Petto, Morello and Inzerillo. This would prove to be a case of wishful thinking. There was, in fact, precious little to go on, apart from one or two reasonably incriminatory clues. Madonia's pocket-watch chain was still attached to his waistcoat, but the watch itself was nowhere to be found in the barrel. The police discovered a pawn shop ticket for the missing watch in Petto's possession, which in itself could only be classed as circumstantial evidence. A sugar distributor with a plant along the East River confirmed that his only customer in Little Italy was Inzerillo's pastry shop. Again, at best a coincidence that would not stand up as conclusive proof of guilt.

When the case came to trial, not a single witness dared to testify against the defendants. This included Madonia's son, who said he was unable to identify his father's watch. Morello and Lupo were given long prison sentences for counterfeiting, all things considered a more attractive option than the electric chair. The gang was cleared of murder, while Inzerillo did a short stretch for doctoring his U.S. naturalization papers. Those who ended up behind bars were at least spared the fate awaiting Petto and Inzerillo. After their release from prison, both men were murdered in 1905 by Mafia rivals. Inzerillo's death, however, remains shrouded in mystery, and it remains unknown if the corpse in the barrel was his. He was reportedly spotted five years later in the company of Morello and Lupo, when the police were tracking down the Morello counterfeiting racket.

The threat of Mafia violence was on the lips of many New Yorkers in the months subsequent to the Madonia barrel murder, which was the first to receive media coverage. The prevailing climate in the city mirrored a feeling of apprehension towards the Italian community, which in the early twentieth century numbered some 400,000, three-quarters of whom were from the Mafia's home territory of Naples and Sicily. This mistrust was due in part to the fact that, unlike the Germans, the Poles and, of course, the Irish, many southern Italian immigrants were either slow or reluctant to adopt the English language, living and working as they did within their own community. The press pulled no punches when it came to stirring up suspicion towards this least integrated of all groups of New Yorkers. 'The barrel murder is one of the many proofs that an infernal system of revenge through assassination, which has prevailed in Italy from the Middle Ages, has been imported here,' said the *Brooklyn Daily Eagle*.[5]

The *New York Times* was not one to be relegated to second division in the scaremongering game. The paper took a different, and indeed more relevant, angle by bringing in the other side of the story. This was the NYPD's purported inability to handle the threat of a rising wave of Mafia criminality. 'This city is confronted with an Italian problem which at the present time it seems unable to cope with,' the paper reported in a front-page story under a banner title that offered its anxious readership little comfort: 'Italian Crime and Police Incompetence'. The subheading read: 'Detectives of the Force Seem Utterly Unable to Unearth Black Hand Conspirators'. The report went on to chronicle how citizens were being sent Black Hand letters demanding extortionate sums of money, with the threat that non-compliance meant 'a pistol shot or dynamite bomb will end their days. Boys have been kidnapped and held for ransom. Homes have been wrecked with dynamite on the failure of their tenants to pay blackmail.'

The *New York Times* held the NYPD responsible for the supposed failure to put a stop to the banditry and racketeering: 'In its efforts to grapple with these forms of crime, the Police Department has shown itself especially incompetent. Officers make a series of theatrical arrests, only to be compelled to let their prisoners go.'[6] The ethnic breakdown of inmates doing time in the city's two main correctional facilities, Sing Sing Prison, 35 miles (56 km) from New York, and Auburn Prison, also located Upstate, would appear to undermine the story's accuracy. At the time, prison inmates of Italian descent numbered two hundred, with 83 Irish and 70 Russians making up the other major groups.

In 1908 Petrosino was sent to Sicily on a covert police mission, one that was fated to end in tragedy. His brief was to gather the prison records of a number of Sicilian criminals who had emigrated to the United States. The federal government had agreed to deport them as soon as proof of their criminal pasts was made available. One afternoon, he was walking through a park in Palermo on his way to his hotel when he took three bullets from an unknown assassin and died on the spot, at the age of 48. He had been gunned down on the orders of Mafia bosses who judged him a traitor to his people. The trip to Italy was meant to have been kept secret, but the news had been leaked to the *New York Herald*. This news was relayed to the mafiosos, who promptly mobilized one of their Old World hit squads. His body arrived in New York aboard a Cunard Line steamship on 9 April 1908. Three days later, funeral rites were held at Manhattan's St Patrick's Old Cathedral in Mulberry Street. More than 250,000 mourners followed the procession behind the horse-drawn carriage as it wound its way through the cobbled streets of Little Italy. Mayor George B. McClellan Jr declared that day a public holiday to allow people to pay their respects to the city's fallen hero. Petrosino's body was laid to rest in Calvary Cemetery in Queens, which, with a pinch of dark irony, is also the burial ground for a number of well-known Mafia chieftains. To further venerate his memory, in 1987 the city dedicated a park in his honour in Lower Manhattan's SoHo District, appropriately named Petrosino Square. The murder was never solved.[7]

Petrosino's name lived on beyond New York City landmarks. In the years following his death, Petrosino's figure was exalted to stardom in literature and cinema. In the 1970s British novelist Frederick Nolan wrote two books based on Petrosino's career with the NYPD, *No Place to be a Cop* and *Kill Petrosino!* Petrosino was also immortalized in four films that centred on his life, starring top personalities like Ernest Borgnine and Gene Kelly. The latest screen version was *The Black Hand*, a 2018 production with Leonardo DiCaprio in the lead role.

Hard Italian Cops

The Italian Squad never numbered more than five officers, yet in its short lifespan the unit attracted a variety of illustrious individuals. Petrosino was venerated by his younger protégé Michael Fiaschetti, a beefy, hard-jawed individual who never shirked from employing the brute force for which his hero was famed and feared. Fiaschetti turned his nose up at traditional investigative procedures. He boasted of his keenness for roughing up suspects, a technique he preferred to that of relying on a stable of stool pigeons. The Italian Squad's activities were gradually wound down after Petrosino's assassination until, in 1918, NYPD Commissioner Arthur Woods resuscitated the unit under Fiaschetti's command.

Two years later, Fiaschetti was sent to Italy in his predecessor's footsteps. His mission as a covert agent – travelling under the alias Don Pasquale, disguised with a goatee beard and luxuriant moustache – was to track down Vito Cascio Ferro, a prominent member of the Sicilian Mafia. Fiaschetti would often adopt the guise of a beggar or, at other times, that of an Italian nobleman. Cascio Ferro had fled New York when Petrosino ordered his arrest for alleged involvement in a particularly nasty 'barrel murder'.[8] While in Naples, Fiaschetti's task was to seek out the identity of the mobster who had ordered Petrosino's death. He took on this duty with much enthusiasm, as Cascio Ferro had been identified as a prime suspect in the assassination. The mission did not have a successful outcome, apart from Fiaschetti managing to get away by the skin of his teeth without having his cover blown, a development that would have brought a violent death. Fiaschetti uncovered evidence that another mafioso, instead of Cascio Ferro, may have been responsible for ordering Petrosino's murder. This put him in a tight spot, all the more so when, while attending a meeting of racketeers, he learned that several Camorra chieftains had been tipped off about his own clandestine presence in Italy. Moreover, he found out that they were attempting to put together a description of this police infiltrator. This was the moment in which Fiaschetti deemed it tactful to put some distance between himself and his homeland.

Back in New York, Fiaschetti became a crusader in the war against the Mafia extortion ring known as the Black Hand. His particular bugbear was Giosuè Gallucci, a numbers racket boss who operated in East Harlem, which was at the time home to some 100,000 Italians. Gallucci was known in gangster circles as the 'King of Little Italy', thanks to the close alliance he kept with Tammany Hall that guaranteed him immunity from police harassment. Gallucci himself was eventually subject to Black Hand extortion and was killed by a rival gang, thus depriving Fiaschetti

Colonel Arthur Hale Woods (1870–1942) who became New York City Police
Commissioner in 1914. In 1917 he became an assistant director on the Committee of
Public Information on foreign propaganda.

of the opportunity to bring Gallucci to justice after years battling to haul
him into court on charges of racketeering.

One of the last cases in Fiaschetti's career on the force was the 1921
kidnapping and murder of five-year-old Giuseppe Varotta. The abducted
boy's body had been dumped in the Hudson River when his parents
failed to come up with the $2,500 ransom demanded by the kidnapper.
Fiaschetti led the team that arrested five suspects, all of whom were found
guilty and sentenced to life imprisonment. Thanks to Fiaschetti's success
in bringing the gang to justice, the Mafia put a $5,000 price on his head.
Treason was at the top of the Mafia's pay rates. It far exceeded the paltry
$10 for a knife slash on the cheek, which served as a warning to anyone
suspected of crossing the mob. For those who failed to heed said warning, $100 was offered for a full-blown murder contract.

In 1922, when many members of the Italian community angrily
demanded to know why there were no Chinese, Polish or English squads,
the NYPD felt obliged to disband the unit. Fiaschetti retired from active
duty with the police two years later. He ran a private detective agency
for a few years and returned to public service for a while in the early
1930s, when Mayor Fiorello La Guardia took him on his team as third
deputy commissioner of markets. His charge was to clean up the city's

racketeer- and politician-dominated markets, in which payment of protection to thugs and solicitation of gifts by city purchase agents were a major feature of business.

The honours bestowed on Fiaschetti were many and diverse, from two gold medals awarded by the mayor of Akron for capturing the slayers of four Ohio policemen, to the title of Chevalier of the Crown, presented by Italy's King Victor Emmanuel for Fiaschetti's testimony against two killers in an Italian court. This most colourful among New York law enforcers of his day, known to his colleagues as 'Treat 'Em Rough Fiaschetti', used this moniker in the title of his memoirs of a career with the NYPD that spanned nearly two decades: *You Gotta Treat 'Em Rough*.

* * *

POLICE CAPTAIN Richard Edward Enright was appointed NYPD Commissioner in 1918, when his predecessor Frederick H. Bugher was forced out of office after only 23 days on the job. If Bugher's career goes down as the briefest in NYPD history, Enright's eight-year tenure was the longest of any commissioner until the appointment of Lewis Joseph Valentine in 1934, who served eleven years under the diminutive, pipe-smoking Mayor Fiorello La Guardia. Bugher was sacked by Mayor John Francis Hylan for allegedly failing to take action against members of the Motorcycle Squad, several of whom were charged with accepting bribes. The Italian Squad was dissolved on Enright's watch, a controversial decision to say the least, as in those days New York's big-time organized crime was almost the exclusive domain of Italian mobsters and hit men, whose job it was to make certain the rackets operated without hindrance.

Death in a Barrel

As a front-page news story, Tammany may have been eclipsed by the Mafia's more eye-catching endeavours, but the Machine's political power was still everywhere to be seen, including in the police. Tammany had high hopes for their mayoral candidate William Jay Gaynor, but it was an ephemeral political marriage, as the bosses were to find out to their dismay. Gaynor won the election and, in 1910, became the City of Greater New York's fourth mayor. The bearded and immaculately attired former New York supreme court justice took office at the comparatively late age of 61. Gaynor also had the dubious distinction of being New York's only mayor to have been hit by a bullet in an assassination attempt. Soon after embarking on an ocean liner bound for Europe, Gaynor survived a shot in the throat by a former dockworker who had been laid off in the city's cost-cutting campaign.

Shortly after taking over at City Hall, Gaynor remarked in a speech, 'The world does not grow better by force or the policeman's club.' It was a clear message to Charles Francis 'Silent Charlie' Murphy, the long-standing head of Tammany Hall and the 'Grand Sachem' who ran New York politics for a generation. Gaynor's point was that he was prepared to break away from the Machine that had backed his candidacy, and instead set his sights on an administration of reform. Gaynor was an austere, strong-minded man. Rain or shine, he marched more than 3 miles (5 km) every day from his Brooklyn home to City Hall. Such acts of fortitude ingratiated him with New Yorkers, which in turn bolstered his defences against Tammany vitriol.

Gaynor endeared himself to voters with his 'the best government is the least government' rhetoric. Newspaper readers ignored the broadsides fired at their fellow New Yorker by the Hearst media machine, whose derogatory editorials failed to tarnish Gaynor's colourful personality. His admirers included many of a social station well above that of the ordinary citizen. After Gaynor's death thirty prominent New Yorkers, bearing such regal names as Astor, Carnegie and Vanderbilt, formed the Mayor Gaynor Memorial Association, which honoured his memory with a bronze bust that stands in Brooklyn's Cadman Plaza.

As mayor, Gaynor was swift to take action against what he denounced as a scourge of professional misconduct within the police rank and file. As a first step, he ordered an end to arbitrary arrests, a time- and money-wasting practice that left one in four suspects released without charge within 48 hours. One of his best-known schemes was to organize the detective force along the lines of London's Scotland Yard. Previous to that, a small squad of detectives operated without a centralized command structure. The deputy police commissioner, who had been accountable almost exclusively to the commissioner, would henceforth answer to no one but the mayor. The upshot of this innovation was to diminish the power and prominence of the commissioner of police. From now on, it was the mayor who would exercise primary responsibility for the work of the detectives in his department in bringing criminals to justice and combatting vice. The prevention and detection of crime had always been in the hands of the police, but from this point on ultimate authority in police matters was vested in the office of mayor.

To Gaynor fell the questionable privilege of overseeing the first trial and conviction for murder of a serving NYPD officer. The unfortunate cop in question was Lieutenant Charles Becker. He was tried, convicted and executed for the first-degree murder of Herman 'Beansie' Rosenthal, a member of New York's Jewish Mafia, who was gunned down near Times Square in 1912. Rosenthal operated several illegal gambling dens – one of which was located in the Hotel Metropole, still in existence as the Casablanca Hotel – in what was Manhattan's disreputable Tenderloin district. Rosenthal was given a free hand to carry on his racketeering business, as he enjoyed the patronage of Tammany boss Tim Sullivan. He also counted on the protection, or so he thought, of Becker, a giant of a man and a former beer-hall bouncer. Becker served two masters: he was collecting bribe money from Rosenthal, reputedly 20 per cent of the casino's take, while simultaneously having to answer to his official boss, Commissioner Rhinelander Waldo.

The events that took Becker and four members of the villainous Lenox Avenue Gang to the electric chair are mired in controversy that starts from the day Rosenthal was murdered outside the Hotel Metropole. Some accounts have it that Becker staged a raid on the gambling den on Waldo's orders, while other reports make no mention of the lieutenant's direct involvement in the bust. Becker was accused of masterminding the shooting, allegedly to stop Rosenthal blowing the whistle hours before he was due to testify to a Manhattan grand jury. Becker was the only police officer in the U.S. to receive a death sentence for murder, in one of the clumsiest executions on record. It took nearly ten minutes for the electric current to put him out of his misery. The hitmen were named as 'Lefty' Louis Rosenberg, Harry 'Gyp the Blood' Horowitz and 'Dago' Frank Cirofici, all of whom went to Sing Sing's hot seat along with Becker, who professed his innocence until the moment he was strapped in the chair.

The Becker–Rosenthal affair gained widespread notoriety across the U.S. The story even found its way into popular literature. In F. Scott Fitzgerald's *The Great Gatsby*, the gambler Meyer Wolfsheim speaks of having been present in the Metropole with Rosenthal moments before the murder. The case was pronounced the 'trial of the century', but more than a century later, conclusive evidence of Becker's guilt is yet to be forthcoming.

Working as a New York City police officer has never been an easy job, but rarely was being part of the force as trying as in the first decade of the twentieth century. 'By now, police reform was no longer just a spasmodic impulse,' James Lardner and Thomas Reppetto explain in their book *NYPD: A City and Its Police*. 'It had become an industry – the seemingly permanent livelihood of an interlocking directorate of citizen activists and advocacy groups. Exposing or decrying police misdeeds was also an accepted way go get ahead in the prosecutorial and journalism fraternities.'[9] The authors argue that, for cops, bribing was the normal state of affairs, tantamount almost to a perk that came with the job. They cite the case of Assistant District Attorney Frank Moss, an eminent anti-corruption lawyer who once asked a veteran police captain, 'But why do you men take this dirty money?' The reply was, 'Wouldn't we be fools if we didn't? Everybody in New York works his job, even the ministers.' Moss asked if the police official really believed that. 'I know it,' the captain declared. Moss persisted, 'But the money was so dirty.' 'We fumigate it,' the captain replied. 'It's clean after we get it.'[10]

The average New York patrolman had earned a reputation for his free-wheeling use of the wooden truncheon. It required little provocation for a cop on the beat to start swinging his club at drunk or rowdy citizens, or those who in any way defied police authority. Early in his administration, Gaynor put out an order to the police to cease deploying brutality and carrying out indiscriminate arrests. Those who clubbed people they suspected of illegal or antisocial activities were summoned to appear before the mayor himself. Gaynor later issued a follow-up directive that did away with the nightstick altogether. In the course of his first year in office, between 1909 and 1910, the mayor's crackdown on police thrashings and arbitrary detention had slashed the number of arrests by more than 30,000.

Within days of his electoral victory, the new mayor embarked on a shake-up of the Police Department hierarchy. Police Commissioner William Frazer Baker, who had been suspected of involvement in the city's gambling racket, was discharged forthwith after having spent a little more than a year in the job. Baker was never formally charged with any wrongdoing, but he had somehow amassed enough of a fortune to purchase the Philadelphia Phillies Major League baseball team, which he owned until his death in 1930. Baker's replacement was the severe, almost cadaverous James Church Cropsey, a Brooklyn lawyer and personal friend of the mayor. Though Cropsey was lacking in police experience, Gaynor appreciated the skills he displayed in the courtroom. A man of great family wealth, Cropsey could afford to accept the appointment despite the 80 per cent cut in salary that went with the job. For his first deputy commissioner, Gaynor shifted his sights from the bar to the press by taking on former newspaperman Clement J. Driscoll. As an investigative reporter, Gaynor believed Driscoll possessed the ability to root out vice rings, from gambling houses to brothels.

By far the most conspicuous appointment was that of William J. Flynn as second deputy commissioner in charge of the Detective Squad, a choice that went hand-in-glove with Gaynor's determination to reform the police. The career of this portly, lavishly moustachioed and incorruptible son of Irish immigrants stood as a testimony to American social mobility. Flynn began his working life as a Manhattan plumber. He then rose to head the New York division of the U.S. Secret Service, where he was sent to tackle Black Hand mafiosos of the Giuseppe Morello mob who were alleged to be behind the murder of Flynn's friend and colleague, Joseph Petrosino. Flynn's international reputation as a top-notch detective went before him. While employed by the Secret Service, he had proven himself remorseless in raiding and shutting down gambling houses that, before he arrived on the scene, were assumed to be impregnable Tammany fortresses.

The Commissioner and the Mafia

Flynn's arrival at the NYPD was greeted with jubilation by the media. 'A real detective bureau – that's what New York is to have,' said the *New York Times*. 'William J. Flynn is to provide it. Scotland Yard is to have nothing on us.' The paper did not attempt to disguise its fervour for the man it considered as nothing short of a Sherlock Holmes alter ego:

> It has taken until the administration of Mayor Gaynor to find a public official who understands the difference between a glorified policeman and a detective. It is unprecedented for a deputy commissioner to go out and do detective work, but that is a precedent that Flynn means to create . . . Flynn's men are to hunt down crooks. They are

to find burglars, second-storey men, yeggmen [safe crackers], murderers. They are to put an end to New York's reputation as the City of Undetected Crimes."

Flynn took over the Detective Bureau in October 1910. On the day he stepped into the domed Beaux-Arts NYPD headquarters at 240 Centre Street, he launched his offensive against Mafia criminals, with some notable successes. The chief detective achieved something approaching hero status when he became the first New York cop to rescue two kidnapped children, eight-year-old Giuseppe Longo and seven-year-old Michael Rizzo, who had been abducted for ransom. Thanks to Flynn's investigations, the Brooklyn Mafia boss Sebastiano Di Gaetano was arrested in connection with the kidnapping, though the charges were subsequently dropped for lack of evidence. Di Gaetano vanished in 1912, never to be seen again. The bold swoop did, however, result in convictions for several members of a kidnapping gang, who were each handed 35- to 49-year sentences.

Clement Driscoll was eventually shunted aside to give Flynn command of the Vice Squad, a job he threw himself into with gusto. In April 1911 Flynn led a contingent of axe-wielding police in a dawn raid on the Hesper Club in Second Avenue, an establishment supported and frequented by the cream of Tammany potentates and known as the haunt that the gamblers treated as their private club. The simultaneous chopping down of the front and rear doors to the club, with the arrest of a clutch of infuriated patrons, made an eye-catching story for New York newspaper readers.

Then, in April 1911, Flynn informed Gaynor he was resigning from the NYPD. He did not make public the reason for his sudden departure, but it was no secret that his frequent clashes with Commissioner Cropsey had come to a head in February of that year. Cropsey was furious with his deputy for refusing to disclose a list of detectives he had sent off on secret assignments, or detail the nature of their work. Flynn was not prepared to put his men in personal jeopardy and sabotage their collective work to hunt down Mafia gangsters. He argued that his appointment as head of the Detective Bureau was a personal matter between himself and Mayor Gaynor.

In the end, Flynn enjoyed the last laugh over his former boss and adversary. Cropsey angrily handed in his resignation after one year as

NYPD commissioner, using the excuse that he had lost Mayor Gaynor's confidence. Cropsey was later selected to serve as a New York district attorney, and was subsequently cited as a potential Republican candidate for mayor and even governor, though he was never selected to stand in either campaign. Flynn, on the other hand, was promoted to the lofty position of director of the Federal Bureau of Investigations (FBI) in 1919. He was also designated president of the World Association of Detectives, and for a few years devoted his time to writing crime novels, most outstanding of which was *The Barrel Mystery*, a thriller based on the 1903 Little Italy barrel murder. His passion for creative writing also took him into the world of scriptwriting for the motion picture industry. His last professional venture was as editor of a literary magazine that bore his name, *Flynn's Weekly Detective Fiction*. The slick publication became the longest-running and most successful journal of its genre.

Gaynor went through three NYPD chiefs during his term in office. As authors Bernard and Jon Whalen put it: 'In selecting his third police commissioner, Gaynor decided not to take any more chances. The last thing he wanted was more conflicts with his head of police. The next commissioner had to be willing to carry out his programmes without question.'[12] In his search for Cropsey's replacement, Gaynor cast his net beyond the NYPD to seek a suitable candidate. After weeks of weighing up a list of candidates, he enlisted Fire Commissioner Rhinelander Waldo to take up the top post. The mayor placed his trust in a man who had successfully tackled corruption in the Fire Department, with the hope that he might achieve a similar clean-up in the NYPD. Waldo soon proved himself an innovator in policing strategy.

The new commissioner's most striking break with tradition was the introduction of a system of fixed-post stations, which he launched in July 1911. This plan involved setting up stationary street posts for patrolmen. One half of the members of this squad were placed on duty at every fourth street crossing. They in turn exchanged places every two hours with the men on foot patrol. One month into the trial, Waldo could report that half as many burglaries had been recorded as in the preceding month. The police themselves were less than happy with what they denounced as forced confinement to the fixed posts of duty. True, they were obliged to stand in the middle of the street for two hours at a stretch, not so enjoyable a pastime as having the freedom to patrol a six-block extent while engaging in conversation with other patrolmen and passers-by. However, this made them accessible to victims of crime and able to respond quickly to situations requiring police intervention. All things said, many people might consider this a preferable way to spend a winter's night in New York than shivering for nine hours on rounds.

The patrolman's working life involved perils other than violent confrontations with drunk and disorderly elements encountered in the street. 'Patrolling tenements around the clock, where tuberculosis and smallpox were rampant, meant that a great number of them succumbed to disease.'[13] The high mortality rate was the impetus for the formation of the Patrolmen's Benevolent Association (PBA), to which officers paid a monthly subscription of 25 cents that guaranteed their widows and orphans a $175 compensation if they were killed in the line of duty.

Waldo began to unveil new projects almost as fast as the NYPD could put them into practice. A fortnight after taking office, the new commissioner set up New York's first police Motorcycle Squad. The team was formed ostensibly to cope with the strain of increased traffic, but its remit was quickly expanded to the pursuit of criminals. Crooks were beginning to pull off heists and other felonies by making quick escapes in their cars. With a spike in robberies involving getaway cars, the department purchased a squad of Ford Model T Runabouts, the forerunner of the Highway Patrol, which were deployed one to each precinct. The

Officers of the police motorcycle machine-gun squad in 1918.

city's first drive-by shooting took place in 1910, when the bullet-ridden body of a Brooklyn gangster, John Lewis, known as 'Spanish Louie' for his Sephardic Jewish background, was found crumpled up on the corner of 12th Street and Second Avenue. He had been gunned down by rival gang members firing a rifle from a sleek Pierce-Arrow saloon. Lewis was a particularly sinister hitman who always wore a black suit over a black sweater pulled up to his chin. James Cagney played Rhinelander Waldo in the 1981 film *Ragtime*, based on the E. L. Doctorow novel of the same title. In 1920 the department made its debut foray into the radio age. The first Radio Motor Patrol (RMP) cars were equipped only with receivers, meaning officers still had to go to call boxes to acknowledge the transmissions. Nearly a decade later, the Motorcycle Squad had been issued with armoured motorbikes for use in fighting criminal gangs.

The advent of patrol cars all but eliminated the familiar face of the neighbourhood police officer. Police were pulled off neighbourhood rounds to fill cars. Criminologist and former police officer Peter Moskos notes: 'The rise of telephone dispatch transformed both the method and purpose of patrol. Instead of watching to prevent crime, motorised police patrol became a process of merely waiting to respond to a crime.'[14]

Isabella the Sleuth

One of the most celebrated police cases of Waldo's administration was the taxi heist of 1912. In keeping with the new trend in motorized gangsterism, in this instance a cab was used as the getaway car. The person who was instrumental in solving the case was Isabella Goodwin, whose thirty-year career on the force began in 1896, when she was hired by Theodore Roosevelt as a police matron. Before long, her extraordinary fact-finding talents were recognized by the NYPD. She was taken on as an undercover agent and sent out to obtain evidence against more than five hundred swindlers, from bogus astrologists and palmists to psychics and quack doctors. During her long years of service, Goodwin was credited with successfully solving numerous cases and was known to fellow officers as the 'Fearless Mrs Goodwin'.

Goodwin was a woman with a stern demeanour and a penchant for dark frocks and flamboyant hats. Her nondescript appearance was a studied art as well as a professional benefit, for she bore no distinguishing marks that would make her stand out from the crowd. She was a reserved person, reluctant to talk in public about herself or her work. In one of her rare newspaper interviews with the *New York Times* in March 1912, Goodwin reveals the composed, resolute temperament of a fearless New York detective: 'Of course, I have made many enemies as a result of my investigations . . . Many people would like to take revenge, but I am not afraid. It is this element of danger that makes the work fascinating.'[15]

Goodwin gained nationwide attention for her role in cracking a robbery committed by the so-called 'taxi bandits'. In February 1912 two bank messengers in a taxi carrying $25,000 in cash to the East River National Bank were attacked by a pair of thieves who forced their way into the cab. They made off with a stash of money equivalent to $675,000 in current purchasing power. The cabbie was brought in for questioning and the police identified two other suspects, but even with sixty detectives on the case the trail went cold for lack of hard evidence. That was when George Samuel Dougherty, an NYPD detective formerly with the Pinkerton National Detective Agency, came up with an idea.

In 1905 Detective Sergeant Joseph Faurot had set sail for England to study and report back on British fingerprinting methods. It took more than five years for Faurot to win over his superiors. That came about when a quick check of his files showed a match between the fingerprints at a burglary scene with those of career thief Charles Crispi. Faurot was applauded for his investigative success, but it was Dougherty who later introduced routine fingerprinting as a tool of the department's crime detection arsenal. He proposed putting Isabella Goodwin on the taxi bandits' trail. Unfortunately, Dougherty was unable to collect fingerprints at the crime scene, which would have enabled him to put the new procedure to the test. Goodwin went into action by impersonating the sister of the landlady of a boarding house frequented by friends of the suspects. She was able to pick up information that led the police to track down the culprits, a triumph that earned her a promotion to first grade in the Detective Bureau, with a salary of $2,250 a year. Goodwin thus became the first woman municipal detective, not only in the NYPD but worldwide.

Mayor Gaynor made a remarkable recovery from his assassination attempt, though his speech was permanently impaired and the bullet remained lodged in his throat for the next three years. During his time as mayor Gaynor was a highly popular figure with New Yorkers and was on several occasions mentioned as a strong candidate for New York state governor, or even U.S. president. Of course, no one was giving odds on

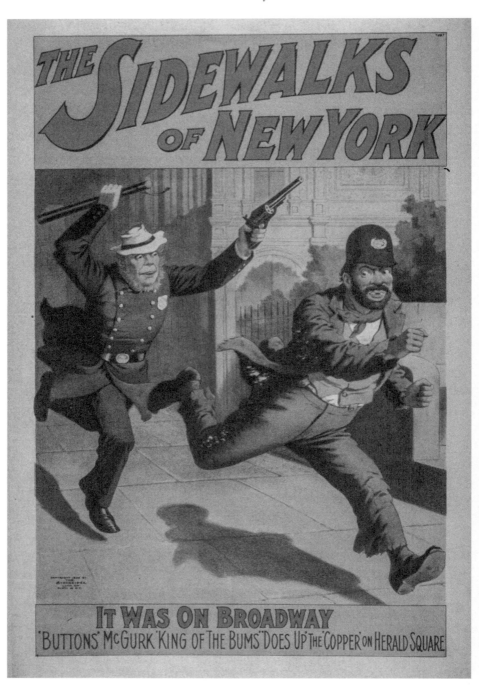

Poster depicting of a police chase through the streets of New York in 1896.

Tammany support for the man they scorned as a traitor to the Machine. It was therefore hardly surprising that the bosses refused to nominate him for re-election to a second term. Gaynor ignored the snub and instead accepted to stand as the candidate for an independent group of voters. In September 1913, wearied by four years of working tirelessly to drill efficiency into the police department and weed out endemic corruption, he set off on a cruise to Europe. One morning, while relaxing in a deckchair, Gaynor died of a sudden heart attack.

On the morning of 12 September New Yorkers were shocked by newspaper vendors crying out the headline splashed across the front page of the *New York Times*: 'Mayor Gaynor Dies in Deckchair on Liner; Stricken While Alone'. The highly principled mayor, who had outfoxed Tammany and was loved by most New Yorkers, was a hard act to follow. City Hall needed to find New York's first acting mayor to fill the gap ahead of the election, which was scheduled for the end of that year. Ardolph Loges Kline was a blunt, bewhiskered retired U.S. Army brigadier general whose most memorable achievement during the three months he served as mayor was to sack Police Commissioner Rhinelander Waldo. Inexplicably for those not conversant with the intrigues of city politics, the mayor accused Waldo of 'childish behaviour' and a proclivity to 'break down the police department in a fit of pique'. Kline did not bother to elaborate on the accusations, but Waldo sensed something was afoot in his strained relationship with the mayor. He was preparing his resignation papers when Kline launched a pre-emptive strike and sacked the police chief. The motive for Kline's hasty action was simple: he argued that a state of confusion and uncertainty permeated the NYPD once news had leaked out that Kline's successor, 34-year-old mayor-elect John Purroy Mitchel, was intending to let Waldo go and replace him with his close friend Arthur Woods. The second part, at least, was accurate.

The 'confusion' and 'uncertainty' Kline had used in his rationale for sacking Waldo might have had some substance, but only in the days that followed the commissioner's departure. Waldo's successor was Douglas Imrie McKay, at 35 the youngest person to occupy the job. McKay held the position for all of five months, until the all-too-habitual antagonism surfaced between the New York mayor and his police commissioner. McKay had served under Waldo's command in 1907, where he learned that an officer had to be quick with his hands to survive. He took an uncompromising approach to lawbreakers, an attitude much to the liking of Waldo, who promoted him to first deputy commissioner.

One of the most controversial schemes of McKay's fleeting time on the job was to enforce a section of the Penal Code that allowed the on-sight arrest of gangsters and other suspected miscreants. This work fell to the forty members of the Strong Arm Squad put together by McKay. When this squad was active, in the early years of the twentieth century, plainclothesmen would go out on routine round-ups of anyone caught disturbing the peace, which mostly involved felonies on public transport. This ranged from clubbing 'rowdies' on a Brooklyn train to wresting firearms from thugs on a Queens tram.

Under McKay's leadership the squad met with some notable achievements in reducing street offences, but this also earned him a reputation for overzealousness and public harassment. Another change he instituted was to restore the daily line-up that Gaynor had abolished. McKay was known as an early 'gangbuster' for his work in breaking up many of the street mobs that had plagued New York since the 1860s. His fervour for cleaning up the city did not stop at the criminal class, however, and he brought reform to the NYPD, above all in his efforts to put an end to corruption. McKay suspended several high-ranking officers known to be on the take, and on one occasion he demoted a police inspector to captain for allowing honky-tonks to operate in the Tenderloin district.

It was the free hand given the police to use their clubs that led Mitchel to regard McKay as a political liability:

> While it was true that he thought that McKay was an efficient administrator, Mitchel, the Bronx-born grandson of an Irish revolutionary, stepped into power on the strength of his sterling anti-corruption reputation. He was looking for someone who saw the police department as more than an organization that simply apprehended criminals. He wanted a visionary to create a department that interacted with society to prevent crime.[16]

The commissioner's militancy in dealing with New York's underworld became a source of concern to local Tammany Hall politicians. For the bosses, this posed a risk of the police muscling in on their lucrative sources of income. Likewise, a number of magistrates took issue with McKay's aggressive policies, as a result of which loiterers and assorted suspicious characters arrested on sight filled up the city's jails overnight. This created a problem by putting the brakes on the legal system, since in many cases charges would be dropped for lack of evidence. So, after less than half a year on the job, out went McKay and in came Woods.

Squire Woods Steps Up to the Post

As later developments were to confirm, Commissioner Waldo's abrupt sacking was not without its compensations. Woods, a Boston-born Harvard graduate and Theodore Roosevelt protégé, was a worthy replacement for Waldo. Moreover, he stood a cut above previous police commissioners in terms of education and worldly wisdom. Woods was welcomed into the upper echelons of New York society, having married the upper-crust Helen Morgan Hamilton, granddaughter of the financier J. P. Morgan. At the Groton Boarding School in Massachusetts, Woods had worked as English teacher to Roosevelt's children, as well as those of his boss's fifth cousin, the future U.S. president Franklin Delano Roosevelt. He was equally adept at hands-on police work, with hands that eschewed the white gloves of the Bostonian aristocracy.

Woods had served as deputy commissioner between 1907 and 1909, when he was in command of the city's Detective Bureau. He was fascinated by the art of stalking and shadowing, and frequently went out with other detectives to take a personal hand in cases. He had travelled across Europe, studying detective work methodology in Britain and other countries. By the time of his appointment in 1914 he was under no illusions about the stirrings of war and the threat that the approaching conflagration posed to the U.S. in general, and to New York in particular. A recent precedent that bore out Woods's fears was the explosion at Black Tom Island, near the Statue of Liberty. This was an act of sabotage by German agents attempting to destroy U.S. munitions that were earmarked for shipment to the Allies. The bombing took place in July 1916 and destroyed some $20 million worth of military goods. Several days before hostilities broke out in Europe, Woods ordered the Bomb Squad to monitor espionage activities by foreign agents on U.S. soil. He was well acquainted with counterterrorism work and had spent much of his time under Roosevelt hunting down anarchists.

The number of changes Woods introduced to the NYPD in less than four years bordered on the spectacular. To a large extent he drew on first-hand observations of European detective forces, whose academic credentials he greatly admired. These visits abroad inspired him to set up a range of bureaus modelled on continental lines. The arrest of more than two hundred criminals in his first year in office was achieved largely by diversifying the department into sectors of specialization, including homicide, robbery and common street felonies. Woods can be credited with the creation of the NYPD's modern Detective Bureau, a department that directs the work of an array of units. For Woods, the bureau's work would consist almost entirely in the detection of major forms of crime, 'felonies as opposed to misdemeanours', as he put it in a report. He set himself firmly against any form of collaboration with criminals in order to obtain information. In the past, police investigating a crime relied heavily on 'stool pigeons', who would barter information about what their comrades were up to in exchange for police protection, coupled with a certain amount of liberty and licence in their own activities. For Woods, this brand of favouritism was 'out of the question'. He encouraged good work by offering his staff salary increases based on a high success rate in crime detection and prevention.

Women on the Force

New York City enacted legislation to appoint female police matrons in 1889 and 1895. In 1895 the first woman to work at Police Headquarters, Minnie Gertrude Kelly, was appointed secretary to the Police Board. In 1912 Isabella Goodwin, who had joined the force in 1896, became the first female 'first grade' detective. Matrons were responsible for the care of the station house and the women and children detained there. During their long shifts they carried out searches on women under arrest, managed rough sleepers and drunks, responded to medical emergencies and tended to lost children.

> The New York police hired mainly working class white women – as the civil service entrance exam discriminated against African-American applicants – and many matrons were widows with a family connection to policing. Immediately, policewomen began to arrest more women knowing they would enter another woman's custody . . . In the 6th precinct, the number of arrests that involved women increased by almost eight per cent in two years.[17]

When the U.S. declared war on Germany in April 1917, a manpower shortage helped to bring more women into the force. Six women joined the NYPD as 'policewomen', a title that was later changed to 'patrolwoman', shortly before the twenty-strong Women's Police Precinct was formed in Midtown Manhattan. The officers' job was to deal with female offenders and runaways, in what was seen as a moral guardianship role. The recruitment drive during and shortly after the war also opened the doors for the first appointments of black women, overriding entrance-exam conventions. In 1919 Cora Parchment joined the force and was placed in charge of welfare work among the black community of Harlem and other areas of the city.

In January 1918, shortly before stepping down, Woods appointed Ellen O'Grady as the NYPD's first female deputy commissioner. This reflected a major step forward in ridding the early twentieth-century NYPD of its image as a club exclusively for men. It was a pioneering event that attracted much fanfare, albeit with a sad dénouement. Less than two years later O'Grady stormed into the commissioner's office and dropped her gold badge on his desk. 'I am leaving, commissioner. I am through with the police department,' she said. O'Grady later claimed, 'I have been hampered in every manner in the performance of my duty. I have been treated like a dog.'[18] She said the end came the morning her authority was undermined when, without prior consultation, two patrolwomen under her charge were put on a case.

In 1912 Isabella Goodwin had already earned renown as the department's first woman detective. Woods saw an advantage in having agents in civilian clothes on the job in place of an easily recognizable uniformed officer, and he encouraged the department to bring more women into the Detective Bureau. Without a doubt, the most intriguing female detective of the day was Mary Shanley, who joined the force in 1931 and, seven years later, was promoted to first-grade NYPD detective. Shanley was attached to the Pickpocket Squad for much of her 26-year career. She became the darling of New York crime reporters, who labelled her 'Dead Shot Mary', a nickname that in 2016 became the title of a one-woman show starring actress Rachel McPhee at New York's Bridge Theatre. Though Shanley was credited with more than 1,000 arrests, not once did she fire her gun at a suspect, though there were a number of close calls. One of these made headlines in 1941, when she fired into the air while dashing through the

Mary A. Shanley being congratulated by Mayor La Guardia, 1937, with Deputy Chief Inspector John Lyons looking on. She is credited with more than a thousand arrests in her career.

Capt. Edyth Totten instructs women police reserve in 1918. The NYPD's Women's Bureau was created six years later.

crowds along Broadway in pursuit of two larceny suspects. Her classic Wild West-gunslinger style cost her a temporary suspension that year when she was accused of discharging her pistol while intoxicated in a bar and grill in Jackson Heights, Queens. In her defence, Shanley swore she had drunk only half a glass of whisky to steady herself 'after a bout of dizziness'.

* * *

THE AMERICAN journalist and satirist Henry Louis Mencken offers some amusing as well as enlightening observations on the police he came across in the early 1900s. Mencken was astonished to learn that, as late as 1941, more than fifty college graduates had been appointed to the NYPD, in contrast to his 'reportorial days':

> In the days of my chief contact with the police . . . there was simply no such thing as a book-learned cop. The force was recruited, not from the groves of Academe but from the ranks of workingmen. The most talented police captain I ever knew was a meat-cutter by trade and had lost one of his thumbs by a slip of his cleaver. All the mounted cops were ex-hostlers passing as ex-cavalrymen and all

the harbour police had come up through the tugboat branch of the merchant marine.[19]

As the century progressed, police were evidently keen to bring in recruits of a higher intellectual calibre to deal with the complex challenges of increasingly sophisticated technology. But the standard patrol officer was still plodding the pavement much as in the past. Mencken humorously points out that 'an ordinary flatfoot' in a quiet residential section had his hands full on his daily rounds:

> In those days he might have to put out a couple of kitchen fires, arrange for the removal of a dead mule, guard a poor epileptic having a fit on the sidewalk, catch a runaway horse, settle a combat with table knives between husband and wife, shoot a cat for killing pigeons, rescue a dog or a baby from a sewer, bawl out a garbage man for spilling garbage, hold the sidewalk rubbernecks back at a funeral on his beat and flog half a dozen bad boys for throwing apples at a blind man.[20]

Tammany contemplated Woods's reformist zeal with disfavour. There were many within the Machine who strongly took issue with the commissioner's almost Messianic determination for tampering with established police procedure. One of the most contentious reforms involved the fixed-post system that had been devised by his predecessor, Waldo. Woods did away with a practice he considered too top heavy in manpower requirements. Instead, he freed up teams of police to patrol neighbourhoods within a demarcated range of streets. The system resembled an early version of the Broken Windows approach that was implemented in the mid-1980s. The idea behind this system was to initiate a crackdown on minor offences that blighted local quality of life while promoting the figure of the neighbourhood cop as a friend in uniform, someone known to local residents who would throw him a cheerful wave when he strode past.

In Pursuit of Corrupt Cops

Placing a meddlesome idealist in charge of the NYPD was bad enough, but one who worked in close collaboration with a Republican mayor?

Well, for the Machine's bosses, that was more than flesh and blood could bear. In the 1917 mayoral election Mitchel was booted from office by John Francis Hylan, the Tammany candidate who took the poll with the support of William Randolph Hearst. The all-powerful press baron, thanks to Tammany support, had twice been elected to Congress. The victory of true-blood Democratic candidate Hylan meant that the Machine was back with a vengeance. Woods followed Mitchel into exile, to be followed by the most transitory of all NYPD commissioner appointees, the hapless Frederick Hamilton Bugher, who held the job for the first 23 days of 1918. On stepping into office, Hylan almost immediately decided to replace the interim police commissioner for allegedly refusing to take 'guidance'. He got rid of Bugher, whom he quaintly decried as 'only negatively honest', though he did not elaborate on what that might mean.

Hylan's choice of Richard Edward Enright brought to the force a talented criminal investigator and well-known author of several works of detective fiction. His first novel, *Into the Net*, written while he was still on the force, was made into a now-lost silent film serial in 1924. He was the first man to rise from the ranks to become commissioner and was

NYPD Deputy Commissioner John A. Leach, watching agents pour liquor into a sewer following a raid during Prohibition in 1921.

famed for his robust criticism of the Mitchel administration, a stance that could not fail to appeal to his new boss. Enright's eight years as head of the NYPD made him the longest serving of any commissioner, until the appointment of Lewis Joseph Valentine in 1934.

Enright served throughout Hylan's term, during which time the NYPD was confronted with a series of complex problems, the foremost of which being the passage of the Volstead Act in 1919 that ushered in thirteen chaotic years of Prohibition. This puritanical calamity coincided with the massive demobbing of troops arriving home from the Western Front. These men arrived in a country immersed in an economic downturn, which by 1920 had plunged the U.S. into full-blown recession. Jobless, and without hope or support, many of these former soldiers turned to a life of delinquency. Enright reinforced the Strong Arm Squad to combat the crime wave that had begun to ravage New York. Enforcement of Prohibition, a cornucopia that fed straight into the hands of Mafia bootleggers and speakeasy operators, was a trickier knot to unravel. The commissioner is also remembered as the man who, in 1925, created a single facility for training NYPD officers. The Police Academy replaced three separate schools: one for detectives, another to train patrolmen and a third which taught the principles of horsemanship. The academy was modelled on training methods in use in five European countries that were observed on visits by Detective Inspector John J. Noonan, who also happened to be the department's chief expert on police bribery.

In 1921 the NYPD's activities came under investigation by a grand jury and the Legislative Investigating Committee, with graft and corruption the chief subjects. Based in part of the disclosures of the committee, the Citizens' Union and the press demanded Enright's resignation. The police commissioner initiated a series of libel suits to defend himself against charges of police bootlegging. In 1924 he brought charges against thirteen inspectors and a large number of deputy inspectors and captains, claiming that they had failed to prevent violation of the Prohibition laws, but he was never able to establish his allegations. Enright will be remembered as the crusading commissioner who introduced several praiseworthy changes in the years he served. He reduced the number of precincts, formed a special division to handle vice and gambling on a citywide basis, granted a day off to the force after every six days on duty, built up a large police relief fund and improved the pension system. Enright was also a fervent promoter of transnational police liaising efforts.

Police on horseback breaking up an anarchist riot in Broadway and 14th
Street in 1908.

To this end, he developed the International Police Conference (IPC) in
1922 to stimulate greater worldwide cooperation among police forces.
The organization was founded two years before Interpol and began as a
meeting forum for police chiefs from major cities in the United States.
With Enright's support, and some generous funding from advertis-
ing tycoon and policing aficionado Barron Collier, the group quickly
expanded to include participants from Canada, Latin America and
Europe. IPC conferences became important venues for police to discuss
and exchange ideas on new developments in crime, particularly regarding traffic control and narcotics. Enright resigned on 30 December 1925,
a day before his contract was due to expire. Both the commissioner and
Mayor Hylan stepped down on the same day, electing to forego one day's
pay rather than jeopardize the validity of their pensions by continuing on
the city's payrolls until midnight of the last day of the year. For the NYPD,
Enright's departure from the force was the start of a near decade-long
roller-coaster ride of instability and rapid turnover at the top.

4

'Don't Be Afraid to Muss 'Em Up'

New York's Roaring Twenties were in full swing in 1926. The famed Palm Restaurant began operating as a speakeasy in Second Avenue, the Savoy Ballroom kicked off as Harlem's focal point for dance, George Gershwin premiered his Concerto in F at Carnegie Hall and New York's 97th mayor, Jimmy 'Beau James' Walker, strutted into City Hall, carrying with him Tammany's blessing.

One of Walker's initial efforts to convince sceptics of his determination to run a clean administration was to offer the post of NYPD commissioner to George Vincent McLaughlin, who at the time held the office of state superintendent of banks. The candidate's ace card was his close friendship with State Governor Al Smith, who had lobbied hard for McLaughlin's appointment.

> Confident, aggressive and just thirty-eight years old, McLaughlin informed Walker that he would take the job only if given a free hand in running the department. Under Hylan the police department had been controlled by political hacks who permitted Tammany district leaders to conduct illegal gaming operations in their clubhouses.[1]

Walker assured McLaughlin he would place no restrictions on launching aggressive raids on these vice dens, adding that in future the NYPD would be run from police headquarters at 240 Centre Street instead of City Hall. What he neglected to mention was that, under Tammany-controlled administrations, the police commissioner served at the Machine's pleasure.

The NYPD's brawny, 6-foot-plus chief cop waded into the rats' nest of New York vice with a pair of Irish fists at the ready. By the end of his first year, McLaughlin could point with pride to having put an extra 1,600 cops out in the streets. He also achieved a 44 per cent reduction in robberies throughout the city. In fact, McLaughlin was no slacker when it came to self-aggrandisement. 'I'm the best police commissioner the city ever had,' he once bragged to a group of business leaders. Tammany was less enthralled with the commissioner's bluster and, in particular, his eagerness to clean up the police force and the city in general.

McLaughlin made his fatal mistake a little more than half a year after taking up the post of commissioner. He had organized a special squad to stamp out gambling, an activity banned in New York until the legalization in 1939 of pari-mutuel betting at horse races. The officer who led the anti-gambling offensive was steely-eyed Lewis Joseph Valentine. Despite his partiality for bow ties and smartly tailored suits, there was nothing genteel about this embodiment of the tough, plain-speaking New York cop. A few years later, Valentine was to loom very large indeed in NYPD annals.

McLaughlin had rescued Valentine from the NYPD wilderness, where he had been whiling away his time as a desk sergeant in the Greenpoint section of Brooklyn. This is where he had been banished after a falling-out with former commissioner Richard Edward Enright in 1918. McLaughlin promoted Valentine to deputy inspector in charge of the Confidential Squad. Valentine set to work by hitting Tammany's heretofore sacrosanct clubhouses. The Machine put its foot down when Valentine's team staged a late-night raid on a Democratic Party gambling den in Brooklyn. The bosses were outraged, and they immediately made their displeasure known to Walker, an issue that provoked a rapid breakdown in relations between the mayor and his police commissioner. McLaughlin's political enemies made the most of this toxic atmosphere by accusing the commissioner of disregarding the safety of his own officers in pursuit of an overzealous crackdown on crime. When confronted with the figure of six policemen killed and eleven others hit by gunfire since he took over at the NYPD, McLaughlin shrugged off the attacks. 'We are getting all the bad breaks so far,' he explained. 'The police are making splendid arrests, but luck is against them.'

After less than a year and three months on the job, in March 1927 McLaughlin handed in his resignation, bemoaning a lack of support from Mayor Walker. He took up a job as executive vice president at telegraph cable services producer Mackay Companies, a position he found hard to resist. The job came with a salary of $75,000 a year, compared with the $10,000 he had been earning as chief commissioner of the NYPD.

Walker appointed four police commissioners during his time at City Hall. The mayor took pains to enlist as McLaughlin's successor a lifelong friend and former law partner, Joseph Aloysius Warren, a Tammany loyalist whom Beau James, one of the mayor's nicknames, believed could be trusted to make no trouble for the Machine bosses. When Warren completed his swearing-in ceremony, Walker took him aside for a discussion about ridding the NYPD hierarchy of troublemakers. Heading the mayor's list was Valentine and his meddlesome Confidential Squad. Warren nodded and said he would see what needed to be done. Beau James was swiftly undermined by the man he assumed to be at his beck and call, for after a lengthy chat with Valentine, instead of packing him off to oblivion, Warren promoted him to deputy chief inspector. Valentine's star was in the ascendant, heading toward the zenith he would reach under the next mayoral administration.

Warren might understandably have expected this act of defiance to set him on a collision course with the mayor. If so, he had jumped the gun, for his career came unravelled as the result of a murder that took place on a winter's night near Lindy's, the Broadway delicatessen famed throughout Gotham for its cheesecake. Arnold Rothstein was a Tammany racketeer and prominent member of New York's Jewish Mafia, which operated a series of gambling dens. In 1928 he lost $320,000 after a bad run at a marathon poker game. Rothstein swore to his pals that the game had been fixed – he had no intention of paying off his debt. That night at Lindy's, he was called to the telephone. After a brief conversation, he grabbed his coat and swiftly departed the restaurant to dash back to his room at the Park Central Hotel in nearby Seventh Avenue. He was about to slip his room key into the door when he was shot in the abdomen by an unknown assailant. He died two days later, refusing in time-honoured Mafia tradition to identify his killer. No one was ever convicted of the murder, and the case remains one of New York gangland's unsolved mysteries.

Walker turned pale when he was told of Rothstein's assassination. He knew this would mean trouble with Tammany. In order to save face, the mayor desperately needed a scapegoat to take the wrap for the police's failure to arrest the killer of a Tammany stalwart. He did not have to look far, for the obvious sacrificial lamb was Joseph Warren. Walker called in his chief commissioner for a meeting. The mayor adopted an affable tone with the man he once hailed as the ideal person for the job, whose head he was about to place on the chopping block. He suggested Warren take early – that is, immediate – retirement. It was not only the Rothstein affair, as Walker tried to explain. In 1928 New York began tabulating the city's annual homicide rate. Rothstein was one of 404 murder victims on Warren's watch that year. The police had made few arrests and obtained even fewer convictions. Clearly the force, as led by Warren, was not up to the task. The commissioner demurred: should he not at least round up Mafia suspects who might shed some light on the Rothstein murder? The affair had by now become a nationwide press story. Walker stood his ground, leaving Warren no choice but to hand over his badge.

Warren left the post with regrets, but also with a sense of having escaped the clutches of a bullying boss and his corrupt cohorts. During the few years he served as commissioner, Warren had come under relentless attack by Tammany district leaders for allowing the Confidential Squad to raid their illegal gambling houses. This became a source of great frustration for the bosses, whose control over the lower courts ensured that few of their cronies were ever handed convictions for felonies. After Warren's departure, Walker came out quickly to praise him as 'an honest public servant'. Eight months later, the mayor who had demanded the police chief's resignation and criticized his alleged inability to see to violent crime joined the procession of pallbearers at Warren's funeral. At the age of 47, Warren, exhausted and suffering from severe depression, had entered a sanatorium, where he soon succumbed to a severe stroke.

A Dandy of a Cop

Grover Aloysius Whalen cut a distinctly dapper figure, even by the standards of the Roaring Twenties. New York City's official greeter was a towering, impeccably groomed and pinstripe-suited Tammany man to the core of his military bearing. As chairman of the Mayor's Committee on Receptions to Distinguished Guests, in 1927 Whalen was put in charge of organizing the city's gala reception for Charles Lindbergh on his return from the first non-stop flight across the Atlantic. It was New York's most elaborate ticker-tape parade ever, at which 60,000 people cheered the young aviator at Battery Park and many fans precariously perched on windowsills and skyscraper setbacks. Lindbergh was driven

Uptown in an open car, alongside Walker, to Sheep Meadow in Central Park, where he was to receive the State Medal of Valor from Governor Al Smith.

Walker was impressed by Whalen's seamless organization of this extravaganza. The mayor's admiration of 'Mr New York', the name which Whalen chose, with singular modesty, for the title of his autobiography, came to the surface a year later when Walker was on the lookout for a police commissioner to step into Warren's shoes. At the time Whalen was employed as general manager of the Wanamaker's Department Store empire, when Walker offered him the NYPD chief commissionership. The mayor had by now had his fill of political appointees. He decided to turn to the business world for help, even if it meant having to match Whalen's $100,000 salary at Wanamaker. Not one to be constrained by protocol, Whalen rang Walker to ask if the mayor would mind dropping into his office at Broadway and 9th Street to discuss the job offer.

At his meeting with the mayor, Whalen held out little hope that Walker would accept the stringent conditions he was about to lay down for accepting the position. In essence, what he demanded was carte blanche to run the NYPD as his personal fiefdom. Whalen insisted on being given a free hand in reorganizing the police department in the manner he saw fit. This included replacing the chief inspector and commanding officer of detectives with candidates of his choice. Walker would also need to abolish the system of forcing on the commissioner requests for appointments, transfers or promotions during his NYPD posting – which, by the way, Whalen stipulated he would accept for only one year. Whalen struggled to disguise his astonishment when Walker blithely nodded his acceptance to all demands.

Whalen lost no time in swinging his scythe around the turquoise-domed NYPD headquarters building on Centre Street. The new chief commissioner announced his General Order No. 1 on 18 December 1928, the day of his swearing-in ceremony. 'I will insist upon absolute loyalty from every member of the department,' the directive thundered. 'When an order is issued it is to be obeyed. No other form of order will issue. Merit and efficiency alone will govern our relationship to each other and to the public. We will be soldiers in a common cause – the maintenance of law and order and public safety in our city.'[2]

The first target Whalen set in his sights was Lewis Valentine. The commissioner could not sanction the Confidential Squad powers that allowed them to take over the authority of commanding officers without notice. The team's privileged status was for him a source of demoralization and buck-passing. He ordered the squad abolished forthwith. Valentine was informed through departmental channels that he was being demoted to the rank of captain and dispatched to a remote precinct in Brooklyn, there to lick his wounds until the moment came for him to take his revenge. On day two Whalen ordered an overhaul of what he decried as the 'slipshod' line-up system. What materialized from his efforts was the popular cinema image of the line-up room, with its platform and blackboard marking a suspect's height.

Next on Whalen's hit list that morning was Chief Inspector William Lakey, the man in charge of the uniformed force. Whalen did not beat about the bush: he accused Lakey of allowing morale to slacken. His subordinate was therefore freed up to pursue his career elsewhere, with immediate effect. Whalen then summoned to his office Inspector James D. Coughlin, commanding officer of the Detective Bureau. The commissioner conveyed his dissatisfaction with Coughlin's handling of the Rothstein murder case, a failure that had unleashed a storm of criticism from the press and an aroused public. Coughlin was sent off to file his retirement papers and gather his personal belongings. The two discredited officers were replaced by John O'Brien, a former patrolman under Theodore Roosevelt, and Inspector Edward Pierce Mulrooney, a cop much respected for having coped with long days of hardship on the Harlem rounds. O'Brien was sworn in as chief inspector, with Mulrooney appointed as his assistant.

Whalen was a resolute believer in the hands-on approach – the heavier the hands, the better – and he never flinched from accompanying his men on dangerous missions. One evening in his first week as commissioner he received a call in his Fifth Avenue home alerting him to a violent hold-up that had just taken place in Brooklyn. In a trice, Whalen ordered his driver to rush to his house and take him to the crime scene. There he found a cluster of detectives and patrolmen standing over the bodies of two masked intruders. The pair had rapped at the door just when a group of friends were in the middle of their weekly Saturday night poker game. The robbers then forced their way into the apartment, only to be confronted by one of the guests who, unfortunately for them, happened to be a former army marksman. He pulled a revolver from his jacket pocket and shot the two intruders dead. The driver of the getaway car was tracked down and arrested that same night. He was tried and convicted of abetting a felony and sent to Sing Sing. It was the sort of neat piece of work the commissioner wanted to see ingrained in the force.

The End of a Nightstick

Whalen was determined to enforce the Prohibition laws by relentlessly targeting what he estimated to be New York's 32,000 speakeasies. In carrying out their nightly raids, his men were quick to take to heart their boss's oft-quoted remark, 'There is plenty of law at the end of a nightstick.' This became an unspoken bone of contention between the commissioner and his City Hall boss. Walker himself was in his private life less than enthusiastic about the anti-drinking laws he professed to uphold. The 21 Club in West 52nd Street is today a classy dining and drinking spot frequented by Gotham's upper crust in search of a perfect dry martini and a dish of caviar. In the 1920s the club's entrance, lined with statuettes of jockeys, led to what was one of New York's most high-flying speakeasies. The club counted among its distinguished clientele the crème of New York society, including its flashy mayor, Jimmy Walker.

The club's basement wine cellar failed to show up on FBI floor plans, even though inspectors came armed with matches for detecting air currents. Access to the cellar was through a row of brick archways used for curing dried meats and cheeses. The first archway on the left had a small hole with an eighteen-inch metal meat skewer hanging beside it, and by inserting the skewer into the hole and a twisting sharply to the left, the lock on the 2.5-tonne cellar door sprang open to reveal a room filled with up to 2,000 cases of wines and spirits. One of the most colourful incidents in the club's history took place in 1932, while Walker was entertaining one of his girlfriends at a table tucked away in the cellar's corner snug. When the Feds chose that night to stage a raid, they never suspected the mayor was wining and dining right beneath their feet. The upshot of the raid was that Walker, who was stuck for five hours in the cellar, became so outraged that he telephoned the NYPD and instructed them to come at once to ticket the FBI cars parked outside the club.

* * *

WHALEN ENTERTAINED no doubts that the Communist Party USA was doing its upmost to turn New York into a hotbed of subversion. He even managed to have fifty officers infiltrate the Party to collect intelligence on the movements and strategies of the organization's leadership. This unhealthy fixation with Party militants, whom he often referred to as 'Tartars', would in the end lead to his undoing. Communist agitation in the streets in the early days of the Depression stemmed mainly from mass unemployment. This was a prime cause of social destabilization and one of the weightiest problems Whalen had to face as NYPD commissioner. Instances of violent police attacks on groups of Communist demonstrators began to escalate following an incident in January 1930 when a striking worker was gunned down in a verbal confrontation with a policeman outside a Bronx cafeteria. The Communists leapt on this killing as a provocation to begin dispatching thousands of their followers into the streets.

The fatal day came two months later, on 6 March 1930, at a huge anti-capitalism rally in Union Square that drew up to 100,000 Communists and their supporters. Whalen pre-emptively ordered the arrest of five Communist Party leaders on charges of organizing a public gathering without a permit. A shouting match broke out at police headquarters between Whalen and Communist Party General Secretary William Foster. The radical labour organizer refused to apply for a permit, saying he did not consider himself bound by U.S. law. In response, Whalen mobilized a small army of 1,000 police reservists, three hundred mounted police and one hundred members of the Motorcycle Squad to tackle the expected outbreak of trouble. The Fire Department was also called to Union Square to stand at the ready next to every fire hydrant in the vicinity, hoses in hand. The outcome was predictable: the massed throng saw this as a provocation. They charged the police barricades, and in a matter of moments Lower Manhattan had erupted into a battlefield. There were press reports of 'screams of women', 'cries of men' and 'bloody heads and faces', all of which roused a public outcry against Whalen. The hard-hitting tactics the commissioner had sanctioned that day were widely condemned as the cause of the violence.

There is no denying that Whalen had made every effort to avoid a head-on battle between the police and the demonstrators. To prevent what he rightly expected to turn into a ferocious clash, with reluctance he had given his consent for the meeting to go ahead without an official permit, which in any case had not been requested. That seemed to do the trick, until one of the speakers began haranguing the multitude to march on City Hall and demand the commissioner's removal. The final ignominy, one that Whalen could not ignore, was when the demonstrators began smashing the windows of Wanamaker's. Whalen interpreted this as a deliberate affront to his years of service at the department store.

The weeks following the street confrontation marked the countdown to Whalen's all but inevitable departure from the NYPD. The media was swarming with rumours of the commissioner's anger at having lost Walker's support. Walker continued to deny the reports until the morning of 21 May 1930. The mayor had been basking in self-confidence after having won a clear majority for a second term, but he was piqued at seeing his name take second place to Whalen's in the daily papers. Whalen sensed the mayor's disenchantment with his police commissioner and realized there was no future for him at the NYPD under Beau James. He therefore tendered his resignation, to return to his old job at Wanamaker's. Whalen's gift for managing events remained in demand after his return to the business world. Walker's successor, Fiorello La Guardia, named him chairman of the Mayor's Committee on Receptions to Distinguished Guests for the second time. In 1939 he was appointed president of the New York World's Fair.

Whalen's legacy is overshadowed by the turbulent police repression of the Communist Party-led protest in Union Square, but it would be wrong to stereotype him as a blinkered, baton-swinging cop. His accomplishments during a relatively short stint at 240 Centre Street were many and diverse. Whalen introduced the Sam Browne belt to give the police the appearance and sense of discipline in an organization he often referred to as the 'city's standing army'. He fought for and won pay increases for the higher ranks, to balance increased pay that had been granted the lower grades at the last mayoral election. Whalen established the Police College and the Crime Commission, both devoted to the study and prevention of felonies. He can also take credit for having established the NYPD Flying Unit in 1928, now known as the Aviation Unit, the country's oldest police flying corps. The inspiration for this undertaking came to mind after his meeting with Lindbergh at the aviator's gala ticker-tape parade and reception. Two years later, Whalen founded *Spring 3100*, the NYPD magazine whose title was taken from the telephone number of police headquarters. The magazine was 'affectionately dedicated' by

Whalen to Mayor Walker. Facing the editorial page of the first issue was a portrait of the humble police commissioner himself, captioned by the artist: 'Grover Whalen is the most inspiring subject I have ever drawn.'

Low-profile Cop

Edward Pierce Mulrooney joined the police force in 1896, along with a group of patrolmen who had answered a 'good government' movement appeal from reformist political groups and police officials seeking a new class of patrolman. He had become known to New Yorkers when, in 1928, he succeeded Inspector John D. Coughlin, chief of the Detective Bureau, by appointment of none other than Grover Whalen. Three years later Jimmy Walker elevated Mulrooney to the role of chief commissioner. The mayor's decision to go back to the uniformed police for a candidate came as something of a shock to Tammany bigwigs. The choice was, in fact, so unforeseen that many Democratic Party politicians objected to the mayor's failure to consult the bosses. Whalen and Mulrooney both turned up half an hour late for the ceremony at City Hall, where Walker simultaneously announced Whalen's resignation and presented his replacement to the assembled officialdom. It was to be the mayor's last appointment of an NYPD commissioner.

Walker was on the lookout for someone who would get the job done without attracting the flood of newspaper stories that had been devoted to Whalen. Walker believed that, by right, the coverage should have accrued to the mayor. In this sense, Mulrooney posed no threat to Walker's sensitive ego. The new commissioner fled from the public light. He rarely granted interviews and, for the most part, adopted a policy of official silence, preferring to throw himself into the policing job he was hired to carry out. Mulrooney was a devout Catholic, endowed with a ready Irish wit, a courtly, almost avuncular mien and a cigar usually clasped between his fingers. He lived humbly in a Bronx apartment with his wife and two daughters, though in his 35 months at the head of the NYPD, the commissioner was to see little of his family.

He worked fifteen-hour days, likening himself to the general manager of a business with 13,143 employees and dozens of branches, a reference to the number of police employed by the force, distributed in precincts across the five boroughs. His working day began at the morning line-up of the felony suspects who had been hauled in over the previous

24 hours. Once that task was done and dusted, he returned to his office to review trial proceedings, often at the rate of two hundred a week. Afternoons were set aside for taking reports and grievances from other officers and receiving the occasional visiting dignitary. Mulrooney had a direct telephone line installed from police headquarters to his bedside in the Bronx. When his wife heard the phone ring after going to bed, she knew her husband would be up and on his way to meet with night patrolmen and detectives at a crime scene.

Mulrooney came to the job when New York was experiencing an upsurge in gangland killings. The number of murders escalated from 421 in 1930, when he took over at the NYPD, to 588 the following year. Some of the homicides carried out during Mulrooney's tenure were sensationalized in the national media. One of the most nefarious of these was the murder of the prostitute and gang moll Vivian Gordon in early 1931. This took place a year before Judge Samuel Seabury put together a bipartisan committee to investigate widespread corruption in New York's criminal justice system, including police extortion of money from ordinary citizens and prostitutes. Some of the incidents brought before the committeemen, specifically those involving gangland violence, were thought to be too horrific for ladies' sensitive ears. Consequently, women were barred from attending the sessions. Disregarding Seabury's directive and knowing that the judge was looking for witnesses to pursue his anti-police corruption campaign, Gordon, a petite forty-year-old redhead, came forward to press charges against Vice Squad cop Andrew McLaughlin. Little did Gordon suspect that she herself was to become one of the victims Seabury wished to conceal from female sensibilities. Gordon asserted she had been framed by McLaughlin as far back as 1923, when he caught her in bed with a man in a Times Square flophouse. McLaughlin had burst into the room, arrested Gordon and charged her with prostitution. For her, there was no doubt that her estranged husband had laid the trap to enable him to sue for divorce.

The lift operator at Gordon's stylish East Side home was the last person to see her alive when she left her apartment on that ill-fated night in February 1931. He described her as wearing an ankle-length mink coat, a platinum wristwatch and a large diamond ring, as she eased herself behind the wheel of a Cadillac. Not long after that, the police pathologist concluded, Gordon was smashed about the head, strangled with a length of rope and possibly dragged from the car for an undetermined length of time. Her bloodied and mutilated body was dumped in a drainage ditch at Van Cortlandt Park in the Bronx. Gordon's connections with the New York underworld were well known to the police. She had established a bustling business selling sexual favours, then blackmailing men who were not keen for their wives to learn of their husbands' infidelities. She used the proceeds from this racket to ingratiate herself with her gangster associates, lending them money and buying property throughout New York as a sort of central banker to the mob.

When Mulrooney sent his men out to search her apartment, what they found were diaries with a list of more than three hundred names of mobsters and shady businessmen. The commissioner instantly put hundreds of police officers on the case and a grand jury was convened to investigate the crime. Prominent religious figures, led by Rabbi Stephen S. Wise and Reverend John Haynes Holmes, demanded a swift probe into citywide corruption, not only in the NYPD but in Jimmy Walker's administration. There were calls for the mayor to resign, an outcry which he casually ignored. The shockwaves of the murder inquiry reverberated as far as the White House, where President Roosevelt issued an order to look into the workings of the New York City government. He vowed that police practices were 'on trial'.

A break in the Gordon case came in the month of March. Investigators found that McLaughlin had deposited $35,800 into his bank account over a period of two years. This raised a few eyebrows, given that his salary as a patrolman came to $3,000 a year. McLaughlin refused to explain where or how he had obtained the money, taking a brazen stand at his hearing by sidestepping the question entirely. He instead bragged that he had made as many as 1,200 vice arrests in ten years, roaming up and down Broadway, detaining suspicious-looking women and even working through his lunch break. In a bombshell verdict, McLaughlin was acquitted and all charges against him for framing Vivian Gordon were dropped. Likewise, the source of the $35,800 was quietly swept under the carpet.

The police eventually dredged up a handful of suspects in the Gordon murder. The Bronx racketeer Harry Stein, who had been advanced funds from Gordon to allegedly commit bank fraud, was indicted. He pleaded not guilty, although the police had collected enough evidence to show that he had disposed of Gordon's belongings the day after her death. In May, Stein's pal Samuel Greenhauer, a tailor, was also indicted. The trial turned into something of a farce when both gangsters came up with what they claimed to be airtight alibis. Stein had gone to the cinema with his sister, after which they went for dinner at a Chinese restaurant. Greenhauer's family swore he was with them at a ceremony of mourning for his mother. After just three hours of deliberation, the men were acquitted of Gordon's murder and Mulrooney's hard work proved to have been in vain.

Mayor Walker applauded Mulrooney's efforts and stated that the arrests and subsequent acquittals were proof that there had been no cover-up by the NYPD or City Hall. The City Affairs Committee, an independent investigative body, was not impressed by the mayor's self-congratulatory rhetoric. They publicly demanded his removal from office. The pressure was mounting on Beau James, who would have good cause to reflect on the Gordon trial and its outcome long after the proceedings had come to an end. Though Vivian Gordon helped to unseat a mayor and tear down an entire political system, her murder remains an unsolved mystery.

The Kidnapping of the Century

Mulrooney was basking in the mayor's praise when, in 1932, the entire nation was rocked by what the press trumpeted as 'The Crime of the Century'. This was the abduction and murder of Charles Augustus Lindbergh Jr, son of the world-famous aviator. On the night of 1 March 1932, Lindbergh had sent his son's nanny upstairs to the second-floor nursery of his New Jersey home to check on the twenty-month-old boy. What she found was an empty cot and a ransom note demanding $50,000 for the child's safe return. Though the case technically fell under the jurisdiction of the New Jersey State Police, which helped in the operation, only the NYPD had the manpower and resources to mount a search-and-rescue procedure of this magnitude. Mulrooney deployed hundreds of patrolmen at all bridge and tunnel entry points to New York. Every car entering the city was stopped and searched. No potential hiding place, including hospitals and hotels, was spared the scrutiny of the Detective Squad.

No sooner had the story broken than the media coverage hit full throttle. Mulrooney rapidly found himself under massive pressure from City Hall, to say nothing of the press, to find the boy and return him

Tribute to honour medal-winning police on parade in 1908.

safely to his distraught parents. In one of the commissioner's daily brief-
ings, it came to light that Lindbergh had been sent two more ransom
demands, both bearing Brooklyn postmarks. This piece of intelligence
sparked a clash between Mulrooney and Lindbergh. The commissioner
jumped on what he considered a valuable clue – he wanted to stake out
every letter box in Brooklyn, giving instructions to his patrolmen to put
a tail on any suspicious-looking characters. Lindbergh flatly opposed the
idea. His fear was that if the abductors sensed the police were closing in,
they would try to save their skins by making a clean getaway, which inevi-
tably meant disposing of a panic-stricken child. It became obvious which
of the two men had the more commanding public profile: Mulrooney
reluctantly scotched his plan.

Lindbergh then decided to bypass Mulrooney altogether. He turned
the hunt for his son's abductor over to Dr John F. Condon, a retired
schoolmaster who had placed an offer in a Bronx newspaper to act as
go-between with the kidnapper. One night, Lindbergh and Condon
were instructed by a cryptic newspaper message to deliver $50,000 in
gold certificates to a man waiting in St Raymond's Cemetery in the

Bronx. Unbeknown to Lindbergh, by that time his son had been dead for two months. The boy's battered and decomposed body was later discovered in a shallow grave by a New Jersey road.

Lindbergh had taken the precaution of making a note of the serial numbers on all the gold certificates in the ransom packet. It was not until two years later that NYPD Lieutenant James Finn, the officer in charge of the case, was able to trace the certificates to Bruno Richard Hauptmann, a German-born carpenter. Hauptmann was a weaselly character with a history of arrests for burglary in his native country, prior to his illegal entry into the U.S. as a stowaway on an ocean liner. Condon was able to identify Hauptmann at his trial as the man who had collected the ransom money at their cemetery rendezvous. The jury handed in a verdict of first-degree murder, which put an end to Hauptmann's career in crime in the electric chair in April 1936.

Beau James Bows Out

During the six-year period in which Beau James was in charge of City Hall, from 1926 to 1932, most New Yorkers were content to turn a blind eye to their mayor's incorrigible boozing and philandering. For those strutting through the Charleston rhythms of his first administration, the mayor's polished, hedonistic ways held up a lifestyle many wished to emulate. With the onset of the Depression, the figure of Walker, the irrepressible bon viveur, helped to dispel the gloom of poverty and hopelessness. His unabashed swagger presented New Yorkers with a source of lavish entertainment. On one occasion, he asserted in an after-dinner speech about being so great a celebrity that his picture was taken at least three times a day. Walker said that if he went off on holiday, it was *de rigueur* for him to be photographed doing things he swore he never did. 'But whether it is a picture drinking water – which I would not do for my life – or anything similar, I do it because it helps the photographer on his job,' he declared. 'I know this fuss that is being made about me is because I am mayor of this City of New York.' 'Gentleman Jimmy', which was the stage name chosen for Walker in the 1959 Broadway musical *Fiorello!*, cast a magical spell over his constituents. This was manifested in the fateful Crash year of 1929, when this dapper son of Irish immigrants easily saw off his firebrand Italian-Jewish rival, Fiorello La Guardia, in the mayoral race. Walker was re-elected by a landslide majority, but his

bloated vanity prevented him from detecting the political warning signals. Gentleman Jimmy was not to serve out his second term.

New York under Walker had the reputation of being a city riddled
with corruption at every level and in almost every echelon of government, the NYPD being no exception. Presidential hopeful and New York
state governor Franklin Roosevelt had for some time been in pursuit of
Walker's impeccably coifed scalp. Once Roosevelt's Democratic nomination had been secured, he turned up the heat on Beau James. In May
1932, with a national election six months away, Roosevelt decided to take
action by summoning Walker to an inquiry. The mayor was subjected to a
barrage of questions about his personal bank accounts, a litany of alleged
bribes and an assortment of other suspect dealings. An embattled Walker
realized he had become a political liability for the presidential hopeful,
who had placed the mayor's back to the wall. He knew he was left with
no choice but to take his leave of City Hall. In September 1932 Walker
departed New York City to sail off on a grand European tour with his
mistress, the Ziegfeld Follies showgirl Betty Compton. Walker was gone,
but far from forgotten. His glitzy life became the stuff of Hollywood
romance, as depicted in the 1957 film *Beau James*, with Bob Hope in the
starring role.

* * *

JOSEPH VINCENT MCKEE, resident of the Board of Aldermen, stepped
in to serve as acting mayor for a brief four-month period after Walker's
departure. In November 1933 the Court of Appeals ruled that an early
election was necessary. The Democratic leaders could find some solace
in the electoral victory of John Patrick O'Brien, but they overlooked one
important fact: nearly 250,000 voters had cast their ballot for McKee,
who stood as a Recovery Party candidate. Nevertheless, the Machine's
man effortlessly thrashed his rival at the polls and Tammany recovered from the crushing blow it had been dealt by Walker's resignation.
O'Brien's inauguration ceremony came off as an outstandingly lack-
lustre affair, in which the Tammany chieftains thought it prudent to
keep a low profile. It became patently obvious from the outset that an
O'Brien administration could not hold a candle to the sparkle that had
characterized the flashy Beau James days. At a news conference after
the swearing-in ceremony, the mayor was asked who was to become his
new police commissioner. A bemused O'Brien replied, 'I don't know,

they haven't told me yet.' Given the feebleness of the opposition, it goes almost without saying that the normal election held later that month was a walkover for the indomitable Fiorello La Guardia.

If the careers of O'Brien and the person who the new mayor – or more to the point, his Tammany overlords – were to select to head up the NYPD, the one thing they had in common was brevity of service. James S. Bolan, known as one of the toughest law-enforcement officers in the force, was a taciturn loner who rose in the hierarchy to serve as police commissioner for nine and a half months. In one way, he had secured his post at an auspicious moment, for Bolan did not have to spend much of his NYPD years grappling with rampant police corruption linked to Prohibition. The repeal of the anti-drinking laws in 1933 was, in fact, to unleash a tsunami of horrors for the police, who now had to lock horns with a Mafia enraged by the loss of their prime source of income. Bolan's 37-year career with the department came to an end with La Guardia's victory in November 1933. Bolan had served as commissioner from April 1933 until January 1934, when La Guardia began his term of office. After his departure, he founded the James S. Bolan Detective Agency, oddly enough the only department of the NYPD in which he had never served.

La Guardia's candidacy had been decided in a primary race between himself and Major General John Francis O'Ryan, both of whom sought the support of the Republican and Fusion parties. O'Ryan, a native Manhattanite and divisional commander in the First World War, possessed a military leader's aptitude for gauging the enemy's strength: he sensed La Guardia would sweep the field. O'Ryan accordingly stepped aside, but there was a reward waiting for him in the wings. It was an open secret in New York political circles that he had been tipped to become police commissioner under a La Guardia administration.

And so it was, but this apparently amicable arrangement did not last very long. The chalk and cheese adage could not better describe the personalities and policies of La Guardia and O'Ryan. The simmering hostilities between the two came to a head less than three months after the commissioner took the oath. On 22 March the *New York Times* reported on an incident of industrial action that went badly wrong: 'Wholesale violence marked the strike of taxicab drivers, when thousands of strikers paraded noisily in Manhattan, the Bronx and Brooklyn, dragging passengers from cabs driven by non-strikers, damaging the machines and giving the police lively tussles.'³ The brawl left Times Square strewn with doors wrenched from their hinges, with other car parts ripped off the cabs of strike-breakers. The protest had its origin in a dispute over working conditions and was directed at fleet owners who refused to recognize union membership for their drivers.

The mayor and police commissioner were left defending radically different positions on the handling of street protests by striking workers, as well as a variety of other issues. There had been mutual discord almost from day one over the commissioner's plans to organize the NYPD along military lines. The disputes at times verged on the mundane, such as whether police should wear coats in summer, the revival of the annual police parade and O'Ryan's insistence that he be addressed as 'general' instead of 'commissioner'. La Guardia reprimanded the commissioner for having allowed his men to deploy what the mayor considered to be excessive force in breaking up the cab drivers' demonstrations. O'Ryan had reacted like the major general he was by ordering his patrolmen to restore order at all costs. In the resultant quarrel with the mayor, rather than submit to what he believed to be the misguided policies of a civilian official, in September 1934 O'Ryan informed the mayor that he was stepping down after less than a year of service. When he was beset by a horde of reporters outside his Lexington Hotel suite demanding to know if there was any truth in the rumours of his resignation, O'Ryan turned and strutted away military style, quipping over his shoulder, 'You shall find out.'

One of the most far-reaching measures taken by O'Ryan, albeit at La Guardia's insistence, was to liberate Lewis Valentine from his Brooklyn backwater. One morning shortly after his inauguration, the mayor summoned Valentine to his Upper Fifth Avenue home. The police official sat on the sofa, perplexed, listening to La Guardia chattering away about his plans to tackle poverty, crime and corruption. When Valentine rose to leave, La Guardia casually remarked at the door, 'Oh, by the way, I'm going to see to it that O'Ryan makes you chief inspector and gives you a free hand on the job.'

Next came a meeting at O'Ryan's office, where the commissioner confirmed Valentine's appointment to the NYPD's second-highest rank. He added that the police department's tarnished soul was in need of cleaning and that Valentine had been entrusted to do the polishing. The first day on the job, Valentine called his commanding officers together for a briefing. 'Be good or be gone,' he thundered. 'I'll stand up for my men, but I'll crucify a thief. And I'll be quicker to punish a thief in a police uniform.'[4]

At the end of 1934 O'Ryan resigned over his disagreement with La Guardia's non-interventionist stance on labour-management disputes. Consequently, Valentine moved one step up in the NYPD hierarchy to become the department's new commissioner. From the outset, it was going to be a hard slog having to cope with a legacy of abusive police practices. The British photographer and diarist Cecil Beaton, who built his reputation in New York in the 1930s, had some shocking observations to report of police misbehaviour towards the public:

> Although there is not much publicity given to police violence, it is still widely prevalent, denials notwithstanding. Many a police-related hospital case arrives at Bellevue with fractured arms and bruises on the upper part of the arms and the head. The police seem especially vicious to non-violent drunks and other arrests: the slightest movement often calls for a blow on the head with the nightstick. Minor arrests are given the third degree, in the hope of pinning other unsolved crimes on them. Innocent bystanders to street crimes are often hauled in for no reason, and passers-by who instinctively dawdle out of curiosity are told to 'Get going! This is none of your goddamned business. Now scram before I run you in too!'[5]

It should be noted that Valentine, a ruthless professional by nature, was only doing his boss's bidding by taking an unyielding approach to racketeering, inside the department as well as in criminal circles. In one of his periodic addresses to the NYPD, La Guardia told the police to put so much fear into the heart of criminals in New York that when one sees a cop 'he'll tip his hat'. The mayor's concern was understandable: the first year of his administration alone saw nearly a dozen officers killed in clashes with mobsters.

La Guardia always maintained a close and amicable relationship with the police. In recognition of their service, he put together a private fund-raising commission to erect a monument dedicated to the NYPD.

> His vision resulted in the creation of the department's most iconic image, a larger-than-life bronze statue produced by the mayor's

long-time friend and sculptor, Attilio Piccirilli. The statue depicts a patrolman holding an American flag with one hand and cradling a young boy with the other. The models Piccirilli used for the statue were slain Patrolman Martin J. Gillen of the 20th Precinct and La Guardia's young adopted son, Eric.[6]

The statue now stands in the Memorial Lobby inside the entrance to One Police Plaza.

By the last months of 1934, Valentine had reached the end of his tether. The breaking point came one morning in an identity parade at police headquarters, when the commissioner came face-to-face with a particularly odious contract killer named Harry Strauss. Valentine flew into a rage when confronted with Strauss's contemptuous smirk, and even more so by the murderer's natty suit and tie, topped by a velvet-collared Chesterfield overcoat. 'He's the best-dressed man in this room,' Valentine sneered. 'When you meet men like Strauss,' he barked at his detectives, 'draw quickly and shoot accurately. Don't be afraid to muss 'em up. Blood should be smeared all over that velvet collar.'[7]

'Muss 'em up' could have served as the war cry emblazoned on the standard carried into battle by Valentine and La Guardia, who served side by side for more than a decade in the crusade against the forces of organized crime in New York. The end of Prohibition had ushered in an unprecedented wave of Mafia criminality, exacerbated by out-breaks of social unrest among people who were being hammered by the Depression. That first year of the Valentine–La Guardia partnership amounted to a dress rehearsal for what was to come. The police com-missioner and his officers were now to set out on a mission to make law and order prevail in New York City.

5

A Valentine for the Mob

Mayor La Guardia sent Commissioner Valentine off to wage war on two fronts. Tammany might have appeared on the wane after the thrashing it took from the Fusion Party in the 1933 mayoral election, a coalition made up of Republicans, disaffected Democrats and independents. There were those who rejoiced at what they interpreted as the downfall of the Machine that had driven New York politics for eighty years, starting with the mayoral victory of Fernando Wood in 1854. As well as the onslaught by La Guardia, Tammany also took a hammering from the New Deal, which helped to alter the demographic landscape of New York by restricting immigration and making people less dependent on the bosses for jobs and assistance. But the reformists' joy was largely unfounded and, in fact, the political mob's fall from power was not truly complete until the early 1960s.

The Machine that commanded the allegiance of more than a few of the NYPD police commissioner's men and women was in no way a spent force. From humble shopkeepers to trade union leaders, large sectors of business people in New York lived in fear of Tammany's intimidation and exploitative machinations. Standing up to the grafters was dangerous and pointless, for little protection could be expected from the police and a cohort of magistrates whose pockets were lined with Tammany kickbacks. The Democratic Party bosses did not have to lick their wounds for long. They soon discovered a willing ally in the Mafia, which was only too pleased to collaborate in crime, to the benefit of everyone.

The Machine's hitherto all-powerful supremos failed to understand the reality that what they envisaged to be an alliance with the mobsters was, in fact, a takeover by a far mightier criminal organization. The story of the mob and the Machine goes back at least to an event in 1931, one that offered a foretaste of just who was to be calling the shots in this partnership. On a July morning the scar-faced criminal mastermind Lucky Luciano sent two gunmen to pay a visit to Harry C. Perry, the co-leader of Manhattan's Second Assembly District. The thugs entered his office with guns drawn to enquire whether Perry might consider stepping down in favour of Albert Marinelli, a veteran Tammany clan leader of the Second Assembly District and close Luciano associate. The *New York Times* reported in unvarnished and somewhat ironic terms that Perry 'had yielded the field to his Italian-American adversary and was stepping out of the Tammany leadership which he held for seventeen years'.[1]

The term 'Zero Tolerance' is associated with the no-holds-barred NYPD blitz on New York's epidemic of criminality in the 1990s. Valentine's crackdown on every type of misdemeanour, from pickpocketing to homicide, was no less assertive than what Broken Windows-enforcer Commissioner William Bratton was to set in motion six decades later. It is no exaggeration to say that La Guardia detested every form of illegal gambling and other underworld activities, which he believed undermined the morals of society. Topping the list of his most despised rackets was the slot machine. Valentine reckoned that up to a staggering 30,000 of these machines had sprung up in arcades and stores throughout New York City. One of the commissioner's first missions was to stage a raid on the True Mint Novelty Company, a firm owned by racketeer Frank Costello that manufactured slots and reportedly earned the mob mogul $500,000 a day. Valentine and his men discovered a cache of four hundred slots along with records that proved the machines were part of a larger Mafia set-up. Valentine immediately dispatched a fleet of Department of Sanitation trucks to round up the slots that had been seized. These were loaded onto barges and dumped into Long Island Sound, where they rest on the ocean floor. Other Mafia enterprises included the policy or numbers racket, bookie parlours, crap games, floating card games, prostitution, loan sharking, control of trade unions, extortion, contract killings and even rubbish collection. No sooner had Costello received news of the raid, he deftly had 15,000 of the machines re-engineered as sweet dispensers. Costello enjoyed many political friendships, all in the right places. The case went to court, whose ruling that chewing gum dispensers were perfectly legal and therefore could not be confiscated was totally predictable.

No sooner had the dust settled on the slots episode than La Guardia directed his commissioner off on another assignment, this time to locate and arrest the gangsters who ran the city's policy game. This was basically an illegal lottery, another Mafia racket that ran afoul of the mayor's high moral principles. Valentine was something of a practitioner in policy game busting. As early as 1926, after being made head of Commissioner McLaughlin's Confidential Squad, he launched an offensive against grocery shops, stationers and other retail outlets that served as numbers collecting locales, most of them in Harlem. Valentine's secret to success in those lightning raids was to keep his plans under wraps, right up to the moment the hit took place. This was to prevent corrupt cops stationed in Harlem from alerting the numbers runners to an impending bust. As Valentine tells the story: 'They could bet hundreds of thousands of dollars on the outcome of a ball game or the turn of a card. But they didn't gamble with their chances of bucking the police. Their easy money purchased politicians and policemen alike.' In 1935 Valentine was able to report to his boss that, for now, the numbers game, as it was also known, had been broken up and that more than 7,000 arrests had been made.

That same year found the crusading commissioner tackling one of the most vexing cases of his career. Samuel Drukman worked as bookkeeper for a haulier, headquartered at the Luckman Brothers garage in the Williamsburg section of Brooklyn. On the night of 3 March 1935, Valentine dispatched one of his detectives to the garage to follow up on an anonymous tip-off of a murder that had been committed on the premises. What the police discovered was the still-warm body of Drukman, his head split open by the weighted end of a billiard cue. He had then been choked to death, shoved into a canvas sack and left crumpled up in the dickey seat of a Chevrolet Roadster. Taken at face value, and given Drukman's almost pathological addiction to betting on the horses, the killing bore the hallmarks of a Mafia revenge attack. It came to light that Drukman had been pilfering money from his employers to feed his addiction to the races, where he had chalked up considerable losses.

It might have been held up as a piece of skilled police work, an open-and-shut case. The police found three men hiding in the garage, two members of the Luckman family and an accomplice, who were summarily arrested, charged with second-degree murder, convicted and sentenced to twenty years to life in Sing Sing. In fact, the story turned out to be far more convoluted, for their conviction was not immediate and the intervening events tell of the gradual development of a wide political scandal. In the first instalment of the saga, no indictments were found at a subsequent grand jury inquiry convened by Brooklyn district attorney William F. X. Geoghan. The prisoners were released and evidence against them was overturned. Detective Charles F. Corbett, who was the officer Valentine had put in charge, came forward to reveal that he had been offered a $100,000 bribe to throw the case. Valentine stepped in to declare Corbett 'an honest and able detective'. It wasn't until Governor Herbert H. Lehman was persuaded to intervene and have Geoghan sacked that the three culprits were finally brought to justice and convicted of the murder. In the resultant political fallout, a cabal of eight Republican politicians, attorneys, a Brooklyn slot machine czar and, to Valentine's fury, Corbett's partner Detective Giuseppe F. L. Dardis were indicted on conspiracy charges.

* * *

THERE WAS ONE criminal activity that neither Valentine nor, in fairness, any previous NYPD commissioner could have declared success in: thwarting terrorism. After the outbreak of the First World War in 1914, a band of Galleanist saboteurs, followers of the Italian anarchist demagogue Luigi Galleani, unleashed a campaign of bombings across the U.S. In 1920 New York became the target of the deadliest of these attacks. On a September afternoon, a horse-drawn carriage drew up in Wall Street, in front of crowds on their lunchbreak across the road from the J. P. Morgan headquarters. A massive bomb filled with dynamite and iron shrapnel was detonated, leaving 38 dead and hundreds more injured. No one took responsibility for the bombing, the police failed to identify the perpetrators and, more than a century later, the case remains unsolved.

La Guardia–Valentine: Crime-busters Duo

Visitors to the British Pavilion at New York World's Fair fled in terror when a blast ripped through the building on the morning of 4 July 1940. The explosion scattered shards of plate glass across the site and blew shrapnel up to 100 feet in the air. New York had been rife with rumours of an impending Nazi sabotage of Allied targets in the city. Tensions had been ramping up in New York, with some four hundred bomb threats being made every week. Pro-Nazi rallies by members of the German

American Bund were held in Madison Square Garden. The anxiety was further fuelled by hostile rhetoric on the part of street corner Nazi sympathizers. On 20 June of that year, a bomb had exploded in a Nazi commercial agency adjoining the German Consulate in Battery Place. The following day, a call was placed to Manhattan police headquarters saying that the Bund was going to blow up the Brooklyn Bridge.

Although the U.S. did not enter the Second World War until the end of 1941, the attack served to mirror the conflict overseas. Moreover, the Germans were fuming over La Guardia's refusal to allot them exhibition space at the fairground. They were particularly unhappy about a display of captured Nazi contraband on view in the British Pavilion, about which telephone threats had already been received from a caller said to have spoken with a German accent. On the morning of America's Independence Day, a small ticking satchel was spotted tucked away in an upstairs room at the pavilion. The warning was reported to NYPD headquarters, which rushed Detective William Morelock to Flushing Meadows to investigate.

Two Bomb Squad specialists, Joseph Lynch and Ferdinand Socha, were sent to investigate. Despite the lack of protective gear, they proceeded to cut a small hole in the wooden case in order to examine its contents. The blast tore the two men to shreds and severely injured five other policemen inside the pavilion, leaving a crater 30 feet (10 m) in circumference. Terrorism had claimed its first NYPD victims. Valentine launched what was, at the time, the most extensive manhunt in the department's history. Despite a massive manhunt and the round-up and interrogation of thousands of known Nazi sympathizers and other potential political enemies, the culprits were never brought to justice and the bombing remains unsolved to this day.

No St Valentine's Day for Crooks

Valentine ranks as one of America's three best-known law enforcement agents of the 1930s and '40s, along with FBI director J. Edgar Hoover and comic strip detective hero Dick Tracy. His talents for waging war on organized crime and his ruthless crackdown on police officers found to be in league with the Mafia acquired an almost mythical status. At the end of La Guardia's first term as mayor, Valentine had personally sacked 221 police officers for corrupt practices or simply on the grounds

Police distributing eggs and bread to the needy at the 104th Street Precinct
during the Great Depression in 1930.

of ineptitude, while another seventy who were under interrogation for
suspected criminal links had committed suicide. Under Valentine's command, and with his relentless pursuit of lawbreakers, by 1939 the NYPD
had made 2,229 arrests, of which 84 per cent brought in convictions. The
following year, the number of arrests had risen to 22,295, with a similar percentage of guilty verdicts. The commissioner never shirked from
pushing New York's penal code to the limit. He once asserted in 1935 that
'barbarians are walking the city's streets'. Shortly thereafter, several hundred people were rounded up under a law that made it illegal for anyone
with a criminal record to assemble in a public place.

Valentine bucked the unhappy trend set by most of his predecessors
by leaving the NYPD commissionership on good terms with his colleagues
and his City Hall boss. His working life had him on radio call and telephone standby 24 hours a day throughout his years in office. Hardships
notwithstanding, he submitted his resignation with 'profound regret',
acknowledging that it was time to end his long and exacting career as
New York's top cop. His tenure officially had four years to run, but he

decided to leave with his mayor, who was stepping down after three terms.

Valentine wiled away the first months of his retirement catching up with his long-neglected family and circle of friends. He also did a stint as narrator on the *Gang Busters* radio show, a popular crime series that began broadcasting in 1936 in response to an alarming upsurge in Mafia activity. The programme brought authentic police case histories to listeners, invariably ending each story with the message that crime doesn't pay. The days of leisure, however, were to be short-lived. Valentine's achievements had received acclaim not only from the mayor he served under and the people of New York City, but at the highest national levels. In September 1946 he took a call from General Douglas MacArthur at the U.S. Department of War. Valentine was sent to occupied Japan to reorganize and modernize the country's post-war police, fire and prison systems. The *New York Times* heralded the appointment as a 'new broom' in modernizing Japan's state-controlled, feudal law enforcement system. 'If he develops a police force there as competent and trustworthy as he built up in this city,' the paper said in an editorial, 'Japan will at last see something new under the rising sun.'[2]

High-flying Achiever

La Guardia's last major act before departing City Hall was to appoint Arthur W. Wallander as NYPD commissioner. In November 1945 Valentine turned over his badge to his successor, a career policeman with nearly 31 years' experience in the department and a man Valentine appraised as courageous and one who would go on 'to make the police department more glorious in the eyes of New York's men, women and children'. At the same time, Valentine hailed the city's mayor-elect William O'Dwyer as a 'number one public official' whose first regard was the welfare of the city's people. With hindsight, Valentine's assessment of the Democratic Party mayor, who by a curious coincidence had been trained by Wallander as a rookie cop when he joined the NYPD, would appear to be a trifle wide of the mark.

Even if the striped tiger symbol of Tammany Hall had, in fact, been plunged into the East River waters, as Valentine asserted was the case when he left the NYPD, Wallander could in no way afford to let his guard down. Tammany may have been a wounded beast, but organized crime was rampant in the city. The new incumbent was to have his hands full taking on the Mafia and its brutal affiliate Murder Inc., the syndicate set up in the early 1930s. Gangland bosses in New York, and indeed around the country, would regularly call on this specialized pack of killers to carry out contract assassinations. Irish-born O'Dwyer might have missed his true calling, for after losing to La Guardia in the 1939 race, he joined the army and swiftly rose to the rank of brigadier general. O'Dwyer chose instead to make his mark in civilian life, and in time he became a significant figure in New York politics of the 1940s. Sadly for O'Dwyer, his tenure at City Hall came to an end when the mayor was found to be embroiled in criminal-linked scandals.

During the time he served as Brooklyn district attorney, O'Dwyer achieved notoriety as a relentless foe of Murder Inc. He came to prominence in 1940 after bringing to justice the ill-reputed killer Abe Reles, a member of New York's Jewish Mafia. Nicknamed 'Kid Twist' for his penchant for completely twisting his victims' necks, Reles was implicated in eleven murders. O'Dwyer was denied the pleasure of sending Reles to the electric chair, which was the fate of his gangland colleagues Martin 'Buggsy' Goldstein, Lepke Buchalter and other mobsters. Reles came within a whisker of saving his own neck by giving evidence against several of his associates. He was placed under protective house arrest in a Coney Island hotel pending trial. One night, he clambered out the bedroom window and managed to lower himself halfway down on a makeshift bed-sheet ladder, falling to his death in the process.

Things began to turn sour for O'Dwyer towards the end of his first term, when links were uncovered between the mayor and several high-ranking Mafia bosses. The Kefauver Committee, established in 1950 to investigate crime in interstate commerce, trained its sights on O'Dwyer for allegedly supporting the operations of Mafia kingpin Frank Costello, known to the mob as the 'Prime Minister of the Underworld'. The committee's findings brought to light a number of unsavoury connections in bookmaking, gambling and narcotics, to name but the most heinous of Costello's rackets. The hearings concluded that the mayor had failed to take effective action against Costello and the top echelons of New York gangsterism. The mayor's fall from grace came shortly after his re-election in 1949. In August 1950 a disgraced O'Dwyer resigned from office, albeit in a burst of glory as the hero of a ticker-tape farewell parade up Broadway. That year, he was tactfully removed from the public light when President Harry Truman appointed him U.S. ambassador to Mexico.

Police Commissioner Wallander's career as the NYPD's top brass, while admittedly lacking in brilliance, stood head and shoulders above that of his City Hall superior. Wallander earned his promotion to the rank of sergeant in 1922, at the NYPD's first ceremony organized by Commissioner Enright. The thinking behind the event was that a promotion should be appropriately observed to reflect the work of officers who, in the past, would merely report to headquarters on a day's shift to collect a new shield. Enright also brought in military-style uniform breast ribbons to reward meritorious service, replacing the inconspicuous metal stars that adorned the cuffs of officers' dress coats. Further along in his career, while working as chief of drill instruction at the Police Academy, Wallander was designated personal bodyguard to Charles Lindbergh on the aviator's triumphal return from Paris. Seeing to the safety of America's number one hero of the day got Wallander bumped up a rank to lieutenant.

In 1929 the future NYPD commissioner took part in another aviation-related event, albeit less dazzling than the Lindbergh extravaganza. In October, Wallander found himself on the first official fight of an NYPD aircraft, which took off that month from the Curtiss Flying School in Queens. They flew to an airstrip in Connecticut, where they were to take custody of a man wanted for murder and fly him back to New York headquarters. The New York airfield became North Beach in 1939, and fourteen years later it was renamed La Guardia Airport, in tribute to New York's former mayor. Two months after his maiden flight, the newly promoted Captain Wallander attended the dedication ceremony of Roosevelt Field in Long Island. Presiding at the ceremony was Commissioner Grover Whalen, who stood shivering in sub-freezing weather while the NYPD band played 'In the Good Old Summertime'. In 1930 Wallander secured for himself further plaudits when he was appointed uniformed head of what was then called the NYPD's Air Services Division (ASD). That same year, the police began flying regular patrol duty over New York City with a fleet of four Italian-made Savoia-Marchetti single-engine biplane flying boats. The new aircraft flew in formation for the first time on the afternoon of 29 March, to the delight of crowds of onlookers standing agape at North Beach and in Manhattan. After the display, the squadron splashed down in the East

River to be met by Whalen, Wallander and a welcoming committee of municipal dignitaries.

Lewis Valentine was always going to be a hard act to follow. The hard-nosed commissioner's successor would need to accept the challenge of emulating a legend. Wallander was an affable type with a ready smile. He was highly regarded by his colleagues and humanely treated by the press. As someone with a rather mellow temperament for the position he held, Tammany Hall and the corrupt network within the police found him untroublesome and easy to work around. His comparatively uneventful four years as head of the Centre Street headquarters came to an end in March 1949. Wallander bade farewell to O'Dwyer with a request that the mayor sign his daughter's autograph book, in his words 'probably the last command' he would receive. Unbeknown to Wallander, he had chosen a fortuitous moment to step down from the commissionership: New York was about to be hit with some of the nastiest police cases of the mid-twentieth century. It fell to his two short-serving successors to deal with these cases.

The immediate effect of Wallander's departure was to drop into the lap of his replacement, William P. O'Brien, in a monumental disaster for the police brought on by gambling racketeer Harry Gross. This became the most devastating exposé of New York police corruption until the shock testimony of Frank Serpico at the 1971 Knapp Commission. O'Brien ended up involved in a mess not of his own making, but which was to hasten his professional undoing. In 1950 the New York papers ran front-page pictures of the tough, cigar-chomping commissioner taking a sledgehammer to illegal pinball machines, looking like a carbon copy of La Guardia's famous photo smashing up the slots. That same year, the police moved in on Gross, whose Brooklyn gambling enterprises were netting him more than $20 million a year. All well and good, until wiretaps revealed that Gross was passing protection payments to the police that added up to $1 million annually. An inquiry set up to investigate police wrongdoings brought in convictions for 22 officers on graft charges, while 240 others were sacked or forced to resign. For some, the shame and dishonour were too much to bear. There were a good many cases of mental breakdowns, and worse. Officer Charles Panarella leapt to his death from the sixth floor of the Brooklyn court building minutes before he was scheduled to go on trial, one of three police officers under investigation who committed suicide.

Gross himself spent eight years in prison, followed by another three on a manslaughter charge for bludgeoning his wife's grandfather to death. His sojourn behind bars did not deter him from pursuing a life of crime. In addition to later arrests for gambling offences, in 1986 Gross was collared at a hotel for attempting to sell heroin to an undercover agent. There was a sense of frustration and concern among NYPD senior officers, who feared more heads could roll if evidence was to turn up of pay-offs to the police. In the end, it became a self-righting problem. Years later, in April 1986, after his arrest on a narcotics charge, Gross took his own life at the age of 69 by slashing his wrists.

> Miles McDonald, the man who had prosecuted Gross so vigorously in Brooklyn and later became a State Supreme Court Justice, said after Gross died that he was 'smart as a whip'. While his own investigation gave the perception that much of the nypd was on the take, McDonald implied that the giver was as culpable as the taker. 'Without Harry, there was no graft,' he said.[3]

As was foreseeable, in the aftermath of the 1986 Gross scandal O'Brien resigned from the force with which he had served for 35 years, acknowledging that the court findings had made his position 'untenable'. His farewell words to Acting Mayor Vincent R. Impellitteri were, 'I find it my regretful duty to turn in my shield. It is a hard thing for a policeman to do.'

The 1950s threw up an assortment of sinister gangland figures in New York, from Harry Gross to Mafia chieftain Albert Anastasia, the boss of the Gambino family, known to the press as the 'Mad Hatter' for his unpredictable and violent temper. Anastasia's stormy life was highlighted by a murder wrap that saw him escape the electric chair on a technicality. He subsequently rose to the rank of sergeant in the U.S. armed forces. Soon after his army discharge, he returned to a life of full-time racketeering. He met his death in 1957, in the barber shop of New York's Park Sheraton Hotel, where he was gunned down by rival mobsters while having his daily shave.

Slick Willie, the Merry Robber

The character who led the NYPD on the merriest of chases in the 1950s was Gross's contemporary William 'Willie' Sutton Jr, a gentleman bank robber who lived life on a grand scale, a crook who carried a gun that was never fired in his forty-year career. Sutton's success as a criminal master-mind was without precedent in NYPD annals. Thanks to his genius for disguise, he managed to keep one step ahead of his police pursuers, year after year. He would variously pass himself off as a maintenance worker, a postman or even a police officer, a skill that enabled him to amass more than $2 million from bank heists. It is not surprising that the police offi-cers assigned to his case referred to him as 'Slick Willie'. Sutton escaped from prison three times by adopting disguises, which, on one occasion, turned out to be a meticulously accurate mannequin of himself asleep on his cell bunk bed. In 1950 Sutton's face appeared on the FBI's Ten Most Wanted list. New York cops carried his photo in their notebooks in the vain hope of spotting their target out of disguise.

In February 1952 it was an eagle-eyed citizen who blew the whistle on Sutton. Officers Donald P. Shea and Joseph J. McClellan were on foot patrol in Brooklyn when Arnold Schuster, a 24-year-old clothing salesman, alerted the pair to a man who had got off the subway at the same stop as himself. His face was a dead ringer for the one on the wanted posters. The police found the suspect hunched over his car, repairing a dead battery near his house, which happened to be a short walk from the local police station. When asked to identify himself, he produced a document with the name of Charles Gordon. The police were sceptical – they summoned Detective Louis Weiner, who placed the suspect under arrest for questioning. When he was taken into the station house for fingerprinting, Sutton knew the game was up and decided to come clean about his true identity. Shea and McClellan were promoted three ranks on the spot to first-grade detectives by Commissioner George P. Monaghan. The NYPD's top cop called the arrest the culmination of 'one of the greatest manhunts in the history of the department.'

Schuster fared less well. A month after tipping off the two patrolmen, he was gunned down in a Brooklyn street, shot in the groin and once in each eye. The assassination was believed to have been carried out on the orders of Albert Anastasia, who had a particular hatred of squealers. Schuster's murder was never solved. Sutton was handed a 120-year sen-tence for his last heist, which netted him almost $64,000 from a branch of Manufacturers Trust Company in the Sunnyside neighbourhood of Queens.

In December 1969 Sutton burst into tears as he was being led from Queens Supreme Court. Justice Peter T. Farrell, the same judge who had convicted Sutton in 1952, moved to suspend the sentence on the bank robbery. The decision was taken on compassionate grounds, as Sutton was by that time in failing health, a sickly convict who had spent 35 of his 68 years behind bars. 'Thank you, your honour. God bless you,' Sutton sobbed as he left the courtroom. In 1970 a separate thirty years to life sentence, handed down in 1952 for robbery, was commuted on similar grounds and Sutton was released on parole. After walking out of prison for the last time, Sutton made good use of his criminal experience by working as a consultant for banks on developing theft-deterrent techniques. He was once asked by a journalist why he decided to devote his life to holding up banks: 'Why did I rob banks?' he said. 'Because I enjoyed it. I loved it. I was more alive when I was inside a bank, robbing it, than at any other time in my life. I enjoyed everything about it so much that one or two weeks later I'd be out looking for the next job. But to me the money was the chips, that's all.'[4] Willie Sutton died in 1980 at the age of 75. As was his wish, his remains were laid to rest in an unmarked grave in Brooklyn. He said he had to put up with too much public attention when he was alive.

Serpico Blows the Whistle

Frank Serpico is the name that dominates narratives of the fight to expose corrupt police practices from the 1960s onward. Serpico is a native-born Brooklynite who joined the NYPD in 1959 at the age of 23. He served with the U.S. Army in Korea and worked as a private investigator in New York and Los Angeles while studying for a degree in police science at Brooklyn College. Serpico never imagined he would go on to become the most celebrated whistle-blower in police department history. Much less did he suspect that act of merit would nearly cost him his life in the line of duty. For Serpico, joining the NYPD represented the fulfilment of a young man's dream. Becoming a New York City policeman was a matter of immense personal pride, hence the anger and bitterness he felt on discovering the graft and crookedness that pervaded all levels of the department.

Serpico was sworn in as a probationary patrolman on September 11, 1959. Before taking the oath, he and the other recruits received their shields. Serpico was given the number 19076. The shield was badly tarnished, and as he pinned it on he was already wondering if he could polish it enough to get the tarnish off. Then he was told that the shield could be re-plated, and after the ceremony was over he raced out to have it done.[5]

During the time Serpico served with the force, the majority of New York police officers turned their backs on pay-offs and other illegal arrangements with racketeers and businessmen, which would place them in the echelons of the corrupt. Serpico was unique, however, in that almost none of these 'honest cops' came forward to denounce the graft they were offered or which they knew existed. He was the most celebrated of the department's whistle-blowers, but he was not alone. Detective Sergeant David Durk became Serpico's partner in exposing some of the most shameful abuses of police power. The two men met in 1966 while attending classes for new plainclothes investigators. They were both against taking 'the nut', pay-offs to police by gamblers and narcotics pushers. The following year Serpico and Durk began working together in an attempt to shatter the NYPD's shameful blue wall of silence that was corroding police morale. Serpico was the one most dismayed by the department's culture of rampant corruption. In precinct after precinct, he began to discover cash 'pads', a gangsterism for lists of pay-offs from gambling organizations, with shares for officers, sergeants and higher-ups.

The two whistle-blowers were like proverbial chalk and cheese in their respective backgrounds. Serpico, the son of Neapolitan immigrants of modest origin, spent his childhood in the turbulent Bedford–Stuyvesant section of Brooklyn. He grew up in a gang environment and was even robbed a couple of times when he earned his living polishing shoes in the street. There he came to regard the cop on the corner as an authority figure, the 'only reality' he knew. Durk, a physician's son, came from a comfortable middle-class Manhattan home. After graduating from Amherst College, he attended Columbia Law School and sold East African carvings before deciding to join the police force, a life he envisaged as 'more exciting' than working as a lawyer. What bound the two officers together was a shared determination to do something about corruption within the department.

Durk was angered by stories of cops on the take, but he was not that close to the graft scene. His chief source of information about police corruption came from his friend and colleague Serpico, a man he came to emulate. In later testimony to the State Supreme Court in the Bronx, Serpico maintained that while most officers wanted to be honest, they could not easily follow that path because of ingrained corruption within the system.

Over the next few years, Serpico and Durk took their complaints to high-ranking police and City Hall officials, including Jay Kriegel, Mayor John Lindsay's police liaison, and commissioner of investigation Arnold Fraiman. They handed over an abundance of names, dates, places and other information, but were told that nothing could be done. Fraiman somewhat unconvincingly lamented that the information they were offering was not specific enough. Kriegel's excuse for inaction was his concern about alienating the police in a period of expected civil disturbances, which in the end never materialized.

In the summer of 1968 New York City held its breath following Martin Luther King Jr's assassination. Everyone anticipated a repetition of the rioting that had broken out in more than a hundred U.S. cities that year. Contrary to the dire forecasts, the city almost totally avoided violence thanks in good measure to the mayor's timely visit to Harlem. Lindsay made an impassioned and persuasive public statement deploring King's murder and promising aid for the residents of Harlem's large black population. His words had a mitigating effect on a community seething with outrage over their hero's murder. As he spoke, the police stood by uneasily, waiting for the streets to explode in riot. It never happened, though a few outbreaks of looting were reported around the neighbourhood and in parts of Brooklyn.

Serpico and Durk had set out to probe the depths of a pay-off system of staggering proportions, one which over the years had spread like molten lava across the city's police precincts. What made their digging all the more difficult was that the vast majority of those implicated in the scandal were protected by lava-resistant armour. Of the nearly 140 cases of police misconduct that were referred to the department between 1967 and 1970, only seven resulted in dismissals from the force. By and large, the judiciary and police higher-ups chose to play it safe by declining to pursue the corruption epidemic with appropriate rigour. A case in point was Arnold Fraiman, the former commissioner of investigation who served as state supreme court judge until 1969. Fraiman opted not to look into charges that Bronx gamblers were passing between $800 and $1,000 a month in protection money to police pockets. New York's Joint Legislative Committee on Crime reported in 1970 that the city's 10,000 small Puerto Rican-owned grocery shops were handing over $6.2 million a year to local cops in weekly payments and gifts of food. This was given as an insurance premium against being issued summonses on minor charges.

After months of investigative work, interviewing sources within the NYPD along with department outsiders, in April 1970 the *New York Times* blew the cover off police graft in a sensational report that put a price tag of $1.5 billion a year in bets on the numbers racket alone.[6] Of this, about $15 million was spent on pay-offs to police and government officials. The newspaper quoted retired NYPD sergeant Ralph Salerno as saying, 'Police officials always talk about the occasional rotten apple in the barrel when corruption comes up. They'd be a lot more honest if they talked about the rotten barrel.'[7]

The paper's investigative reporters found that building contractors were paying local patrolmen up to $400 a month to make sure no trouble befell their sites and that construction premises enjoyed immunity to parking fines. Police were also reported to be extorting vast sums from the city's drug dealers. The extent of this line of corruption came to light in February 1970, when three detectives were charged with pocketing $1,200 in cash, along with 105 packets of heroin and a variety of personal possessions taken from five pushers. More than 2,000 off-licences would routinely pass 'Christmas presents' to local patrolmen, ranging from $5 to $50 according to rank, along with a bottle of spirits. In return, customers and suppliers were allowed to double-park in front of the shop, and as an added bonus the shopkeeper knew he could expect a speedy response from the police if help was needed. Another source of illegal money was the 'reward' large retailers paid for the return of stolen goods. On one occasion, an NYPD detective and a lieutenant assigned to Manhattan's Lower West Side were indicted on charges of extracting $5,000 from a Montgomery Ward department store branch, on the promise the cops would be able to locate two vans filled with stolen radio equipment.

When word of these criminal activities swept through the precincts, Serpico embarked on a campaign to uncover and denounce corruption inside the NYPD. The chief whistle-blower soon found himself cold-shouldered by his colleagues. Durk reported that his life was once threatened by a fellow officer at the police pistol range. For Serpico, however, who was the first NYPD officer in the department's history to openly condemn corruption and testify about it in court, things got a lot worse. Serpico was always going to be perceived as something of an oddball by his fellow officers. The image of the NYPD patrolman as a conformist and almost staid individual clashed sharply with the bearded, Greenwich Village-living, hippie-attired Narcotics Squad officer so masterfully depicted by Al Pacino in the 1973 neo-noir biographical film *Serpico*.

On the night of 3 February 1971 Serpico joined several officers on a narcotics raid in the Williamsburg district of Brooklyn, a neighbourhood in those days notorious for gangland activity and drug trafficking. Serpico had wedged himself in the half-opened door of a known heroin dealer when suddenly he saw a gun pointed at his head from the dark interior of the flat. 'He simultaneously heard the roar as the gun went off and saw the flash – an enormous burst of colours, merging reds and yellows – and felt the searing heat in his head, as if a million white-hot needles had been plunged into it. He had been shot in the face.'[8] Serpico returned fire, hitting his assailant before falling to the floor, bleeding profusely.

For reasons never officially clarified, the other officers standing in the hallway when the shot was fired failed to call for assistance. Serpico was rushed to Greenpoint Hospital only when an elderly neighbour called the police. When the news was radioed to police headquarters, the initial fear was that Serpico had been gunned down by one of his colleagues in the drugs bust. If true, this could have been in retaliation for Serpico's testimony six months previously. He had come forward as a central witness in the perjury trial of a plainclothesman convicted and sent to prison for taking thousands of dollars in bribes. Had retaliation been the case, it would have surprised few in the department, for Serpico had already been threatened with violence by other cops, even at knife point.

After much prevarication, in 1970 Mayor Lindsay had agreed to put together a panel to investigate the widely shared allegation of corruption within the police department. The committee became known as the Knapp Commission, whose chairman, Judge Whitman Knapp, was a jurist of impeccable credentials. The judge was a one-time prosecutor with the Manhattan District Attorney's Office, which added legitimacy to the endeavour and offered the commission a unique law enforcement perspective. The committee was a five-member panel, composed of well-known figures like Cyrus Vance, who served as secretary of state under Jimmy Carter, and philanthropist Franklin Thomas, former chairman of the Ford Foundation. Knapp and the commission members knew that their task of investigating an opaque brotherhood of police officers was never going to be an easy one.

Though they had compiled a list of nearly 1,700 citizen complaints by the time the commission convened its opening session, the most credible evidence was to come from inside the police department. Most of the testimony by patrolmen conformed to a pattern of gradual induction into a life of dishonesty on the job. Patrolman Edward F. Droge Jr, a witness at the proceedings, said that for him the real education of a rookie policeman came not at the Police Academy, but in the streets of Williamsburg in Brooklyn. Droge was assigned to the 90th Precinct and, within a short time, he was introduced to the custom of receiving free meals from shopkeepers. It became a routine of petty graft, sometimes picking up boxes of hot dogs from 'friendly' grocers, and once even watching his colleagues make off with armloads of shirts from a factory where the police had been called in after a burglary. The retinue of accusations and revelations of corruption was like turning over a rock and seeing what lay underneath. Droge told the commission that all but two of the 70 to 75 policemen he worked with in Brooklyn regularly took small bribes from gamblers, tow truck operators, cheque cashers and supermarket operators. As for his personal involvement in bribery, Droge estimated his take while assigned to a patrol car was between $60 and $100 a month.

The commission learned that corruption was by no means confined to the lower ranks of the force. Daily evidence revealed that the top brass ignored and even abetted dishonest dealings.

> The chief inspector, the department's highest uniformed officer, acknowledged accepting gifts from businessmen. The chief of detectives refused to turn over his files of suspect detectives to the Chief of Inspectional Services. A confrontation in the chief of detectives' office ended in a fistfight. The chief of internal affairs left, bruised and empty-handed.[9]

The commission got a lucky break and simultaneously achieved a higher public profile when, during the investigation, Manhattan Patrolman

Police officer Frank Serpico gives testimony on police corruption before the
Knapp Commission in 1971.

William Phillips was seen taking a bribe from Xaviera Hollander, a prostitute who ran a brothel on the Upper East Side. Phillips agreed to testify before the commission to avoid prosecution. Yet the most hard-hitting evidence of all came from Serpico. One of the most memorable and damning of his statements to the commission was: 'Ten percent of the cops in New York City are absolutely corrupt, ten percent are absolutely honest, and the other eighty percent – they wish they were honest.' There is no doubt that Serpico's testimony served to enrage some of the less honourable members of the force. In July 1971 NYPD officials confirmed there had been threats of violence against that 'bearded policeman' and that detectives had been assigned to protect him from further retaliation.

Serpico spent six weeks in hospital, returning on 15 March to his Greenwich Village home to begin a long period of convalescence from his near-fatal wounds. In May, still beset by blinding headaches that struck without warning, he reluctantly paid a visit to police headquarters to be presented with his detective gold shield by Commissioner Patrick Murphy. Serpico was less than enthusiastic about receiving the award. For him, it was foreseeable that little would be done to address the issue of dishonest behaviour in the ranks.

As for Durk, in 1973 he went off to advise a federal investigation on underworld influence in New York's Garment Centre, a mission that was called off after eighteen months. He was then banished to a small police office in Queens, and subsequently took a year's leave of absence at the United Nations to study crime issues, retiring from the force in 1985.

Cops on Cops

The 1894 Lexow Committee had disclosed police involvement in vice operations and identified a number of officers responsible for rigging elections and police brutality. The 1930 investigation led by Samuel Seabury uncovered rampant corruption and a relentless practice of harassment of innocent women by police vice squads. Periodic scandals sparked attempts to reform and bring professionalism to the force, but these efforts proved slow and largely ineffective. One of the measures to come out of the Knapp Commission was the creation of the NYPD's Internal Affairs Division (IAD), with units stationed in every borough command. By the late 1970s about a hundred officers were assigned full-time to the IAD and another two hundred to the Field Internal Affairs Units (FIAU). One segment of this strategy to reduce opportunities for corruption and misconduct at the precinct level was the designation, in 1973, of an integrity control officer (ICO) with the rank of lieutenant. He became a key member of a commanding officer's management staff, to serve as the 'eyes and ears' of the department.

The IAD composed about one-third of the Inspectional Services Bureau, which included the Inspections Division, the Intelligence Division and the Internal Affairs Division. The IAD reported through channels and their information was filtered up and down the chain of command. When the Internal Affairs Bureau (IAB) was born in January 1993, it became a stand-alone bureau reporting directly to the police commissioner. This was deemed an important step in being able to fight corruption and get the support it needed to work independently within the NYPD. No deputy commissioner or chief could influence the IAB because its officers worked directly for the commissioner.

Charles Campisi headed the IAB from 1996 to 2014, working under four police commissioners, where he gained the reputation of a hard-fisted and incorruptible cop. During Campisi's IAB tenure, the number of New Yorkers shot, wounded or killed by NYPD officers every year declined by 90 per cent, and the number of police failing integrity tests also shrank to an all-time low. 'It might not be so bad if the IAB had a reputation for rooting out serious corruption and misconduct,' says Campisi. 'But it doesn't. In the rank-and-file view, the IAB seems more interested in busting cops for administrative violations – not wearing their hats when they get out of a patrol car, calling in sick so they can go to their daughter's dance recital, that sort of thing – than in spending the time and effort to go after really bad cops.'[10] Campisi considers it unfortunate that many people believe the Internal Affairs Bureau is out to hurt good cops just doing their jobs.

'The IAB in New York is not interested in minor violations,' says Campisi. 'It concentrates on criminal activity committed by an extremely small segment of the men and women that make up the NYPD.'

Serpico takes the view that there is very little reward for those who make a serious effort to expose and punish bad cops. 'What has not changed is the negative response to those who expose or wish to expose corruption,' he says. 'There is an attempt to belittle, demonize and undermine their credibility, instead of exalting them for coming forward and presenting an opportunity to improve the status quo. The anti-corruption commissions set up over the years have not been of much use. They have brought about at best some exposure and a change of tactics. The real players move up in the hierarchy food chain.'[11]

While Serpico was arguing for a radical shake-up within the police department to combat corruption, outside the great chamber of the City Bar Association events were gathering pace that were to stretch the department's policing resources to its limit. The breakdown in order of the 1970s, from senseless acts of vandalism to brutal homicide, had New York in its grip, to the point that the city's social order looked to be on the brink of wholesale disintegration. Criminality and general fear enshrouded the streets. Polished metal panels were installed next to subway staircases to give commuters a glimpse of assailants who might be lurking in the shadows. Gangs of muggers lay in wait for unwary shoppers coming out of department stores along fashionable Fifth Avenue. Rapes and robberies at gunpoint were routinely reported in Central Park, by now out of bounds even in daylight hours.

Crime Hits the Big Screen

The cinema offers a revealing starting point for those who may wish to experience the flavour of New York in its grimmest days. Several films depicting life in the city in the 1970s may strike the cinemagoer, and especially one who lived through that era, more as documentaries than screen fiction. Ernest Tidyman's 1971 action thriller *The French Connection* tells the story of two NYPD detectives in pursuit of French heroin smugglers in New York. The film is based on Robin Moore's non-fiction account of the outbreak of drug trafficking in the city in the late 1960s. The author did not have to probe very deeply for factual evidence to support his narrative. At that time, heroin usage was spiralling to record highs, with 28 deaths of young addicts reported in a ten-day period in June 1968. A city medical examiner described this as the worst upsurge of heroin-related deaths in memory. Hard drugs were directly linked to a near 25 per cent increase in youth homicides in that year alone, as police fought a running battle to stave off violence between rival New York drug gangs.

Coming hard on the heels of *The French Connection* is Martin Scorsese's *Taxi Driver*, with Robert De Niro in the starring role as New York cabbie Travis Bickle. He haunts the streets at night, retreating ever deeper into detachment from reality, a dark story set against the city's darkest recesses. Travis ends up shooting several gangsters in the seedy environment of a brothel, in what was formerly the no-go area of the East Village.

In February 1965 New York riot police were placed on high alert after the assassination of human rights activist Malcolm X at the Audubon Ballroom in Broadway. It became a murder that inflamed tensions between rival black Muslim groups. Harlem was still reeling from the previous summer's rioting, brought about by an NYPD patrolman's fatal shooting of a black youth. Later that year, a citywide power failure left hundreds of thousands of New Yorkers trapped in lifts, subways and commuter trains during rush hours. Those days composed the backdrop for Sol Yurick's novel *The Warriors*, a book that in 1979 Walter Hill adapted for the cinema under the same title. The film tells the story of New York gang members who meet to discuss an alliance that would leave New York in their hands, as together they outnumbered the police by three to one. The truce breaks down in an orgy of killing and the

Warriors embark on a 30-mile (48 km) journey from the northern tip of the Bronx to Coney Island in southern Brooklyn, leaving in their wake a trail of arson, murder and fierce clashes with the police.

Taken together, these films portray a city drifting from a state of law and personal security into a maelstrom of social disorder. New York had become a metropolis teetering on the brink of chaos, staring into what law enforcers, politicians and the media alike envisaged to be an approaching apocalypse. The full impact of the meltdown was yet to make itself felt.

6

Fear City

Police corruption scandals in abundance, a financial crisis auda-
ciously ignored and even scorned by U.S. president Gerald Ford,[1]
great swathes of New York City streets rendered unsafe for shoppers and residents – the general sense of impending doom was summed
up in New Yorkese vernacular by the cab driver taking Leslie Charteris's
fictional anti-hero the Saint to Grand Central Terminal: 'I can't figger
what dis city is comin' to,' he remarks in *The Saint in New York*.

In the decade and a half between Mayor O'Dwyer's resignation in
1950 and Lindsay's first electoral victory in 1965, one name stands out
as New York's most influential political leader since La Guardia. Robert
F. Wagner Jr shares a place in the pantheon of great New York mayors
with the 'Little Flower' (La Guardia), and also the superstar mayor of
the twenty-first century, Michael Bloomberg, who can be credited with
having served three successive terms of office at City Hall. Wagner's
soft-spoken manner and kindly smile concealed a resolute determination
to break Tammany's grip on municipal politics. It was paradoxically the
patronage of the Machine's political kingmaker Carmine De Sapio that
put Wagner in the forefront in the 1953 mayoralty race. Five years after
taking office, Wagner began distancing himself from De Sapio and the
Machine, with the final split coming in 1961. That year Wagner stepped
forward as a reformist and, by 1969, a fallen De Sapio was languishing
in jail on a petty bribery charge – the Machine's stranglehold on the city
and its police force had come to an inglorious end.

Of the three police commissioners who served under the Wagner
administration, the toughest years by far fell to Michael J. Murphy. New
York's scholarly, widely admired chief cop spent many days under extreme

pressure at the 240 Centre Street headquarters. This was during the tumultuous 1960s, an era punctuated by riots and bitter accusations of police brutality. The trying events with which he had to deal followed in quick succession in 1963 and 1964. First came the sensational story of the murders of Janice Wylie and Emily Hoffert. In August 1963 the bodies of the two young Manhattan socialites were found in their swanky Upper East Side apartment, their corpses bound together by strips of bedsheets. This was sensationalized in the media as the 'Career Girl Murders'. An eight-month manhunt by hundreds of officers and involving thousands of leads failed to yield any results. Finally, a mentally disturbed nineteen-year-old by the name of George Whitmore was arrested and convicted of the murders. It took nearly ten years of legal entanglements for Whitmore's conviction to be overturned, an ordeal that served as the basis of the 1973 television film *The Marcus-Nelson Murders*, which in turn became a pilot for the crime drama series *Kojak*. During this time, the police picked up Ricky Robles, a heroin addict, who was interrogated, put on trial and confessed to murdering the two women. Robles has to date spent more than fifty years behind bars, where even now he continues to press for his release.

See Nothing, Say Nothing

Murphy scarcely had time to lay the Robles case to rest than New York was stunned by the horrific death of bar manager Catherine 'Kitty' Genovese. For half an hour in the pre-dawn hours of 13 March 1964, dozens of residents of Queens stood by and watched a killer stalk and stab Genovese in three separate attacks in the Kew Gardens district. The murderer was twice frightened off by shouts and lights from bedroom windows. Each time he returned, sought out his victim and stabbed her again. The third attack left her lying dead next to a car park. According to newspaper accounts, not a single person telephoned the police to report the assault.[2] Ignoring the 28-year-old woman's cries for help, neighbours shut their doors to silence her screams.

The police officers who went about the neighbourhood interviewing local residents were outraged by people's refusal to get involved. It is not surprising that ordinary people would want to distance themselves from the police. This was when narcotics dealers, gamblers and businessmen alike were making illicit payments of millions of dollars a year to NYPD officers. One West Side shop owner said he paid the police about $2,000 a year in cash tips and free or cut-rate alcohol. Rampant corruption had the effect of imposing a massive secret tax on the citizens of New York, while diluting law enforcement and undermining public faith in the justice system.

This reflected a pattern of collective fright, confusion and apathy that became known to psychologists as the 'bystander effect', and in the media as the 'Genovese Syndrome'. Assistant Chief Inspector Frederick M. Lussen, who at the time was in charge of Queens detectives, expressed shock at the failure of those who had witnessed the murder to intervene, or at least report the incident. 'If we had been called when he first attacked, the woman might not be dead now,' he said. A suspect named Winston Moseley was arrested during a house burglary six days after the murder. While in custody he confessed to killing Genovese, as well as stabbing two black women to death, one a fifteen-year-old girl. Moseley said he wanted to see if there was a difference between the two races. He was found guilty of first-degree murder and condemned to die in the electric chair. His sentence was later commuted to life in prison, where he remained for 52 years until his death in 2016.

Crime was on the ascendant in the last years of the Wagner administration. In 1961 the NYPD reported 390 homicides in the city. By 1964 that figure had risen by nearly two-thirds, to 636. The public apathy on that night was condemned as being as much responsible for Genovese's death as Moseley himself. 'I didn't want to get involved' was the mantra voiced by many witnesses interviewed by the police. The story of Genovese's death quickly took on a life of its own. It became symbolic of an ominous change taking place in the city's life, showing that 'a worrisome number of New Yorkers were no longer prepared to take the responsibilities or follow the rules that bound the city together.'[3]

After the Genovese murder, the NYPD spearheaded a national drive to introduce the 911 emergency call system, which was established in 1968. At the time of her killing, the only option for emergency callers was to phone the operator or call the local precinct. The Genovese case provided the crucial impetus for the roll-out of the nationwide 911 number, which now handles more than 11 million calls per year. There is a pinch of grim melancholy in one of Moseley's pleas for parole, in which he expressed his belief, perhaps to gain favour with the police, that the establishment of the 911 system warranted favourable consideration.

If ever a police case brought on a deluge of commercial spin-offs it was the murder of Kitty Genovese. The year after her brutal killing, a Perry Mason television episode portrayed a young woman whose screams for help when she was attacked by an assailant were ignored by neighbours in her building. Fully ten television serials and cinema productions have since been based on the Genovese homicide, while six novels and non-fiction accounts of the murder have been published.

* * *

THE NYPD, like all metropolitan police forces, is burdened with the challenge of controlling public gatherings by peaceful methods, above all when an orderly demonstration disintegrates into mob violence. By the mid-twentieth century New York's law enforcement agencies, in their various historical guises, had accumulated many years of expertise in handling the entire panoply of criminal activities, from illegal gambling and prostitution to robbery and homicide. In the decade from 1954 to 1964, the NYPD added more than 7,000 men and women to the ranks, bringing the total manpower to 29,407 well-trained, and for the most part honest, officers. For more than a century, taking as the starting point the Astor Place Riot of 1849, the police had met with limited success in containing public insurrection. In a word, the dilemma consisted of confronting overwhelming numbers of angry citizens while doing the utmost to restrict the severity of the response. This operational handicap left the NYPD ill-prepared to tackle the civil disorder that exploded on a steamy July night in 1964, in the centre of Harlem and the Bedford–Stuyvesant neighbourhood of Brooklyn.

Cops and Rioters

Off-duty Lieutenant James J. Gilligan, a 6-foot-3-inch Marine Corps veteran, was strolling along East 76th Street in Manhattan's Yorkville area, when he spotted a black youth brandishing a knife. Gilligan shouted at the boy to drop the blade, while at the same time he whipped out his badge and service revolver. The boy, fifteen-year-old James Powell, turned and dashed into the dark hallway of a building behind him. Finding himself cornered with no escape route, Powell ran out and lunged at Gilligan. The officer fired off three shots, killing his assailant on the spot. When Gilligan put in a call for assistance, the squad cars that

Police with guns drawn stand watch at the Harlem riot of 1964.

rushed to the scene were greeted by a barrage of bottles, tins and paving stones, pitched from across the road by some three hundred black youths attending a summer school. The news of Powell's killing by a white cop spread like a bushfire through the streets of Harlem. Two days later, a large crowd was gathered outside the 123rd Street police station to protest the slaying. The demonstration quickly deteriorated into a full-scale riot, with thousands of people spreading chaos across Harlem and the predominantly black district of Bedford–Stuyvesant. Turmoil and disorder engulfed the two neighbourhoods for six days, while gangs roamed the streets smashing windows, looting shops and attacking any police officers found within range of their missiles.

Many rioters clambered to nearby rooftops, hurling loose bricks, tiles and masonry at the beleaguered cops who were struggling to contain the mob. The police attempted to disperse the crowds into smaller groups, but this only served to intensify the general anger. The stakes were dangerously ratcheted up when Molotov cocktails were sent flying at patrol cars. Commissioner Murphy, who was directing the anti-riot operations, gave the Tactical Patrol Force permission to draw their firearms. The NYPD's Tactical Patrol Force (TPF, or Tough Police Force, as it was called by its members) was an elite unit set up in 1959 to deal with rising crime in New York. TPF recruits were all volunteers, but they had to be young, at least 6 foot tall and have high activity records as police officers. By the late 1960s there were nearly 1,000 members of this special squad. They almost immediately drew criticism for an alleged excess of zealousness. On one occasion, a TPF officer captured the actor James Coburn while he was filming a chase scene for the 1967 satirical comedy *The President's Analyst*. People often complained that they acted with equal force against litterbugs and jaywalkers as when moving in on dangerous criminals. Their original mission was to combat mugging and supplement regular precinct officers between the peak crime hours of 6 p.m. to 2 a.m. The TPF had been hailed as the police force of the future, as well as an example of how protection is more to do with a physical police presence than a precinct. The controversial unit drew much criticism, including from within the NYPD, before it was disbanded in 1984.

In the mayhem of the Harlem and Bedford–Stuyvesant riots, the police let off a volley of shots into the air. A few minutes later, one protestor was found lying on the pavement, mortally wounded by a .38 calibre bullet, the ammunition used by NYPD officers. When the clashes finally abated and calm had been restored to the streets, the best estimate of the final tally was one dead protestor, more than a hundred injured, including nearly thirty police officers, and 465 people taken into custody.

The incident that touched off six nights of turmoil in Harlem and Brooklyn was to incite further anger when, in November 1964, the NYPD's Civilian Complaint Review Board (CCRB) absolved Lieutenant Gilligan, who had been temporarily suspended during a departmental investigation, of any wrongdoing in the fatal shooting of James Powell.[4] The NYPD established the CCRB in 1953 to investigate civilian complaints against New York City police officers. Forty years later, the board became an all-civilian agency independent of the department. The James Powell shooting prompted church leaders, civil rights activists and members of the legal profession to unite in indignation over the alleged police 'whitewash'. Murphy announced that the CCRB had 'unanimously concluded there were no violations of the rules and procedures of the department'. He also pointed out that, in September, a New York grand jury had already cleared Gilligan of criminal responsibility. It is arguable whether the NYPD had closed ranks around what amounted to a cover-up, but what is certain is that the CCRB ruling achieved two things: for many this served as further evidence of police 'immunity' from public scrutiny, while, to the benefit of the NYPD, it avoided what would certainly have provoked extreme demoralization within the department.

The gruesome execution-style killing of two glamorous Manhattan socialites, the stabbing to death of a young woman in full view of bystanders who refused to get involved, a week of pitched street battles between police and rioters – horrific as these incidents were, they served as mere scene-setters for the decade that nearly saw New York City consigned to the rubbish heap as a hopelessly bankrupt, crime-ridden and ungovernable metropolis.

Former IAB head Charles Campisi joined the NYPD in 1973. He was assigned to the 73rd Precinct in Brooklyn's Brownsville and Ocean Hill area, in what was at that time a three-storey building which fellow officers baptized as 'Fort Zinderneuf', after the remote desert outpost featured in Percival Christopher Wren's 1924 novel Beau Geste. There was even a flag with a 'Z' printed on it hanging over the arched granite entrance. 'Those were terrible days for New York,' says Campisi.

> The precinct radio never seemed to stop. We were short-staffed, thanks to the fiscal crisis of the mid-1970s, when more than five thousand cops were laid off. For the police, we were swimming against the tide. The scourge of lawlessness that swamped the city in the 1980s was due to the combined effect of near fiscal disintegration and an epidemic of crack cocaine and other hard drugs. We did our best to combat and contain the violence, but it was like talking one step forward and two backward.[5]

As the decade progressed New York began to acquire an uglier, more menacing face. It was an era of economic hard times and drug-fuelled violence, with its attendant climate of fear. Hostage-taking and terrorist bombings were far from unknown in the city's history – one has only to recall the deadly Wall Street bombing of 1920 and the Lindbergh kidnapping twelve years later, two incidents that stand out as particularly odious examples of criminal brutality.

The incident that drove home the need to refine police tactics in the response to criminal acts involving the taking of hostages was a Brooklyn bank robbery that took place in August 1972. The assault on a branch of Chase Manhattan Bank turned into the heist of the decade, one which had the entire nation riveted to television screens, and three years later was adapted for the cinema as *Dog Day Afternoon*, with Al Pacino in the starring role. The botched bank heist was the brainchild of John Wojtowicz, a young, married Vietnam War veteran who secretly kept up a stream of homosexual affairs. It is believed he organized the hold-up to pay for his lover's sex-change surgery.

Wojtowicz's two accomplices were Salvatore Naturale and Robert Westenberg, the latter of whom got cold feet and fled as they were about to move in on the bank. The Chase Manhattan Bank was chosen as

The aftermath of the Wall Street bombing of 1920. More than thirty people died in the attack, and the perpetrators were never brought to justice.

their target after seeing the film *The Godfather*. The two robbers stepped casually into the branch in the Gravesend district of Brooklyn, where Wojtowicz handed the clerk a note that read: 'This is an offer you can't refuse.' The next thing the teller saw was the barrel of a shotgun pointed at her head. The pair held seven bank employees hostage while they seized more than $200,000 in cash and traveller's cheques. The heist almost immediately turned into a media circus, during which, at one point, Wojtowicz ordered a takeaway pizza and then tossed fistfuls of stolen money to the cheering crowds outside. Fourteen hours later, with only two shots having been exchanged, the police agreed to drive the robbers to John F. Kennedy Airport and put them on an international flight. The two men naively fell for the ruse, never suspecting that police agents were in waiting at the airport, where Salvatore was shot dead attempting to escape and Wojtowicz was arrested and subsequently given a twenty-year prison sentence. The NYPD came under reproach for the heavy-handed tactics employed with what were obviously a pair of inept comedians. There were calls for departmental innovation in dealing with hostage situations. With seven people held at gunpoint by two nervous amateurs, the attempted robbery could have had a tragic outcome. Five months later, a second, far more serious robbery involving hostages was to drive home the point.

'Talk to Me'

On 19 January 1973, in sub-freezing weather and with a blanket of fresh snow on the ground, New York got its first taste of deadly jihadist terrorism. The scene was Brooklyn's Williamsburg district, home to tens of thousands of Hasidic Jews and not far from where Frank Serpico had been shot two years previously. Until then, the worst of the anarchy was believed to be concentrated 13 miles (20 km) to the north, in the derelict slums of the South Bronx. In that month alone, and in the span of one week, the NYPD had recorded the killing of a drug pusher, shot by six bullets that shaped a cross across his chest; the hijacking of a bus whose driver was held at gunpoint while passengers were relieved of wallets, watches and other valuables; and the crippling of a runaway young girl who was savagely thrashed with belts and chains. Those were only the most recent of more than eight hundred violent crimes linked by the police to the gangs that proliferated in the South Bronx. Police

Inspector Robert H. Johnson, who was in charge of the ninety-strong youth gang task force in the Bronx, said at the time that in the previous year, that is 1972, 130 of these bands operating in the district accounted for more than thirty murders, 22 attempted homicides, three hundred assaults, ten rapes and 124 armed robberies. Even with their resources stretched to the limit, the police were able to make some 1,500 arrests. Johnson added that the highest number of youth gang homicides for the entire city until then had amounted to twelve, which were recorded in 1962.

That January night in Brooklyn it was armed assault with a twist. The action unfolded at a Brooklyn sports equipment shop, where four young Muslim men brandishing pistols burst into the shop, aiming to steal a cache of firearms and ammunition. Their plan was to launch a jihad against churches and synagogues in the neighbourhood. Unnoticed by the gunmen, an employee had tripped a silent alarm, bringing hundreds of armed police to the streets around the shop. Police sharpshooters crouched behind vehicles, rooftops and the elevated BMT subway tracks overlooking the premises between Myrtle Avenue and Melrose Street. Eleven employees and customers were taken hostage. Without warning, the four terrorists began firing at the police, sparking a 47-hour stand-off that left one policeman, Patrolman Stephen Gilroy, dead and two fellow officers wounded. The contingent of heavily armed officers maintained a massive but impotent cordon of firepower around the shop. Inside, the gunmen rejected repeated appeals for a peaceful surrender. An imam from a local mosque was summoned to try to reason with the gunmen. He was harangued with the fanatical rhetoric that was to become all too familiar in future Islamist campaigns. One of the terrorists cried out: 'This is the end, this is glory – we'll go out in a hail of bullets.'

Fearing for the lives of the six men and three women being held inside, the police told the terrorists no attempt would be made to storm the shop. The siege became one of the longest such dramas in the city's history, as well as a signal moment in the NYPD's approach to hostage situations. Instead of brute force, the police used psychology, firearms discipline and patience to end the stand-off. This was a modus operandi that would be codified in the department's hostage-negotiating training programme which came into effect later that year. 'We know some of you are hurt,' boomed a bullhorn on top of an armoured police vehicle outside the sports equipment shop. 'We want to help you. Please come out with your hands on your heads and you will be well treated. There is no place for you to go. The building, the block and the entire area is surrounded.'

By Sunday afternoon, 43 hours after the siege had begun, the exhausted terrorists lost their leverage. The nine remaining hostages (two had been released and a third was let go in exchange for a doctor bringing medical supplies) were left unattended by the gunmen when they suddenly heard footsteps in the adjacent furniture shop. Led by a shop manager, the six men and three women tore through a half-inch plasterboard wall to run to a hidden staircase that took them to the roof. They came into view, one by one, their hands clasped above their heads, and were escorted into the vans of the police officers standing guard. Four hours later, the hostage-takers surrendered. One came out waving a letter that read: 'O Muslims! Unite against the oppressive infidels whose aim is the destruction of Islam.' In 1974 the men were tried in state supreme court in Brooklyn. A jury found them guilty on 41 counts, including murder, kidnapping and robbery. They were sentenced to thirty years in prison and were released on parole five years later.

The Brooklyn Islamist episode set a precedent in police hostage-taking methodology, which in turn gave rise to the creation of the NYPD's Hostage Negotiation Team (HNT). According to police sources, this was the first law enforcement hostage negotiation unit of its kind in the world. It was founded under the motto 'Talk to Me', an axiom intended to emphasize communication as an essential police negotiation practice for crisis negotiators. Harvey Schlossberg, a clinical psychologist and former police officer, set out the behavioural, emotional and cognitive framework for the newly formed unit. Detective Captain Frank Bolz Jr added his tactical experience and became the unit's first commanding officer. For a decade after the HNT was formed in 1973, Bolz served as the team's chief negotiator until his retirement in 1982. During that time he handled about 285 incidents, which brought the safe release of 850 hostages from aeroplanes, buses, supermarkets and banks. This elite unit is today made up of some 250 officers. Bolz says that, in his career, the toughest hostage situation was always the next one. 'Each one is a life-and-death job,' he says. 'No matter how good your record has been, it's a new roll of the dice. You don't know who you're dealing with.'[6]

Bolz's baptism of fire came in his first year on the job. He and a team of negotiators responded to the report of a bank robbery in East

Harlem. By the time they arrived at the scene, one of the perpetrators had been shot and killed by the police and was lying in a pool of blood in front of the bank. Two others were still inside the bank holding a number of employees and customers hostage. The tactical perimeters had been set up, however the outer perimeters were very porous, so that many civilians were walking around the incident area, including school-children. The description of the robbers was 3/B/M (three black males) armed with handguns. Two of the negotiators were black and were also walking around with unholstered guns inside the loosely set perimeters. After prolonged negotiations, the bank incident ended successfully with all the hostages released, the negotiators talking and no further injuries.

Stay Away from This City

Anyone strolling along Manhattan's bustling shopping streets today would find it hard to believe that this was, well within living memory, once known as 'Fear City'. The late-night television host Johnny Carson once remarked on his *Tonight Show* programme: 'It was so quiet in Central Park last night you could have heard a knife drop.' It is worth noting that this biting comment came from the safe remove of Burbank, California, where Carson had shifted his studio in 1972 from its origi-nal headquarters in New York's Rockefeller Centre. By early 1975 New York City owed almost $6 billion in short-term debt, out of an operat-ing budget of $11.5 billion. That year, the Wall Street banks and the bond market that lent New York money to pay bills decided that the days of binge spending had at last made it a bad risk. They summarily switched off the tap, leaving the city's finances high and dry. New York could no longer serve as both poorhouse and cash machine for the nation. The city turned to Washington for help, asking the federal government to back its bonds while it put its fiscal house in order, by making swinge-ing budget cuts and reforms. It was then that President Gerald Ford decided to advance his own political prospects by holding New York up for ridicule to the rest of the nation. Ford insisted that the city's 'day of reckoning' had come and promised he would 'veto any bill that has as its purpose a bailout of New York City to prevent a default'. The city was effectively cut adrift without a hope of receiving outside aid.

Starting on the morning of 13 June 1975, tourists and other visitors arriving at the city's airports, bus terminals and Midtown hotels were greeted by off-duty policemen who were handing out leaflets entitled 'Welcome to Fear City: A Survival Guide for Visitors to the City of New York'. The four-page pamphlet was being distributed by disgruntled patrolmen of the NYPD, along with colleagues of unions representing 60,000 members of the Fire Department and other public safety officers. The cops offered anyone who stopped to listen a lecture about the need to stay away from New York because of the prevailing wave of crime and violence. The pamphlet's cover bore the image of the hooded skull of Death. The text contained such stark warnings as, 'Until things change, stay away from New York City if you possibly can.' Inside was a list of nine 'guidelines' that *might* allow you to get out of the city alive and with your personal property intact. These titbits of advice painted a nightmarish vision of New York. Visitors were advised not to venture outside of Midtown Manhattan, not to ride the subway under any circumstances and not to walk outside anywhere after 6 p.m. Tourists were also instructed to personalize their possessions with special metallic pens, to clutch their bags with both hands, to hide any property they might have in their cars and not even to trust their valuables to hotel vaults. In fairness, it must be noted that the campaign was carried out almost entirely by rank-and-file patrolmen. The majority of New York's municipal unions condemned or distanced themselves from the Fear City campaign, including those representing police sergeants, lieutenants and captains.

A frightening truth lurked beneath much of the pamphlet's calamity-howling. Crime, and most markedly violent crime, had been increasing rapidly for years. The number of murders in the city had risen more than twofold over the past decade, from 681 homicides in 1965 to 1,690 in 1975. Car thefts and physical assaults had also more than doubled in the same period, while the number of reported rapes and burglaries were three times higher, and robberies had shot up an astonishing tenfold. The historian, novelist and New York City resident Kevin Baker tells us:

It's difficult to convey just how precarious, and paranoid, life in New York felt around that time. Signs everywhere warned you to mind your valuables, and to keep neck chains or other jewellery tucked away while on the subway. You became alert to where anyone else might be in relation to you, augmented by quick looks over your shoulder that came to seem entirely natural. Worst of all was the idea that anything could happen, anywhere and at any time. Female colleagues working in Midtown routinely found their handbags had somehow been rifled during lunch hours, their credit cards and wallets gone.[7]

Lindsay left office in 1973 after taking the decision not to seek a third term. The tall patrician of upper middle-class English and Dutch descent lacked the showmanship, so beloved by New Yorkers, that characterized the likes of Jimmy Walker and Fiorello La Guardia. Lindsay was moreover held largely responsible for excessive borrowing to finance municipal expenditures, which was a major cause of the city's 1975 fiscal crisis. Six months before stepping down, the mayor appointed Donald Francis Cawley as the thirtieth commissioner of the NYPD. At 43, Cawley took office in the same year police headquarters was moved to the fortress-like One Police Plaza, across the street from City Hall. He was the youngest person since Theodore Roosevelt to head the force of some 20,000 uniformed patrolmen. The swearing-in ceremony offered the first indication of Cawley's resolve to launch a programme of reform and tackle corruption. Speaking softly, so that the audience of colleagues, family and newsmen found themselves leaning forward to catch his words, Cawley said, 'We've got to break away from tradition.' The fight on corruption, he asserted, would be his principal concern.

Cawley's innovations kicked off with a regulation that eliminated minimum height requirements for officers and culturally biased questions on police civil service exams. He also persuaded City Hall to raise the age limit for those aspiring to higher ranks from 29 to 35, in order to bring in more mature senior officers. Cawley established performance standards to encourage officers to make more arrests and issue more traffic violation fines. He posted detectives to precincts, making them responsible to station house commanders. He also ordered 1,000 members of the Detective Squad out on patrol to acquire a first-hand knowledge of neighbourhood issues. Heavy fines were levied on top of dismissal for any officer found guilty of accepting even minor gratuities, while funds were made available to build new police precincts in Manhattan and Queens.

Cawley was given little opportunity to bring his reformist initiatives to fruition, however. In November 1973, Abraham Beame, a 5-foot-2-inch London-born son of Polish Jewish refugees, defeated Senator John Marchi to become New York's 104th mayor. With Beame's election to City Hall, Cawley found himself out of a job. His replacement was Michael Joseph Codd, a strapping career officer of 36 years' experience who towered nearly a foot above his boss. Codd was known in New York precincts as 'Chief Straight Arrow', a testimony as much to his ramrod military physique as to his reputation. The commissioner looked the part of the old-fashioned paternal policeman, and whatever the crisis he was famed for keeping a gentlemanly calm throughout.

Codd's talent for maintaining his poise would stand him in good stead, for calmness was in short supply in New York's Fear City days. The commissioner's four-year term in office was marked by draconian lay-offs without parallel in the history of the NYPD. Mayor Beame swinging his scythe through the department became the trigger for the 1975 scare campaign, when police protestors were joined by the fire brigade and sanitation services. It can rightly be said that Codd's major contribution during this turbulent period was his almost miraculous ability to hold the force together and keep it performing a semblance of its duties. His popularity among department officers was rigorously tested when, as part of the citywide financial cutbacks, he laid off more than 5,000 officers and slapped a freeze on salaries and promotions. At that time, the department's total strength numbered 32,000 officers. In reality, it was acknowledged the commissioner was only acting on orders from City Hall, which he found distasteful and self-destructive. He publicly stated there 'was no earthly way to reduce our force by five thousand people without it having a noticeable impact on crime prevention'.

Codd was an affable type, one who was never known to raise his voice in a crisis. But he was also a no-nonsense son of Irish immigrants and never shirked from cracking the whip when he saw the need to impose discipline. The high esteem he inspired in fellow officers was put to the test when he threatened severe measures against those police who joined the strike action. Codd followed through on this warning by placing Ken McFeeley, the president of the PBA, on one-year probation. McFeeley was also served a $7,500 fine for refusing an assignment and manning the picket line while on duty.

As if mass insubordination in the force was not a heavy enough cross to bear, Codd's years at One Police Plaza were fraught with a number of infamous murders. On a January afternoon in 1975, as tourists and bankers were enjoying lunch in a Lower Manhattan landmark tavern, a deafening blast left four people dead and more than sixty injured. For much of the media, it was the fulfilment of the Fear City prophesy. The shockwave propelled a wave of cutlery about the dining room with such ferocity that knives and forks had to be surgically removed from those who moments before had been enjoying a relaxed lunch. The Fuerzas Armadas de Liberación Puertorriqueña (FALN), a terrorist group seeking Puerto Rican Independence from the U.S., claimed responsibility for the atrocity. It wasn't until 1978, a year after Codd's departure, that a suspect was taken into custody. William Morales had just lost an eye, six teeth and nine fingers when a homemade pipe bomb exploded in his Queens flat. In this state, he was unable to resist arrest. Though Morales was arrested, tried and convicted, he managed to escape from prison and is presumed to still be at large in Cuba. The most frustrating thing about the Fraunces Tavern bombing is that the culprits eluded punishment by Codd and his successors.

Sam's Son on the Loose

Codd's casebook of the number of brutal homicides perpetrated in 1970s New York was filled to the brim, but of the lot, none was so macabre as the 'Son of Sam' serial murders.

> Serial killer – the two words that NYPD detective supervisors absolutely hate to hear. And yet, during the spring of 1977, those very words not only were being whispered throughout the corridors of power within the NYPD, they were being shouted virtually from every rooftop in the five boroughs by terrified citizens.[8]

New York City was being terrorized by a psychopath. He called himself the Son of Sam, a furtive creature who could have leapt from the pages of a Gothic horror tale. His calling card was a note written in block capitals, a document that after each killing was sent to the newspapers. The wording of one reveals the twisted cynicism of its author: 'Please inform all the detectives working the case that I wish them the best of luck. Keep 'em digging, drive on, think positive, get off your butts, knock on coffins, etc. Upon my capture I promise to buy all the guys working on the case a new pair of shoes, if I can get up the money.'

Over the course of 1977 six people were shot to death and another seven were wounded by this phantasmagorical assailant who left little behind in the way of clues, apart from a fondness for young brunettes with shoulder-length hair and the fact that his weapon of choice was a .44 calibre Bulldog revolver. Codd assembled a three-hundred-strong Omega Task Force to hunt down the murderer. The commissioner deployed male and female decoys to dark rendezvous spots where the killer sought out his victims. Son of Sam became a tabloid feast of gory detail to arouse their readers' prurient fascination. Many brunettes dyed or changed their hairstyle, thereby hoping to escape falling victim to this bloodthirsty serial killer.

Son of Sam's stalking grounds were the boroughs of the Bronx and Queens, though he chose Brooklyn to carry out his final murder. One of the central command centres for police operations was the 109th Precinct in Flushing, Queens, the borough where the killer had claimed most of his victims. The 8 p.m. to 5 a.m. detective shift was deluged with reports of sightings from neighbours, patrolmen, parole officers and even astrologers and assorted cranks. A squad of sixty police made the rounds at night, knocking on doors and stopping cars, all in vain. 'Everyone knows someone who looks good, someone who looks like the composite,' said Detective Sergeant Edward Dahlem, one of the officers in charge of the precinct's evening shift. 'The problem is that there have been different composites since last March. But you've got to check out each lead, each clue. You'd hate to let the right one pass you by.'[9]

The spree carried on until July 1977, when Son of Sam claimed his last victim in the Bensonhurst area of Brooklyn. That was when the police finally made their breakthrough, thanks to the testimony of a woman who reported seeing a police officer issue a fine to a car illegally parked in haste close to the murder scene. A check threw up an address in the Bronx and a name: the postal worker David Berkowitz. Following this lead, a cordon was set up around the suspect's apartment block. A search of Berkowitz's Ford delivered pay dirt: on breaking open the car, the police discovered a semi-automatic rifle and a message for Deputy Inspector Timothy Dowd, head of the Omega Task Force, threatening to carry out more homicides. Later that night, Berkowitz was arrested when he approached his car. He gave himself up with no resistance. Instead, he asked the police in a soft-spoken voice what had taken them so long to find him.

Son of Sam turned out to be a Korean War veteran who worked in New York as a security guard. He was determined to be mentally fit to stand trial and was found guilty. He was sentenced to 25 years to life for each of his crimes in Attica Correctional Facility, a maximum-security prison in Upstate New York. Explaining his deadly binge of serial killings, Berkowitz claimed to have been sent commands to go on the rampage by a neighbour's pet Labrador. The figure of the psychopathic killer is a staple of Hollywood melodramas, so it was almost inescapable that a Son of Sam crime thriller would hit the cinema screens. That came in 1999 with the release of *Summer of Sam*, a film by Spike Lee, with Michael Badalucco of *Raging Bull* fame in the starring role.

Once Commissioner Codd closed his last big case, he awarded promotions to the 25 members of his team who had tracked down Son of Sam. This was the year in which the commissioner would hand over his badge to a successor, who was to come in with the election victory of Mayor Edward Koch. But the closing weeks of Codd's term left him no time to contemplate his planned retirement. While the search for the serial killer was in full swing, the commissioner found himself having to deal with yet another calamity that befell a battered New York.

On the night of 13 July 1977 a dinner was underway in Harlem for local police agents. The East Harlem Community Corporation had invited the commanders of the 23rd and 25th precincts to a Spanish restaurant in Third Avenue to thank them for their help in organizing a local festival. Suddenly, the lights went out in the restaurant. Within a few minutes a scratching, twisting sound was heard outside: a looter was ripping the iron gate off the shop next door. Two electrical substations had been struck by lightning, and at 9.27 p.m. the hulking power plant on the East River waterfront in Queens went down, plunging the entire city into darkness. It looked at first like a replay of the power failure that had caused major disruption in 1965, only this time it proved to be far worse. For a start, the blackout hit at night, leaving the city wide open to vandalism and looting. Codd ordered all off-duty cops to report for work immediately to confront what was quickly swelling into a wave of anarchy, which in the end left 550 police injured, eighteen of them seriously. An estimated 10,000 in the NYPD ranks, mostly those who were furious over the departmental staff cutbacks, refused to heed the commissioner's orders.

The north Brooklyn neighbourhood of Bushwick was particularly hard hit that night. When the lights went out, hundreds of people began breaking into shops along Broadway, the southern boundary separating

Bushwick from Bedford–Stuyvesant, pulling down security gates, smashing windows, stealing furniture and TVs, whatever they could carry off. Forty-five shops were set ablaze, 134 were looted and fifty cars were stolen from a Pontiac dealership. That night, the sum total of police that were on hand in the area to respond to what resembled full-blown Armageddon was fourteen.

It was well into the following day before those police officers who had responded to the call to duty managed to restore a semblance of order in the city. Codd was exhausted and far from happy with the chaotic performance of the officers who, in theory, were under his command. For the commissioner, Beame's failed bid for a second term of office in December was probably greeted with a sense of liberation. There was little hope of re-election for a mayor who, albeit through no fault of his own, had presided over a city besieged by a serial killer, rocked by violence during the blackout and now facing financial collapse. Codd knew that a new face at City Hall meant his time was up at One Police Plaza. His colleagues in the NYPD's upper echelons spoke unanimously of their praise for Codd's undaunted fortitude and composure in tackling nearly four years of back-to-back crises while at the helm.

Mayor and Showman

Abraham Beame, New York's first Jewish mayor, was succeeded by the city's second, Edward Koch, who stepped into office in January 1978. If the incoming mayor's appointment marked a break with ethnic tradition, not so with his choice for NYPD commissioner. Like Codd, Robert Joseph McGuire was the descendant of Irish immigrants, the suppliers of the backbone of New York police officialdom since 1901, when Michael Cotter Murphy served as the NYPD's first commissioner. For many in official circles, it was somewhat astonishing that on 15 December 1977, on the eve of taking office, Koch named bespectacled, bookish McGuire to succeed Codd. The odds, including among several members of the mayor's selection committee, had been on Lindsay's former police chief Donald Cawley. It was a strong recommendation from special prosecutor John Keenan that helped to clinch McGuire's appointment. At 41, McGuire had now superseded Cawley as the youngest person since Roosevelt to hold the commissionership. Like Roosevelt, McGuire came to the job as an outsider, having made his career as a lawyer. On announcing McGuire's appointment, Mayor Koch said he had chosen a person from outside the department because he wanted 'a fresh approach' from someone who would not be bound by the way things had always been done in the NYPD.

For McGuire, becoming New York City's police commissioner entailed a radical change in lifestyle. The commissioner took a hefty cut in income when he accepted the $54,000-a-year post. He went from driving a Mercedes-Benz and a Porsche in his legal practice to a Volvo saloon as NYPD commissioner. It also meant being buffeted by a never-ending bureaucratic and organizational storm. The 25,000-member police department was reeling from heavy lay-offs and the city streets were perceived to be overrun with criminals. Add to that the persistent financial crisis, which was compounded by damage from the power failures, which in turn conjured up a widely shared perception of New York as a city in irreversible decline. The tone of his first year in office was set when a brawl broke out at the Borough Park precinct in Brooklyn. In that incident, 62 policemen were injured by a rampaging crowd of Hasidic Jews who assailed the station house to protest the stabbing of one of their brethren in a pre-dawn street robbery. It took the police half an hour to eject the mob, in what turned into a bloody free-for-all of screams, punches, nightsticks swinging and rocks hurtling through the air.

Riding herd on the world's biggest metropolitan police force soon began to take its toll on the new commissioner. The baptism of fire came during his first summer on the job, when McGuire had to fight off demands from black city officials to suspend fourteen cops who were at the scene of a violent episode in Crown Heights, Brooklyn. That day, thirty-year-old Arthur Miller, a black community activist, was choked to death while resisting arrest for allegedly driving with a suspended licence. About the same time, McGuire came under fire from City Hall bean counters for publicly calling for 'real dollar' pay increases for the police. A scandal over lack of discipline erupted a few months later, when in November 1978 six officers were found sleeping in a forested army training area in Queens. Shortly afterwards, a convicted murderer out on parole gunned down, stripped and set alight Bonnie Bush, a nurse whose call to the 911 emergency number had failed. Reflecting on his early experiences, McGuire said: 'One could sit back and consider that you are responsible for the security and safety of seven million to twelve million people. It's like contemplating death. You do it periodically, but you don't dwell on it for very long. It's not healthy for the psyche.'[10]

McGuire endured these tempests without gathering much tarnish on his shield. At a time of extensive industrial action and an escalation of public questioning of police methods, the department continued to function smoothly under his supervision. To the cop in the precinct, the commissioner projected an image of a man who cared for the patrolman's welfare. McGuire also achieved notable progress in streamlining the department. He staffed more desk jobs with civilians, which allowed precinct captains and area commanders to exercise greater authority. The 911 emergency call system was made fail-proof after the Bonnie Bush tragedy, while the use of sick leave by chronically ill officers was put under more rigorous supervision. One of McGuire's most important undertakings was the Neighborhood Stabilization Program, which in essence meant taking cops out of the radio car and putting them back on the beat, where they would be in touch with community residents. This became a forerunner of the neighbourhood policing strategy deployed by future commissioners.

Rampaging Hasidic Jews attacking the Borough Park precinct, the police strangling of a black community activist in Crown Heights and the failure of the 911 system that resulted in the diabolical murder of a young nurse – these were but three of the numerous cases that virtually held McGuire captive at his desk without a let-up. From the commissioner's appointment in 1978 to his departure from the department six years later, McGuire was kept hopping from one high-profile crime to the next, with barely a moment to catch his breath. He had stepped into a hornets' nest of diverse and headline-grabbing cases almost from the day he stepped across the threshold of One Police Plaza.

It is a matter of speculation whether McGuire would have taken on the commissioner's role had he known what awaited him in his first year alone, which turned out to be one of the most tumultuous any NYPD commissioner ever had to tackle. The start of 1978 was marked by the Willie Bosket case and the icy indifference shown by this fifteen-year-old killer, whose eight-day orgy of violence led to the enactment of the Juvenile Offender Act. In the space of little more than a week, Bosket shot dead two people, injured another and pulled off two armed robberies. With this law on the books, police had the satisfaction of knowing that their efforts to go after juvenile offenders would no longer be in vain, since those as young as thirteen could now be arrested and charged with murder.

Several weeks after the Bosket affair, the NYPD Detective Bureau took an urgent call from the fire brigade asking them to examine the human remains discovered smouldering in a wooden crate in the Bronx. On arrival, the police found the bullet-ridden body of Jack Tupper. The victim, according to witnesses, had been tossed out of a yellow Cadillac and set alight. The car was traced to Tupper's killer, a horse trainer named Howard Jacobson. It turned out to be a revenge murder for Tupper having absconded with Jacobson's girlfriend, Melanie Cain, a dazzling cover girl regularly featured in several celebrity magazines. This became an instant cause célèbre, and even more so, to the embarrassment of the Department of Corrections, when Jacobson escaped in disguise from the Brooklyn House of Detention. He was tracked down several weeks later hiding out in California, and returned to police custody in New York, where a court sentenced him to 25 years to life.

Then, in October, a blockbuster homicide hit the headlines: John Simon Ritchie, known to the punk rock world as Sid Vicious, was taken into police custody after the corpse of his twenty-year-old girlfriend, Nancy Spungen, was found in their bathroom at the Chelsea Hotel with a knife plunged into her stomach. The tabloids got to work in time-honoured style: the police found themselves vying for space with a swarm of reporters at the West 23rd Street hotel, famed for its catalogue of idio-syncratic guests of the literary world, from Dylan Thomas to Tennessee Williams and Allen Ginsberg. Under interrogation at police headquarters Sid admitted stabbing his girlfriend but denied meaning to kill her. After his release on $50,000 bail, Sid promptly attempted to commit suicide, then got himself arrested again, this time for assault, and finally, in February 1979, he fulfilled his death wish with an overdose of heroin.

No sooner had the NYPD extricated themselves from the celebrity spotlight than McGuire and his team became entangled in another tab-loid jamboree. That was when Oscar-winning actor Gig Young shot dead his wife along with himself in their fashionable West Side apartment. This was all particularly tiresome work for the commissioner and the department. The sequence of celebrity murders, brimming with the sala-cious details that boost ratings and swell circulation figures, meant having to manage a media onslaught while getting on with the job of criminal detection.

It caused no surprise at the department when, in October 1983, McGuire called a news conference to announce his decision to step down in December. He had served as commissioner for six years, the longest term since Lewis Valentine's years of service from 1934 to 1945. For McGuire, the last few years on the job had become an exhausting marathon of dealing with front-page scandals: the abduction and murder of a six-year-old boy, a $5 million airport warehouse theft, a female violinist slain between acts at the Metropolitan Opera and, the most shocking of all, the assassination of former Beatles member John Lennon at the Dakota Apartments on the Upper West Side. McGuire chose his words carefully when he said the decision was prompted by the desire 'to ease the pressures' on his family. His next role in the private sector was that of chairman of Pinkerton's, the world's leading private security company.

7

Get Those Broken Windows Fixed

Most New Yorkers who lived through the Ed Koch years would undoubtedly consider him a strong contender for the title of feistiest mayor in living memory, and possibly the most ebullient chief of City Hall in the Big Apple's history. Koch could regularly be found perched atop a park bench shouting to the assembled crowd, 'How'm I doin'?' This display of showmanship became his trademark, even into retirement. Two years before his death in 2013, the Queensboro Bridge was renamed Koch Bridge in his honour. At the age of 87, the former mayor would flag down cars at the approach to the bridge, shouting to the startled passing motorists, 'Hey, welcome to my bridge!'

There was another exceptional twist in Koch's tenure at City Hall: he was the only mayor to have sworn in four NYPD commissioners during his years in office. In 1983 McGuire had appointed career cop William J. Devine first deputy commissioner, the department's second-highest posting. Two days before McGuire tendered his resignation, Koch handed over the job to Devine, a promotion designed purely as an honorary salute to his years of distinguished service. Devine was gravely ill and had to give up the job two days after accepting the commissioner's shield, in order to undergo brain surgery. He died two years later at the age of 55.

Devine's replacement was Brooklynite Benjamin Ward, who joined the NYPD in 1951 as a patrolman, combining his police duties with evening university classes that earned him a law degree with honours. In 1966 Ward left the uniformed ranks to become executive director of the CCRB, and from there he went on to hold high-ranking positions in the force before his appointment in January 1984 as New York's 34th

NYPD commissioner. So far, one might be tempted to conclude that he was an obvious choice for the job. The surprise factor is that Ward was the NYPD's first commissioner of colour. He was assigned to Brooklyn's 80th Precinct, where he was no stranger to racial resentment from white residents and white fellow cops. For three years, he was not assigned a locker at the precinct, forcing him to dress at home and ride the New York City Subway to work in his uniform before he was appointed commissioner.

Koch picked Ward because, as he explained with characteristic bluntness, he was black. There was also the fact that Koch was in political trouble with New York's black community after the death of Michael Stewart, a young man who lapsed into a coma while in police custody, a year earlier. Stewart, a model and artist, had been detained for scrawling graffiti on a subway station wall. He was taken bruised and bound to hospital, where he died without regaining consciousness. The transit police officers in the dock were acquitted on all counts before a raucous crowd in state supreme court in Manhattan. The three arresting officers had been charged with criminally negligent homicide, assault and perjury. In a perverse twist of legalese, since no witness was able to point the finger at the officer who might have delivered the blows, the defendants were accused not of striking Stewart, but of allowing him to be beaten while in custody. His death sparked an outcry against racism and police brutality, which placed Koch in the political hot seat. Numerous black activists and their supporters contended that city officials had engaged in a cover-up for the transit police. Ward's nomination handed the mayor a tool to help him mitigate black activist anger.

Ward's good-humoured countenance camouflaged a rough and gruff character. His booming voice more than once landed him in trouble with Koch, and even black New Yorkers. The commissioner made few concessions to those who expected a liberal administration. He was once jeered at a black journalists' conference for stating, 'Most crime in this city is black-on-black, committed by young blacks under thirty.'[1] Here was a cop who unabashedly spoke his mind, a handicap for anyone in public office and especially a law enforcement chief who came out with remarks about what he called 'our dirty little secret', a reference to black crime statistics.

Even Ward's staunchest supporters often took issue with his proclivity to trivialize serious situations. The commissioner had suffered an abundance of discrimination during his early years in the department,

Mayor Ed Koch looks on as Benjamin Ward, the NYPD's first commissioner of colour, examines a collection of weapons and drugs confiscated in raids and seizures, January 1984.

but he also found himself facing more politically risky race issues city-wide. In one such incident in the Bronx, in 1984, a police officer shot and killed a 66-year-old black woman, Eleanor Bumpurs, who was resisting eviction for non-payment of rent. Ward defended the officer for following the laws and guidelines about use of force, but he could not help remarking that the slain woman reminded him of his mother. His guiding principle was to implement police policy to the letter of the law, irrespective of race or colour. He set out his philosophical and moral compass in a news conference after his appointment: 'Many people make the mistake of thinking that black people are liberal because they are black. I'm very, very liberal when it comes to race relations, but when it comes to law enforcement, I am very, very conservative. I certainly believe bad guys belong in jail.'[2] At the same time, Ward fought for equal rights for non-white officers by pushing for the integration of people of colour, Hispanics and women into NYPD supervisory roles. By the time of his retirement in October 1989, the percentage of black people serving in the department had increased by 17 per cent and Hispanics by 60 per cent, while the number of women police officers had nearly doubled.

NYPD statistics for 2019 show that white people make up about 51 per cent of the department, Hispanics 26 per cent, Asians 6 per cent and black people roughly 16 per cent of the force, so the balance is in the range of fifty-fifty white versus non-white officers. That said, there is still a disparity in the top ranks, where almost 80 per cent per cent of the NYPD's chiefs, deputy inspectors and inspectors above the rank of captain are classified as 'non-Hispanic white'. Factor in captains, and the department's leadership is still 72 per cent white. While the racial and ethnic diversity of rank-and-file patrol officers has grown substantially over the previous thirty years, the upper echelons have not come close to keeping pace. There were around 20,000 civilian and uniformed women members of the department as of 2020, with some in high-ranking positions. In that year, Chief Martine Materasso became the first woman to lead the NYPD's Bureau of Counterterrorism.

Commissioner James O'Neill, who served under Mayor Bill de Blasio from 2016 to 2019, once praised Ward as one of the first NYPD commissioners to recognize the importance of community policing. Ward was in this respect more a torchbearer than an initiator of policing tactics. Returning the cop to the neighbourhood had made its comeback in the late 1970s under Koch's first commissioner, Robert McGuire.

That was when the NYPD's newly recreated Neighborhood Stabilization Program were redeployed, after having been disbanded as a casualty of city budget cuts. By 1978 more than six hundred officers had been assigned to patrol duty, in an endeavour to deter a crime epidemic. In some of the most badly affected areas, the wave of lawlessness was wiping out small businesses and emptying the streets of pedestrians and shoppers. This strategy brought a major uplift in the number of patrol officers, who in 1977 accounted for only a third of police on regular street duties, most of them behind the wheel of the radio cars that were introduced in the 1920s.[3] Moreover, these officers were told to travel to their foot posts by bus or subway, so that even en route to work they would send out a reassuring presence. To make sure these neighbourhood officers were not merely displacing crime to other sectors, the department deployed additional police in civilian clothes or as decoys to adjoining areas. Ward's contribution to the community policing programme was to assign a patrol team, consisting of a sergeant and twelve patrolmen, to a majority of New York's 76 precincts to carry out these duties. Nevertheless, the project's effectiveness was significantly constrained by the department's manpower shortage, while the city's streets were still ravaged by crack dealing and the constant threat of assaults against local residents.

There was a less savoury side to Ward's commissionership, however. This came to light during an event that took place four months into his term, though the sordid details would not be known for a full year afterwards. The tragedy took place on a rainy Palm Sunday night in 1984, when ten women and children were gunned down execution-style at a house located in Brooklyn's 75th Precinct. The shooting of the Hispanic family and their friends was at first believed to be a crack-related vendetta. The drug motive seemed right on the mark when police found out that the shootings had taken place at the home of convicted cocaine dealer Enrique Bermudez. A suspect named Christopher Thomas was tracked down, arrested and charged with the murders. It turned out instead to be a crime of jealousy, as Thomas believed his wife, one of the victims, was having an affair with Bermudez. Thomas avoided a murder wrap and was sentenced on reduced charges of 'extreme emotional disturbance.' He served 32 years and walked free in 2017.

To the astonishment of police brass and City Hall officialdom, at a press conference called to explain what had achieved media notoriety as the 'Palm Sunday Massacre', Police Commissioner Ben Ward was nowhere to be seen. The highest-ranking official in the NYPD was incommunicado. According to crime reporter and author Leonard Levitt, 'Koch and First Deputy Mayor Stanley Brezenoff played dumb. It turned out Ward was on a three-day bender out of the city.' This fact was reportedly covered up by nearly everyone in city government.[4]

The Commissioner Storms the Alamo

Ward served through some traumatic times in policing the Big Apple. This was brought on to a large extent, but not exclusively, by the scourge of crack cocaine addiction that fuelled almost constant outbreaks of violence and general lawlessness. In the 1980s crack was responsible for as much as 40 per cent of the city's murders, which by now had some 600,000 regular users of the drug, according to NYPD sources. Unfortunately for the commissioner, some of the most shocking felonies involved members of the department. In the early 1980s, Brooklyn's 77th Precinct in Bedford–Stuyvesant was known to members of the force as the 'Alamo', a Wild West breeding ground for what became the 'Buddy Boys' scandal. Cops assigned to this station house had gained a reputation for activities that stagger the imagination, from stealing money from murder victims to pocketing cash from drug busts and scouring crime scenes for anything of value left behind by burglars. On days when takeaway activities might have slumped to a low ebb, the crooked cops created opportunities of their own. These included anything from after-dark shop break-ins to staging raids on drug dens, solely for the purpose of stealing cash on hand. The radio signal 'Buddy Boy' was used to alert fellow officers who might want to take part in one of the raids. Several of the cops involved became so emboldened that they began roaming the streets of their own precinct with other officers, taking part in armed robberies, burglaries and drug deals.

The first officers of the 77th to be taken into custody for their bare-faced felonies were Henry Winter and Anthony Magno. In May 1986 Internal Affairs Division officers found Winter in possession of cocaine and strong-armed him into informing on his fellow cops. The resulting tapes and testimony were used to indict thirteen cops and to have another ninety relocated, in an attempt to purge the precinct's toxic culture. Winter and Magno jumped on the chance to escape punishment by becoming the first police officers in NYPD history to deliver virtually their entire precinct to a magistrate. Less fortunate was Patrolman Brian O'Regan, who committed suicide on the day that eleven of his fellow officers were arrested and indicted on charges of corruption, theft and illegal distribution of firearms. Winter never managed to come to terms with his personal disgrace, for several years later he was discovered hanging from a bungee cord in a wardrobe in his mother's suburban home.

The Knapp Commission issued a report in 1972 which defined two types of corrupt cops: the 'meat-eaters' and the 'grass-eaters'. The former were the more rapacious of the species, those who 'aggressively misuse their police powers for personal gain'. The latter were no less unscrupulous, but their misdemeanours consisted more in 'accepting the pay-offs that the happenstances of police work throw their way'. The rogue cops of the 77th Precinct answered with precision to the description of 'meat-eaters'.

Among the most testing episodes of Ward's career with the force, and one which would almost certainly have given rise to thoughts of retirement, was the Tompkins Square Park riot of August 1988. The park, located in the East Village and Alphabet City neighbourhoods of Lower Manhattan, was at that time occupied by a permanent troupe of drug pushers, homeless people and squatters, to the chagrin and physical peril of local residents. On 6 August, the police decided to take action. The battle that neighbours applauded as a swoop on anti-social elements was for veterans of that night a merciless felling of protestors, like so many trees. The police onslaught sparked a riot that swept over the park like a tsunami, with bystanders, activists, residents, journalists and, it must be added, police officers caught up in its wake.

Ward was fast off the mark to humbly acknowledge that the police deserved no praise for their more than obvious lack of restraint. The commissioner issued a fair and candid report on the incident, making it clear that what had taken place that night was indeed a 'police riot', as protestors had claimed. The report's step-by-step analysis describes how a panic-stricken police captain had issued a '10-85 forthwith' radio call, in NYPD vernacular an emergency code to request immediate backup. Hundreds of police responded to the call, flooding the park and surrounding streets, although the report states that they had arrived at the square without being properly briefed and lacking the supervision of a superior officer. In other words, it became a baton-swinging free-for-all. Some plainclothes-men even tried to conceal their identity as they randomly attacked the multitude. Ward took swift action against those he considered responsible for the police debacle, first by ousting Deputy Chief Thomas Darcy, who had hurriedly left the scene. Deputy Inspector Joseph Wodarski was transferred to another borough, while Captain Gerald McNamara, who had issued the 10-85 call, was assigned to retraining. Ward also created a crowd-control training programme for police, in an attempt to avoid a repetition of the Tompkins Square Park fiasco.

In spite of the occasional peccadillo and off-the-cuff remark, Ward departed the NYPD in good odour, at least in the eyes of his boss and the general public. He can be credited with having transformed popularly held assumptions of who can lead the NYPD. He worked assiduously to clean up corruption and malpractice wherever it reared its head in the department. Ward retired in October 1989, leaving behind the legacy of a criminal justice visionary, while taking with him a plaque that sat on his desk bearing the inscription: 'Lord grant me patience . . . but hurry.'

*　*　*

IN 1965, ED KOCH was employed as a district leader in Greenwich Village. New York's future mayor had put in a request for heightened police protection in MacDougal Street, a prized hunting ground for pickpockets and muggers to prey on unwary tourists. On a meander along the café-crowded street one afternoon, Koch ran into the leading light of Beat Generation poets Allen Ginsberg and his partner, Peter Orlovsky. A passing patrolman was invited to join in the discussion and the four men retired to a local coffee house to continue the debate on how to make one of the Village's most quintessential streets a safer place. The policeman was Richard J. Condon, who six years before his Greenwich Village coffee klatch had joined the force as a patrolman in the rough Bedford–Stuyvesant streets of Brooklyn.

On an October morning nearly 25 years after that Greenwich Village encounter, Condon stood in the Board of Estimate Chamber in City Hall to take the oath as Mayor Koch's fourth NYPD commissioner. With his hand on a family Bible held by his wife, Charlotte, Condon exclaimed he had 'no way of knowing what the future holds', while taking it as read that he was stepping into a normal five-year term as commissioner. His words were to prove prophetic, for his tenancy at One Police Plaza was to last one day short of three months. The white-gloved officers keeping watch over the pageantry beamed with joy when Koch spoke of plans to add 3,220 police to the department by June 1990, although he neglected to explain where he was to find the $27 million needed to cover the hiring and training costs for the first year alone.

Unfortunately, Koch did not stay around long enough to carry out his promise to invigorate a worn-down police force. The mayor lost the primary in his bid for a fourth term, which was then allowed, to Manhattan borough president David Dinkins. Koch's defeat was partly the result of a backlash by black voters, many of whom were angered by the mayor having accused black activist and U.S. presidential candidate Jesse Jackson of antisemitism. In the mayoral election on 7 November 1989, Dinkins scored a narrow but historic victory over his rival Rudolph Giuliani to become New York City's first black mayor.

Whatever regrets Condon may have harboured over his short-lived career as police commissioner, he could be grateful for having been relieved of his command at a timely moment. The year of his appointment turned out to be the bloodiest in New York City's history. In all, 1,905 people were slain in 1989, though this marked only a 0.5 per cent notch up from the previous twelve months. The tempo was mounting: killings in the first two months of 1990 had soared by 20 per cent compared with the same period in 1989. Robberies, generally considered a barometer of street violence, rose almost 8 per cent to 93,337 in 1989, making New York the nation's worst city for muggings and burglaries.

Dinkins has been described by those who knew him as 'a soft-spoken, courtly gentleman' and the man he selected to become NYPD commissioner, Dr Lee Patrick Brown, as being 'cut from similar cloth, easy-going, cautious and careful by nature'.[5] In choosing Brown, the Oklahoma-born son of sharecroppers, Dinkins passed over the incumbent Condon and rejected the advice of Governor Mario Cuomo, the Archbishop of New York John Joseph O'Connor and other civic leaders, who had thrown their support behind Condon. On 22 January 1990 the Oklahoman Brown, popularly known as 'Out of Town Brown', became the second person of colour to head the New York force after Benjamin Ward, who notably had also advocated retaining Condon. Dinkins, meanwhile, issued a statement refuting claims picked up in some quarters that race had been the motivating influence behind his choice of commissioner. More enlightened voices called attention to the fact that, by bringing in Brown, Dinkins was sending a strong signal to his core constituency. The mayor was sensitive to non-white communities' concerns about justice from a police force that, at the time, was more than 75 per cent white, in a city whose population was estimated to be more than 50 per cent black, Hispanic and Asian.

Brown brought an impressive set of qualifications to the job. He had earned a doctorate in criminology at the University of California and made a career of taking over police departments in racially troubled metropolitan areas such as Houston, Texas, where he later became the city's first black mayor. He was credited with putting more patrolmen into the neighbourhoods and bringing about a notable improvement in relations between the residents and the police. Brown was taking on an enormous test of his professional capabilities: the 26,000-member NYPD was seven times as large as the force he had headed in Houston. There was also a noticeable undercurrent of resentment among some officers about having a non-New Yorker for a boss, though in this respect there had been a number of precedents: Arthur Hale Woods was a Bostonian, Joseph Warren was from New Jersey, so too Edward Pierce Mulrooney, while several others had hailed from outside Gotham. Brown con-founded his opponents in a very short time on the job. He earned high praise for implementing a community policing programme that quadru-pled the number of police officers on foot patrol. He also sought to create a partnership between police and citizens, striving to create a side-by-side working partnership to combat crime.

From the 1970s onwards there was never what might be remotely considered a 'good' time to take on the stewardship of the NYPD. The city's crime wave continued on an upward spiral year-on-year, mirroring the onset of the crack epidemic in 1985. That was the year drug-related crime began to gain momentum, coinciding with municipal budget cuts that had left police resources stretched to the limit. By 1980, the depart-ment had lost nearly 8,000 officers to attrition. In the five-year period from 1980 to 1985 the number of reported murders in the city fell by 545 to 1,683. But by 1990, that number had risen to an alarming 2,605 hom-icides. That was more or less when violent offences peaked, after which they began to subside in the mid-1990s. In 1994 the number of murders in New York fell by one-fifth compared with the previous year. Brown likened the spread of killings to a public health crisis that needed to be treated as an epidemic. Lesser offences like vandalism and vagrancy pro-liferated largely unchecked, contributing to an overall sense of disorder and chaos. The commissioner and his successor, who served in those critical years, can take credit for the cut in murder rates, which had been achieved largely through the tried and tested uncompromising system of imposing mandatory sentencing on drug offenders and giving the police a more visible presence in the streets.

In this sense, realism had prevailed over budgetary worries and the disquieting comments uttered by Dinkins, who had spoken of the possible need to postpone the promised hiring of 1,848 police recruits. In March 1990, three months after Dinkins put out his warning of a delay in beefing up the force, the cracks began to show in what had been a relationship of mutual understanding between the mayor and his police commissioner. Brown had already made known his concerns about understaffing. While urging the U.S. Congress to enact strong anti-gun legislation, as quixotic an undertaking then as now, he insisted that a force of 25,000 officers would be far too thin on the ground for effective policing of New York. In this, the commissioner found backing in Thomas Reppetto, the president of the Citizens' Crime Commission, who echoed Brown's claim that the shortage of officers was making it hard to maintain law and order in the streets. 'Until you can get cops out there to challenge these drug groups and the other violent people, the figures will not be rolled back,' Reppetto said. 'They will escalate and the streets will be chaos.' Manhattan District Attorney Robert M. Morgenthau emphasized that crime statistics confirmed what his office had realized years ago, that the drug trade had changed the nature of violence in the city. More than two-thirds of the killings in Manhattan in 1989 stemmed from shoot-outs among thirty drug gangs operating in the borough. 'I don't know how we can say we've got to wait for social change,' Morgenthau said. 'We've got to aggressively police, arrest and prosecute people breaking the law. We're going to pay for this one way or the other. I don't buy the argument that we can't afford it.'[6]

Racial Warfare Sweeps the Streets

On a brutally hot August night in 1991, almost exactly a year before Dinkins and Brown parted company, the mayor and police commissioner found themselves confronting one of the worst outbreaks of street violence the city had experienced since the race riots of the nineteenth century. Crown Heights in west central Brooklyn was settled in the 1830s by freed slaves, and well over a century later immigrants from the Caribbean continued to move into the neighbourhood, which by the 1960s began to show the signs of neglect and decay. On that night, Dinkins's work on community policing was thrown into disarray when a mob of local residents surged at police who had responded to a fatal road accident. The flare-up came after a car span out of control down Utica Avenue and hit two black children on the pavement. The boy, Gavin Cato, was crushed to death under the wheels, while his sister Angela was taken to hospital with serious injuries.

The driver of the car was a Lubavitcher, a sect of Hasidic Jews who lived in uneasy cohabitation in Crown Heights with black Americans and Caribbean immigrants. No attempt was made to flee the scene – on the contrary, the driver, Yosef Lifsh, struggled alongside bystanders to pull the children from under the car. One of his co-religionists who was in the car put in an emergency 911 call. Before the first squad car sped to the scene, however, all semblance of order had melted away. The situation went into free-fall as the frenzied crowd attacked and beat both men. The situation deteriorated even further when a private Orthodox Jewish ambulance arrived and its paramedics approached the occupants of the car before they turned to the children. That, at least, was the version put about by the rabble-rousers who were egging on the crowd from the sidelines. The fact is that two ambulances turned up at roughly the same time. As the rumours spread, a shot was fired, a police car was set alight, and the air was thick with rocks and bottles. During the night, another Hasidic man was pulled from his car and fatally stabbed.

Dinkins lost no time in taking action, though many saw his efforts as being too little, too late. The mayor and Commissioner Brown rushed to the hospital, where they tried to comfort the parents of the two children. They also visited the Hasidic stab victim, then still fighting for his life. Brown put together an emergency task force at Brooklyn's 71st Precinct in Empire Boulevard with the mayor, Deputy Mayor Bill Lynch, Criminal Justice Coordinator Milton Mollen and a handful of other officials. They conferred with leaders of the black and Hasidic communities and listened to both sides' grievances until 4 a.m. The plan that emerged from the meeting called for enlisting support to reduce tensions and avert more violence. After four nights of disturbances between both ethnic groups, it was blatantly clear that the city's race relations remained dangerously strained, despite the election of a mayor who had campaigned on his ability to ease such tensions. The Crown Heights upheavals acquired an even uglier veneer when Dinkins was slammed by accusations, mostly from Hasidic Jewish quarters, that as he was black he had ordered the police to stand back and refrain from arresting the rioters. This was a first step in the mayor's eventual undoing.

The NYPD did not come out of New York's worst incident of racial unrest in more than twenty years smelling of roses. The final toll, apart from the one death, came to 43 civilians and 152 officers injured. A 371-page report into the disturbances issued by New York State Director of Criminal Justice Richard Girgenti reads like a litany of failures by the mayor and his police commissioner. It states that Dinkins was misled by Brown who, in turn, was allegedly unaware of a breakdown in the performance of the police and their inaction in responding in good time to the emergency call. The report found the department had failed to control demonstrations, did not effectively prevent acts of violence, muster sufficient resources or respond adequately to 911 calls. There was, it says, a total lack of assessment on how the police were doing or any review to see if tactics should be changed.

Cops Score Well With Mollen

The Mollen Commission to investigate police corruption, which Dinkins set up less than a year after the riots, effectively made all but inevitable Brown's departure from the NYPD. This independent panel represented the most extensive external inquiry into the police since the Knapp Commission of the 1970s. It was by insinuation a slap on the wrist for the person in charge of the department under investigation. Mollen, the mayor's friend and former deputy mayor for public safety, was named to head the panel. Brown maintained that his departure was for family reasons, without mentioning his wife's fatal illness. He went on to become President Bill Clinton's 'drug czar' when he was appointed director of the Office of National Drug Control Policy. It was a subject he had come to know well in his dealings with New York's wave of crack dealing.

The commission's report, released in July 1994 after 22 months of investigation and witness testimony, stood as the most damning indictment of corruption in the department to date. A vital fact to emerge from the findings was how corruption had evolved in the twenty-year period before the commission began its work. The final document spelled out that corruption was far more criminal, violent and premeditated than traditional notions of police corruption suggested, and a good deal more invidious than the level of corruption of the previous generation.

In the 1970s the most common form of corruption was of a relatively minor variety. Officers took bribes to allow gamblers, prostitutes and other lawbreakers to avoid arrest. By the 1990s, the situation had been reversed: minor corruption was no longer systemic in the ranks. Virtually all the corruption uncovered now involved groups of officers, called 'crews', who protected and assisted one another's felonious activities. This was accomplished by identifying drug sites, planning raids, looting crack-trafficking locations and sharing the proceeds. These crews varied in closeness, purpose and size. For instance, in Brooklyn's 73rd Precinct, whose motto was 'Where Angels Dare Not Go', a tightly knit group of eight to ten officers routinely conducted unreported raids on drug dens, sweeping up all cash and valuables in sight. There were times when these squads would attend clandestine meetings in desolate locations within precincts, including in one case an abandoned coffin factory called the 'Morgue', to drink, avoid patrol duties and plan future raids. The 75th Precinct, also located in Brooklyn, had a gathering spot called the 'Pool', where Michael Dowd and as many as fifteen other officers from his crew would meet while on duty to drink, fire their weapons, meet their girlfriends and agree raid strategies. The commission found that Dowd and his associates did not just permit drug dealers to operate , they became dealers themselves and ran large drug rings. Like much of NYPD folklore, the sleaze and venality exposed by Mollen and his fellow commission members spilled over the media boundaries and were pounced upon by the film industry. Dowd's infamous misdeeds and corruption in the 75th Precinct were portrayed on the big screen in the 2014 film *The Seven Five*, directed by Tiller Russell. The documentary starred none other than Dowd himself, who was released from prison in 2006 after serving twelve years and five months on a charge of narcotics conspiracy. Dowd's chief partner in crime was fellow officer Ken Eurell, who received a more lenient sentence for testifying against his colleague.

Ken Eurell is known as one of the dirtiest cops in the history of the New York Police Department. While in uniform, he doubled as security for drug dealers. Later, using police connections for protection, he sold kilos of cocaine. In 1987, he was partnered with Michael Dowd.

He stole drugs and cash from crime scenes and allowed crooks to bribe their way out of arrests. Yet none of his colleagues would turn him in. 'You don't rat on your own,' Eurell said. 'That was the attitude.'

Eurell moved to Florida's Tampa Bay area, and in 2014 he stepped back into the limelight when he featured alongside Dowd in *The Seven Five* documentary.[7]

Those who expected the Mollen Commission to issue a blanket denunciation of the NYPD as a corrupt and immoral organization were to suffer disappointment. The report states in its preface:

> Part of what we found was disheartening, part was uplifting. But our fundamental conclusion is that this city has cause for faith in the future of our police department. Unlike the situation a generation ago, this commission can confidently report that the vast majority of New York City police are honest and hard-working and serve this city with skill and dedication each day.[8]

Some observers believe the correct posture for Brown in the Crown Heights riots, if he wanted to stay on as commissioner, would have been to express outrage and take charge, demoting top commanders while railing against the malfeasance of those he had inherited from the previous regime.

> Brown was too much of a gentleman to adopt this approach. Insisting on the need for a thorough investigation, he moved slowly, defending the Internal Affairs Division and minimizing the dimensions of the scandal. Soon the papers were full of allegations of cover-ups and warnings of yet more revelations to come.[9]

The Man of Vigilance Steps Onboard

It took Dinkins two months to come up with a worthy replacement for Brown. The person chosen in October 1992 was Raymond W. Kelly, a Marine Corps combat veteran of the Vietnam War and a police officer of 29 years' standing, who had served as the previous commissioner's first deputy. Dinkins's search had been abruptly put on hold in September, the month Brown stepped down, when the mayor was obliged to tackle a demonstration by the police that turned into something akin to an outright insurrection. An estimated 10,000 off-duty officers stormed through police barricades in front of City Hall in a rowdy protest. The main issue, however, was not the Mollen Commission, but was directed at Dinkins's plan to make the CCRB a totally independent body using civilian investigators. The system in place at the time was a civilian board which made the final decisions, while cases were investigated by NYPD detectives. The protestors argued that the use of civilian investigators was wrong because they had no police experience and did not understand police work.

There were outbursts of racial slurs, and several thousand cops blocked traffic on the Brooklyn Bridge for nearly an hour. It was tantamount to a replay of the police riot 135 years previously, between the dissolved New York Municipal Police and the newly formed Metropolitan Police. In the aftermath, Dinkins resorted to placing the choice in the hands of a five-member screening panel to re-interview the top candidates, in light of the issues the demonstration had raised. The main concerns were racism among some white officers, overall discipline in the department and a rift that had arisen between the mayor and many members of the police union, the PBA. It was hoped the appointment of Ray Kelly, as he is known to all, would help rectify this falling out between the PBA and Dinkins, who had himself only little more than a year left to serve as mayor. Unfortunately, the wounds failed to heal, and the PBA mounted a vigorous campaign against Dinkins's re-election by running a series of virulent newspaper ads attacking the mayor.

Kelly was thrown in at the deep end almost from the outset. On 26 February 1993, when he had been police commissioner a little more than four months, something happened that no one was remotely prepared for – not the city, not the police department, not the FBI or the Central Intelligence Agency (CIA). 'The modern age of Islamic jihadist terrorism came to New York,' says Kelly. 'An explosion occurred in the parking garage below the World Trade Center at 12:18 p.m. I was in my office at One Police Plaza when the call came in. I jumped in my car and reach the Trade Center by 12:25.'[10] Within fifteen minutes of the explosion that tore open a near-100-foot crater in the car park, hundreds of officers, as well as firefighters and first responders, were at the scene. Helicopters of the NYPD's Aviation Unit plucked people off the tower's roof, while Kelly put the Office of Emergency Management into action and called for multi-agency meetings to come up with a strategy.

The commissioner immediately ordered a security cordon thrown around airports, hotels, business centres and tourist attractions. Extra police were stationed on bridges, tunnels and the subway. It was nothing short of a miracle that only six people died and little more than 1,000 were injured in the blast of the 1,500 pound (680 kg) bomb.

Trudging through the rubble a few days later, Bomb Squad Detective Donald Sadowy found bits and pieces of a vehicle that had been torn apart, including a severely twisted section of the frame. As he began to swab it for chemical residue, a series of raised dots emerged, forming letters and numbers. This enabled him to determine that the demolished vehicle was a Ford van. Officers of the Auto Crime Division found the Vehicle Identification Number (VIN) plate, and with that in hand they were able to trace the vehicle to a rental firm in New Jersey. The name of the person who had hired the van was Mohammed A. Salameh. One by one, Salameh's three accomplices were tracked down, arrested and put on trial. They were convicted and sentenced to life in prison. Four years later, two more terrorists were brought to justice and imprisoned for their involvement in the bombing. It emerged that Ramzi Yousef was the mastermind behind the plot, and Eyad Ismoil the driver of the van carrying the bomb.

The 1993 World Trade Center bombing was the only successful terrorist attack Kelly had to deal with on his watch. It stands as a testament to his swift and determined action in taking on the jihadist threat that he was able to foil another sixteen plots in the years he served as commissioner. 'I learned some larger lessons from the 1993 World Trade Center bombing,' Kelly says. 'We learned how dangerous the threat of Islamic terrorism could be. We learned that the these weren't random individuals in solo acts of violence . . . I also learned how little information the NYPD had about these and similar threats.'[11]

During his tenure, Dinkins had opted to throw his weight behind Kelly, facing off deepening racial hostility caused by an appointment that had antagonized a number of leaders of black and Hispanic officers' associations. They questioned the new commissioner's commitment to easing tensions both within the NYPD and between the department and the people it is charged with policing. In the first working hour of his first full day as Dinkins's commissioner, Kelly endeavoured to assuage these concerns by visiting the black-owned New York radio station WLIB-AM to stress his determination to recruit more ethnic minority officers to the force. He said his goal was to 'break the back of the 11.5 per cent African American representation' within the NYPD ranks that had stagnated as the department's maximum level for nearly a decade. The city's black population at that time hovered slightly above the 25 per cent mark.

Kelly held the post of commissioner for only fifteen months, until Dinkins's defeat by Giuliani in December 1993, yet he went on to claim the longest tenure of any NYPD commissioner to date. After a gap of eight years, in 2002 Kelly was put back in charge of One Police Plaza by Mayor Michael Bloomberg, under whom he was to serve until January 2014.

In November 1993 voters reversed the New York mayoralty results of four years previous by handing victory to Republican candidate Rudolph William Giuliani, who had lost to Dinkins in the 1989 race. Brooklyn-born 49-year-old Giuliani, 'Rudy' to all, had risen from his humble origins as a bar owner's son to become a federal prosecutor famed for challenging Wall Street, political corruption and the Mafia. Having promoted his candidacy along Republican and Liberal party lines, a strategy that invoked memories of La Guardia's Fusion Party legacy, Giuliani campaigned for back-to-basics municipal services. He pledged to crackdown on crime, improve New Yorkers' quality of life, reshape City Hall bureaucracy and contest the hegemony of municipal unions and entrenched Democratic politics.

Whole Lotta Shakin' Up Going On at the NYPD

The business of policing the Big Apple entered a momentous era on 3 December 1993, when Mayor-elect Giuliani chose Boston's feisty police commissioner, William Joseph Bratton, to take over the leadership of the NYPD. Bratton stepped into a much larger and more complex position than in his previous role as head of the New York City Transit Authority Police. He was now in charge of some 30,000 police officers responsible for the public safety of more than 7 million New Yorkers. Dinkins had smoothed the path by expanding NYPD resources through his 'safe streets' policies and having authorized the hiring of about 6,000 officers. This provided the new commissioner with the tools he required to introduce a programme of innovation.

Bratton took on the job with high confidence, given his track record in supervising the subway system. 'Quality-of-life policing in the transit system worked,' he said.

From 1990 through 1993, crime rates underground fell by 39.9 percent. Observers, academics, and pundits had difficulty with the idea of concentrating on fare dodging when violent crime was as predominant as it was. But we proved the conventional wisdom wrong, first in the transit system and then, starting in 1994, in New York City as a whole the first time I served as Police Commissioner. With my leadership team – particularly Deputy Commissioner of Operations, the late Jack Maple, and Chief of Department, Louis Anemone – we established the crime accountability system known as CompStat.[12]

Giuliani had launched an aggressive electoral campaign buoyed by promises to wage war on crime. He vowed to sweep the streets clean of drug dealers, make schools safer and protect New Yorkers from violence. The man tasked to do the job had already won wide praise during his 21 months at the Transit Authority Police, often riding the subway himself to check on the morale of his officers. At a news conference in Giuliani's transition headquarters, Bratton said, in his Bostonian accent, that he accepted the mayor-elect's challenge to 'restore order, to bring back to the streets of the city of New York a sense of well-being, to begin to improve the quality of life in this great city'. He concluded his remarks with a Churchillian flourish: 'I did not come here to lose. We will fight for every house in the city. We will fight for every street. We will fight for every borough. And we will win.' It was not only the mayor who greeted Bratton as a breath of fresh air. The commissioner was able to count on the support of the Grand Council of the Guardians, a black police officers' organization, while the PBA as well as the Transit Authority Police union also added their congratulations.

As part of his drive to bolster police efficiency, one the first missions Giuliani entrusted to Bratton was the eventual consolidation of the 4,000-strong Transit Authority Police into the NYPD. Mayors Koch and Dinkins had also proposed, and subsequently failed, to merge the two departments. They had been confronted by clamorous opposition from elected officials, commuter groups and even uniformed members of the department, who viewed subway policing as an unattractive assignment. The amalgamation was finally achieved in April 1995, more than sixty years after La Guardia had authorized the hiring of a small squad of special patrolmen for the New York City Subway. Under Bratton, the Transit Police were reintegrated as the Transit Bureau of the NYPD.

By agreement with the Metropolitan Transportation Authority, the state agency that runs the Transit Police, Giuliani pledged to keep on average more than 1,000 officers on duty every day on what was at that time the subway network's 469 stations. Bratton went all-out from day one to set an example of a commander who leads from the front. In his first week in office he took to the streets to physically remove a panhandler from a subway carriage, and then travelled to Harlem's 30th Precinct to confiscate the badges of a number of officers accused of corruption.

In the 1990s Harlem's 30th Precinct in West 151st Street was at the heart of New York's cocaine trade. In 1994 alone, police inspectors confiscated $900,000 in drug money, more than double the average recovered in all of Manhattan's twenty other police precincts. The volume of business conducted at the 30th was nothing short of colossal. This was a place where officers stumbled across cardboard boxes stuffed with cash – $80,000 one day, $230,000 the next – and stacks of Colombian cocaine worth millions, all warehoused in networks of apartments rising along the streets that flank Broadway and Amsterdam Avenue. The precinct became known as the 'Dirty Thirty', a reference to the rogue cops assigned to this ward whose sphere of operations extended over roughly a square mile, from West 133rd to West 155th streets.

Dealers would pitch up from neighbouring boroughs and even other states to buy the drug, known as 'blow', in bulk at heavily guarded pre-war buildings. They also did their shopping straight out of the 30th Precinct headquarters. Bogus radio calls were sent out to provide cover for illegal raids on drug dens, the spoils of which were either pocketed or resold in the streets. The Harlem market was so saturated with stolen drugs that a gram of coke sold for $20–25, a snip compared with the going rate of $50–90 in the rest of the city.

It took a two-year investigation by undercover officer Barry Brown to bring down the corrupt crew. Brown testified under the alias 'Officer Otto' during the Mollen Commission hearings on police corruption, his face hidden behind a screen and his voice disguised, for fear of retaliation from the colleagues he was identifying. Thanks largely to his testimony, 33 officers were arrested on charges ranging from extortion and civil rights offences to grand larceny and narcotics distribution. Fourteen police officers were accused of accepting pay-offs to permit wholesalers and others to operate freely in the precinct. Three officers from Harlem's 30th Precinct were caught on videotape attacking local residents and stealing drugs and cash. Eventually, eleven more cops from the same precinct were arrested when Commissioner Bratton threw himself personally into the campaign to weed out corruption and criminal doings in the department.

Get Those Little Guys

Bratton put his enormous stockpile of personal energy into shaking up what he judged to be a culture of entrenched lethargy and demoralization within the NYPD. Less than a year after marching into his Downtown Manhattan office, he had empowered the police for the first time in decades to take a hard line on drug trafficking, still the root of the most violent felonies in the city. As a result, by the end of 1994 drug arrests had risen 25 per cent, though the tough-fisted policies deployed by the police raised more than a few objections among civil liberties advocates. They expressed concerns over Bratton's efforts to improve New York City's quality of life by the use of such radical procedures as arresting windscreen washers perched on street corners, squeegees at the ready, or confiscating the cars of men caught soliciting prostitutes by the kerbside. On the whole, these anxieties were not shared by New Yorkers and business leaders. They were exasperated after many years of having to look over their shoulders when walking the city's threatening and under-policed neighbourhoods. Influenced by the desires of people who wanted key urban areas, in particular Times Square, the Big Apple's ultimate public space, cleansed of graffiti and vagrants. The policing of non-violent behaviour and offences eventually became the bedrock of the NYPD's war on crime across the metropolis. Thus was born the era of Broken Windows policing.

Bratton boosted the optimism level of an anxious citizenry when, in November 1994, he could proudly report that compared with the same period in the previous year, robbery and car theft in New York had been cut by almost 15 per cent, with a similar decline in shootings. The commissioner stood staunchly behind department officials who argued that criminals were carrying far fewer guns out of fear of being snared in the increased number of police sweeps. The commissioner advocated the principle that the most effective way to address disorder in the streets and bring down the crime statistics was to increase the number of misdemeanour arrests. He was thinking of the type of policing that focuses on minor disorder transgressions. Giuliani gave Bratton carte blanche to enforce municipal ordinances against minor wrongdoings like group loitering, nuisance begging, graffiti, turnstile jumping and drinking in public. These offences could result in arrest, detention and criminal charges. On the other hand, breaches like vandalism and vagrancy had for years proliferated largely unchecked, contributing to an overall sense of disorder and chaos.

This became a principal component of the Giuliani administration's crime strategy: arresting people for lesser offences and then tying them to more serious ones. 'The Bratton revolution was to transform what was largely a reactive police department into a proactive force,' says Jeffrey Kroessler, a professor at John Jay College of Criminal Justice. 'The strategy shift was from containing to reducing crime.' Kroessler highlights the fact that turning the NYPD into a more professional organization actually brought a decrease in the use of police firearms. 'New York police officers fired their weapons ten thousand times in 1970,' he says. 'This was reduced to 120 firearms discharges in 2019.'[13]

A Clean Sweep Underground

After his appointment in 1990 as chief of the New York Transit Police, Bratton began rolling out what was to go down as an almost legendary approach to crime-busting. It was known as Broken Windows, a theory of policing techniques in which a close link was identified between fear, disorder and crime. CompStat formed an integral part of this method, as well as the first real test of the thesis that if disorder causes crime, bringing disorder under control could prevent it. The year Bratton took on the job, crime statistics for the New York City Subway system were staggeringly high. Robberies had soared 48 per cent in the previous two years, far exceeding the figures for the city as a whole. Lawlessness underground was fomenting a climate of fear, which in turn was putting the public off using the transit network for their daily commute or shopping journeys.

'The New York City Subway system was a horror,' Bratton says. 'Crime was skyrocketing, fare evasion was epidemic, graffiti was rampant, the fear underground was overwhelming and, as a result, ridership and public confidence were plummeting.'[14] Bratton began to apply the Broken Windows concept to the subway. 'We were going to fix that broken window and see that it didn't get broken again,' he vowed on assuming the Transit Police leadership.[15] For the first time in many years, cops were put on the offensive to begin arresting offenders, starting from the bottom of the felony ladder. Ten or twenty turnstile jumpers would be pulled over in one go, handcuffed and lined up on the platform. In this way, passengers were able to view a line-up of fare evaders as they were marched out of the station into waiting vans, for processing at the nearest precinct. Bratton had succeeded in bringing subway mayhem under control and he achieved a cut in crime. The knock-on effect of applying Broken Windows policing from the bottom up brought a dramatic drop in major felonies, defined as homicide, rape, robbery, assault, burglary and grand larceny. In less than five years from the time Bratton took charge, these offences fell from more than 15,000 to 5,000.

Gentleman Jack Maple

Bratton is routinely credited with having devised the Broken Windows strategy, but it was by no means solely a product of his design. The flamboyant NYPD detective Jack Maple was instrumental in putting together the plan, which he worked out over evening cocktails at the now-defunct celebrity bar and restaurant Elaine's, on the Upper East Side. Elaine's in Second Avenue was a favoured watering hole of writers, film stars, musicians, media types and also, to lend some grit to the glamour, men with pistols holstered on their ankle or a badge pinned to a topcoat.

'Maple was a well-known eccentric within the Transit Police,' recalls his former boss William Bratton. 'A solidly built, stocky five-foot-eight, he cultivated a taste for sartorial display. He actually wore a carnation in his lapel.'[16] In his bowler hat, two-tone brogues and bow tie, Maple cut a colourful and exuberant figure, a throwback to the more extravagant police officers of earlier days. He was a bon vivant who frequented New York's better-known night spots, sipping champagne and recounting tales of his zestful life. 'Jack Maple looked like he pined for the days of Damon Runyon's *Guys and Dolls*. But whatever Maple's sartorial predilections, his greatest passion was catching crooks and, more importantly, developing systems for catching crooks. He did that like no one else in living memory.'[17]

Maple began his career as an undercover detective, at 27 the youngest in the department. His patrol beat covered Times Square and the 42nd Street subway station in Eighth Avenue. While making the rounds of

New York's decaying public transport network of the 1970s and early '80s, working at a job that was disparagingly known in the department as a 'cave cop', he assembled his 'Charts of the Future', paper maps into which he stuck colour-coded pins to track crime. It was a simple and obvious procedure, but no one in the NYPD had come up with the idea until Maple formally devised it. He was soon locking up dozens of gang members, which earned him a promotion to the rank of lieutenant. That was when he met Bratton, an encounter that led to a tragically short-lived but powerful partnership. At the end of 1993, the now NYPD commissioner Bratton took Maple on as his top anti-crime strategist.

Maple was a larger-than-life character whose reputation transcended NYPD circles. He was adopted as the model for the main character in *The District*, a crime and police-procedural television series that aired on CBS from 2000 to 2004. Maple did not answer to the description of an armchair detective. Late on a February night in 1996 he waded into a brawl taking place on the Upper East Side, in which three men were exchanging insults and punches. Maple, who worked out on a regular basis with a punch bag, thought he was witnessing a mugging in progress. In his Beau Brummell suit and bowler hat, he broke up the fight and arrested the three men on charges of disorderly conduct. Shortly before Maple died of colon cancer at the age of 48, Giuliani paid tribute to the man Bratton had assigned the special role of deputy commissioner for crime control strategies as 'one of the truly great innovators in law enforcement who helped to make New York City the safest large city in America'.

The four objectives Maple jotted down on a napkin at Elaine's one evening while sipping his third glass of champagne were 'accurate, timely intelligence', 'rapid deployment', 'effective tactics' and 'relentless follow-up and assessment'. Those principles were soon disseminated through weekly meetings held at police headquarters. 'Downtown, the numbers I had been pulling out of the chiefs and the data keepers were telling me that throughout the city, the detective squads weren't earning superlatives in all aspects of their game,' Maple recalls in his memoirs.

> Their record on fugitive apprehension was just one example. In the previous two years alone [1992–3], at least twelve thousand people who had been positively identified as the perpetrators of violent crime in New York City hadn't been arrested for those crimes. These crimes

weren't page-one material so the suspects, instead of being hunted down and thrown in the poky, had suffered no further inconvenience than that their names were on index cards and filed in drawers marked wanted. In the 5.6 square miles of the Seven-Five [75th Precinct], which had logged a record 125 homicides in 1993, having three hundred of these characters running around free was like declaring open season on more killings.[18]

A keen student of military history, Maple compared the system to Britain's use of radar against Luftwaffe bombers in the Second World War. At the time of his appointment as deputy commissioner for crime control strategies, the task of seeking out information was largely limited to what had happened the previous day. Maple required each of New York's 76 precincts to compile statistics and map crime locations on a daily basis, then fax the information to headquarters to collate into a larger data set. This was intensive, time-consuming work. It needed to be done by computer, but the NYPD's mainframe technology staff said it would take six months to design a longer-term statistical database. Time was not on the department's side, with an average of six murders being committed every day. With the help of the Police Foundation, an organization set up by the business community to provide assistance to the police, the NYPD purchased a Hewlett-Packard 360 computer to kick off the CompStat revolution.

The system allowed the police to act, rather than just react, against crime. CompStat may not sound like a revolutionary development, but Bratton saw it otherwise. As Maple went about introducing technological changes, the commissioner turned to the department's management. He devolved unprecedented authority to precinct commanders, who oversaw two hundred to four hundred officers serving some 100,000 residents each. This marked a radical departure in crime-fighting techniques. Bratton once said that the best-kept secret in the U.S. was how ineffective the police had been in combatting criminal activity. One reason for CompStat's success was that it now allowed top officials to interact with and question lower-level commanders directly. CompStat, or versions of it, were widely heralded and frequently imitated as a ground-breaking step forward in police tactics. The system was adopted by police departments in scores of other cities, including New Orleans, Newark and Baltimore. Within five years of its application in 1994, one-third of the nation's 551 top police departments had implemented a program modelled on CompStat.

The NYPD Goes Digital

How did it work? As Maple describes the process:

> One way to look at a CompStat meeting is as a live audit of overall police performance, one in which the leadership's goals sometimes border on the unreasonable because that's the only way to assure at least reasonable results. But before that, a CompStat meeting is a way of sharing crime data that recognizes why the first step to crime reduction itself – the gathering and analysing of accurate, timely intelligence – has to be quickened by the heat of accountability. The reason is simple: most people in the world learn things faster when they know they're going to be tested on them. Cops are no different. If we had been satisfied to just sit in a circle and chat about the intelligence we all had . . . a lot of cases in New York would never have been solved and a lot more people would have been victimized.[19]

The third member of what might be termed the 'CompStat Trio' was Chief Louis Anemone, the NYPD's third-highest-ranking official, known to his enemies as 'The Dark Prince'. Anemone's forceful voice first made itself heard in 1991, after the department was criticized for its mishandling of the outbreak of racial violence in Crown Heights. Following the incident, Anemone became an instrumental figure in overhauling police strategies for responding to civil disturbances. Bratton admired the aggressive style Anemone implemented in shaking up the department and jolting commanders into finding innovative ways to keep crime down. Bratton, who promoted Anemone to chief of patrol, once commented, 'He was not shy and he was willing to go the extra mile. He was not in it to make friends.' Anemone became one of the architects of the department's CompStat strategy. His pugnacious style was buttressed by a soldierly appearance. As the highest-ranking uniformed member of the department, Anemone cut a truly martial figure. He was always to be seen sitting ramrod straight at CompStat meetings, wearing a Sam Browne belt with a shoulder strap on his uniform. It went well with his motto: 'Walk tall, hold your heads high and never back down.'

Anemone's retirement in 1999 elicited exceptional praise from Bratton's first deputy commissioner, John F. Timoney: 'There are very few people who are irreplaceable. Chief Anemone is one of them.'[20]

In a nutshell, the CompStat program's main functional components were up-to-date computerized crime data, analysis and advanced mapping, all of which served as the basis for regularized, interactive strategy meetings. A map projected at the front of the room used dots to indicate crime incidents. In what became common CompStat jargon, precinct commanders were held accountable for 'putting cops on the dots'. Managers were given responsibility for providing results of crime strategies and solutions in their respective areas of operation. The underlying rationale can be summed up as the application of business-orientated managerial reforms to modern policing. Enhancing accountability for performance by adopting professional business practices emerged as the holy grail of this system. The orchestral score for these changes was baptized 're-engineering', which in essence meant an overhaul of the NYPD's working structure.

Each of the department's twelve re-engineering teams was dedicated to a specific topic and asked to determine what was broken and how to repair it, or, alternatively, what could be used to replace it. Slow, continuous movement from the top was no longer acceptable. In order to hold precinct commanders accountable for crime prevention, Bratton decided that the new system must grant them more discretion. Instead of headquarters determining staffing and deployment on a citywide basis, the task of reducing crime, fear of crime and disorder would flow from patrol borough and precinct coordination of selected enforcement plans.

And did it work? Maple cites a homicide that took place in mid-1995, a little more than a year after CompStat became operational. The victim was a 46-year-old prostitute, found bound and gagged in a room at the New York Inn, near Times Square. She had been strangled with a pink towel, which was not part of the hotel's linen stock. In a CompStat meeting Sergeant Gene White produced the file of an unsolved murder of a prostitute from several months previously. She had also been strangled with a pink towel. Five months later, the killer struck again. This time the victim was a 21-year-old prostitute discovered in the bathtub of a hotel in East 27th Street. The woman miraculously survived her ordeal and was able to describe the client she had accompanied to the hotel. He was a man with a pock-marked face, wearing a beret and carrying an orange sports bag. Maple deployed officers to interview prostitutes in Midtown and Lower Manhattan. One woman told them how she had been taken to a hotel by a man of the same description, who was also carrying an orange bag. He assaulted her at the hotel, wrapped a rope round her neck, sodomized her and left her for dead. Several days later, this woman flagged down a patrol car and shouted to the officers inside that she had spotted her assailant. When he was arrested, the police found a rope and gun in his orange bag. In many of the country's large police departments, the executive corps and detective commanders would not have had any knowledge about these three attacks, distant as they were from one another in time, circumstances and locations. Maple's strategy was widely considered a success.

8

Zero Means Zero

Once it had put into practice a procedure of cross-departmental management, statistics and accountability, CompStat was able to successfully drive down crime in New York. Most notably, the first three years of the NYPD's CompStat program showed a dramatic decline in felonies across almost all categories. The cut in index crime, which is one included in the yearly crime statistics of the Federal Bureau of Investigation, alone was 12.3 per cent in 1994, compared with a below 2 per cent national average.[1] By the end of that year, index crime in New York City had marked a sharp decline from the previous year, exceeding Bratton's promise of a 10 per cent cut. Nationwide it dropped a scant 1.1 per cent in the same period. In the decisive crime reduction years of 1993 to 1999, New York City felonies were down 50 per cent.[2] In 1995 Bratton told the department he would accept nothing less than a 15 per cent decrease for the year. The final figure for the year came in closer to 20 per cent, most notably with 21 per cent fewer murders.

As a tribute to the architect of a safer city, *Time* magazine featured on the cover of its 15 January 1996 issue a photo of William Bratton alongside the banner headline: 'Finally, We're Winning the War Against Crime. Here's Why.' The report lavished praise on Bratton's undeniable success in slashing New York's crime rate: 'CompStat has become the Lourdes of policing, drawing pilgrim cops from around the world for a taste of New York's magic.'[3]

It was almost inevitable that sharp differences were to surface between two strong personalities like Bratton and Giuliani. The discord came to a head with the publication of the *Time* story, which ostensibly gave Bratton primary credit for having slashed New York's crime rate. This sparked an undeclared War of the Titans. On 26 March 1996 this head-on rivalry for the limelight prompted Bratton to hand in his resignation. The popularity of a nationally known crime fighter whose approval in opinion polls exceeded that of Giuliani was too heavy a weight for the mayor to bear. 'To Giuliani, it didn't matter that Bratton created the successful anti-crime strategies, such as Zero Tolerance or CompStat,' says veteran crime writer Leonard Levitt. 'Giuliani wanted the billing.'[4] A few days prior to Bratton's resignation, the commissioner took Giuliani aside at a funeral being held for a police officer to request a meeting with his boss. Giuliani knew what was on the commissioner's mind: the mayor had let slip at a news conference that Bratton was actively seeking a private sector job. In April of that year, Bratton announced his decision to bow out.

Giuliani began casting about for a replacement commissioner, one who would not attempt to compete with him for the media spotlight. It did not take him long to come up with a candidate. Three days after Bratton made public his departure from the NYPD, a dark horse appeared on the stage: Howard Safir, a person with 26 years of federal law enforcement experience and, more importantly, a close personal friendship with the mayor stretching back to the 1970s. Giuliani poached his nominee from the New York Fire Department, where he had served for two years as commissioner. Standing alongside a beaming Giuliani the day the nomination was made public, Safir expressed in discreet terms that he planned to follow a less confrontational style than his predecessor: 'I do not believe that the New York City Police Department ought to be identified by personality.' Safir has been described as a man with a 'stainless-steel backbone', a cop with a pugnacious cleft chin and a granite bearing, who became the NYPD's first Jewish police commissioner.

Safir brought to the job a colourful background in law enforcement. As a bearded undercover drug agent for the federal government in the 1970s, he had organized busts in New York's East Village and the Haight-Ashbury district of San Francisco. While working as operations chief of the U.S. Marshals Service during the 1980s, he helped capture noted fugitives like Juan Ramón Matta-Ballesteros, a trafficker wanted for the murder of an American drug agent.[5] He also nailed Edwin Wilson, a CIA officer who fronted companies for the purposes of spying, and Christopher Boyce, one of the Soviet agents involved in the Falcon and the Snowman case. This political scandal became an American spy drama film, *The Falcon and the Snowman*, based on the 1979 Robert Lindsey book of the same title. It tells the true story of two young Americans, Christopher Boyce and Andrew Daulton Lee, who sold U.S. security secrets to the Soviet Union.[6]

The task Safir and Giuliani took on in combatting what was historically a spiralling homicide rate had already been set on a roll by the time the new commissioner took over. In less than seven years, New York witnessed roughly a two-thirds decline in murders, from 2,245 in 1991 to 770 in 1997. Commissioner Safir and Mayor Giuliani saw eye-to-eye on the need for a free hand in controlling their respective territories. Consequently, one of the first heads to roll at the NYPD was the exquisitely coiffured pate of Jack Maple, the one man most likely to pose a threat to his boss's authority. This was big news for Gotham's citizens, who had come to regard their extravagant deputy commissioner with admiration and gratitude. The *New York Daily News* reported his departure with the front-page banner headline 'Jack Hits the Road'. Maple left to set up a CompStat unit in New Orleans where, over the course of nine months, crime statistics were slashed by 22 per cent and kept declining for more than four years thereafter. Maple and his business partner, former Bratton aide John Linder, went on to introduce their systems in Newark, Baltimore and even Istanbul.

High on the commissioner's agenda was the need to address and strive to repudiate an extensive wave of charges of police brutality. Civil liberty groups and neighbourhood activists were levelling charges of trigger-happy behaviour against cops. They alleged the police considered themselves empowered by the Broken Windows policy to act with arbitrary violence. To give Safir his due, during the commissioner's four-year term of office crime in New York dropped precipitously in all categories, and the murder rate fell to its lowest level since 1964. But there were incidents on the negative side to strengthen the widely held perception in many neighbourhoods that aggressive police policies unfairly singled out minorities. As a consequence, police–community relations in those years sank to a low point. Two incidents in particular drew the loudest outcries against police misconduct.

Abner Louima was a young Haitian who worked in New York as a security guard. In August 1997 he was arrested and hauled into Brooklyn's 70th Precinct on charges of disorderly conduct and assault. While in

detention, Louima was sodomized by a broken broomstick that pene-
trated his bladder and perforated his intestine and colon. He was taken to
nearby Coney Island Hospital, where he was handcuffed to his bed. From
his hospital bed, Louima described how a broken stick was shoved into
his rectum and then into his mouth, while his attackers shouted racial
slurs at him. It was an act of animal brutality, except that animals are not
known to exhibit that sort of perverse behaviour. Louima's 'crime' was
having been present at a brawl between two women outside a Brooklyn
nightclub frequented by Haitian immigrants. In the midst of the fracas,
an officer who rushed over to intervene was punched to the ground, but,
as it later emerged, not by Louima. In court proceedings that lasted three
years, four cops were convicted on charges of violation of civil rights and
making false statements, leading to a $5.8 million settlement, the highest
in New York history for police brutality.

'We lost no time in getting on top of this case,' says Charles Campisi,
who at the time was serving as chief of the IAB. 'Louima was arrested in
the early hours of Sunday. We responded that afternoon and the investigation commenced. By Monday morning we had set up crime scenes and
I was waiting outside Safir's door to put the commissioner in the picture.
He was astounded by what I told him and he assured me I could count on
all the resources I needed. We went to City Hall to brief Giuliani, who
immediately snapped into his investigative and prosecutorial role. Safir
and Giuliani were well aware of what needed to be done and working
together, we had indictments within two weeks.'[7]

The next terrible incident to hit the headlines broke in February
1999, when a 23-year-old Guinean immigrant was shot dead in a hail
of 41 bullets fired by four plainclothes officers. The killing of Amadou
Diallo took place shortly before 1 a.m. in the South Bronx, outside the
victim's home, which he shared with a friend and two cousins. Diallo
earned his living as a stall keeper in Union Square, selling videotapes
and items of clothing.

The Diallo shooting resonated among New Yorkers, ethnic minorities and white people, in ways the city had never seen before.

There was the starkness of his death. Four police officers had killed an
unarmed civilian. They had fired forty-one shots at someone having
no criminal record, who was standing by himself, minding his business. For reasons they could not explain, the cops had believed he

might have committed a crime. They had believed he had a gun. The sole explanation for these misjudgments was that the man was black.[8]

This was grist for the media mill. It consequently became the catalyst for civil rights groups to spring into action. Mass protests broke out in front of NYPD headquarters a few weeks after Diallo's death. For a fortnight crowds numbering in the thousands kept up the campaign. One after another, spiritual leaders of the black community, people like Reverend Al Sharpton, Jesse Jackson and others, stood up to hurl accusations of racism against the police. The demonstrations ended with more than 1,000 arrests, including that of the former mayor David Dinkins. Diallo's death even inspired a 2001 Bruce Springsteen song, 'American Skin (41 Shots)', with lyrics contending that being a black American was enough to get you killed, which would have sat uncomfortably with the NYPD. Sharpton in particular has continued to be involved in direct activist interventions. A colourful and popular figure in the black community, he embarked upon controversial protests that gained wide coverage in the national media and sometimes precipitated confrontations with police. Sharpton took a lead role in organizing protests against the police-related deaths of Michael Brown in Missouri and Eric Garner in New York. He worked with Garner's family to request his death be investigated as a civil rights violation on a federal level. In June 2020 Sharpton spoke at the memorial for George Floyd, who died in May of that year after a police officer kept his knee on Floyd's neck during arrest. Sharpton has been a steadfast champion of police reform and accountability, calling for the elimination of unjust policies like the stop-question-and-frisk programme.

United States Founding Father Alexander Hamilton famously said, 'When the sword is once drawn, the passions of men observe no bounds of moderation.' The same principle could be applied to mass public outcries, when 'the other side of the story' is almost invariably relegated to the category of minutiae. There is no denying the facts: an innocent, unarmed man was gunned down by four police officers. That is the 'What', while the 'How' and 'Why' take on a different hue. The police are under the constraint of having to wait for a judicial review to present their version of events. The plainclothesmen who opened fire on Diallo were members of the NYPD's Street Crime Unit (SCU), which was set up in 1971 by Commissioner Patrick Murphy. This elite squad, which bore the menacing motto 'We Own the Night', was dispatched into New York's most crime-ridden neighbourhoods to apprehend rapists, murderers and other violent felons. The command-style team achieved a considerable degree of success. The four-hundred-strong unit comprised less than 2 per cent of the department's manpower, yet by the time it was disbanded in 1999, largely in response to protests following Diallo's death, SCU operations accounted for some 40 per cent of the illegal guns confiscated in New York City.

'The four officers involved in the Diallo incident were not seasoned investigators on the beat,' says Charles Campisi.

They were simply patrolling a neighbourhood notorious for its high rate of sexual assaults. They spotted a man standing on a corner of Wheeler Avenue, who fit the description of a rapist wanted by the police. The officers jumped out of their car to question Diallo. He most likely thought he was going to be mugged, so he ran for the doorway of his home. At the door, he nervously fumbled for his keys and in doing so, he drew a black wallet from his trousers pocket, just as he was confronted by the police, who shouted, 'Police. Don't Move. Show me your hands!'[9]

At the same time, says Campisi, two of the officers slowly began to approach the front doorsteps. When they spotted the wallet in Diallo's hand, one of the cops, believing it was a weapon, gave the required shout of 'Gun!' What followed was a sequence of tragic errors, each one compounding the other. The first officer tripped and tumbled down the steps. His colleagues thought he had been shot, and in a few seconds they respond with a hail of gunfire. The flash of bullets hitting the glass and metal door made them think Diallo was returning their fire. In fact, a ballistic impact from a ricochet was found in a car parked behind the officers.

Safir was hamstrung by not being able to release these details ahead of the trial. Had the media published the police version, the commissioner would have come under attack by the judge and prosecutor. The verdict announced on 26 February 2000, after a month-long trial, came in a tense and racially charged courtroom. The twelve jurors, four of whom were black, including the foreman, acquitted the defendants of all charges. On hearing the judgement read out, the officers hung their heads, wiped their eyes and hugged each other and their lawyers. As they left the courthouse without speaking to reporters, the men walked silently past a crowd of jeering protesters. That marked the end of the Diallo case, but as events were to attest, it was only the starting point in a long-running series of protests, charges of racism and accusations of police brutality towards minorities that have beleaguered the NYPD ever since.[10]

Technology on the Move

The NYPD can be a bit slow in embracing change. For instance, an officer at a Lower Manhattan precinct says that, until 2016, typewriters were still being used in the office to write up crime reports. Strategic and Tactical Command (SATCOM) was to a large extent the brainchild of First Deputy Commissioner Joseph P. Dunne, a long-serving officer who joined the force in 1969. Dunne began his career patrolling the perilous streets of Brooklyn's 75th Precinct. He was promoted to deputy chief in 1995, and in the following year he rose in the ranks to assistant chief. One of Dunne's most successful achievements was the creation and implementation of the SATCOM Brooklyn North concept. This accomplished the redesign of several traditionally separate command jurisdictions into a single cohesive structure.

SATCOM had the advantage of being brought in on the back of CompStat, an existing technology platform. The new system, in fact, traces its origins to the advances brought about by CompStat. It was first conceived in 1994, when Bratton was serving as commissioner, but it took another two years for it to become operational under Safir. SATCOM is essentially a geographically based system for crime detection, one that replaces the multi-departmental division of labour that assigns narcotics to one bureau, detective and street-control operations to others, and so on.

> SATCOM is NYPD writ large – an amalgam of past accomplishments and weaknesses, promises and pitfalls, reform impulses and bureaucratic caution, managerial vision and political infighting. To understand SATCOM's development, operations and future is to grasp the complexities, commonalities and contrasts embedded in the NYPD's reform saga.[11]

The new system put all 4,680 detectives and narcotics officers under a single commander, who had complete authority to dictate geographical coverage. This started in Brooklyn North, which encompassed ten of the borough's toughest, most drug-ravaged precincts. It was a vast area that accounted for more than a quarter of New York's drug offences and firearms homicides. It was therefore the logical place for SATCOM's unveiling. Jack Maple, who was on his way out of the department, predicted it would be the definitive law enforcer's tool for breaking the back of the cocaine racket. The system made it possible to share information and organize manoeuvres by bringing together detectives and officers on patrol, deploying police where they were needed at any given moment. The concept appeared to be on its way to achieving success, as officials channelled resources and many of the NYPD's best supervisors into the new command to fight drugs, historically the culprit responsible for most crimes.

SATCOM did not come into being without inciting criticism from some quarters. There were those who questioned the wisdom of launching the scheme in April 1996, when the charts were showing a levelling off, if not a clear drop in felonies, even in hardcore criminal lairs like Williamsburg and Bedford–Stuyvesant. SATCOM triggered a rift in the NYPD between those who favoured geographical decentralization and the empowerment of precinct-level policing, and those on the other side, who were proponents of citywide operations. In the end, the nays had it. In 2005 the NYPD disbanded SATCOM, while at the same time the department recreated Patrol Borough Brooklyn North and transferred command of specialized units, previously a part of SATCOM, to the bureaus and divisions of units in other boroughs. At the same time, the CCRB reorganized its five-year tables to reflect the department's new organizational structure and to set up a five-year comparison of data systems, from year to year, for all commands.

The Cops Ratchet Up the Stakes

Safir was not given an easy ride in his tenancy at One Police Plaza, which lasted four years and four months. In early August 2000 Safir announced that he would take up a job in the private sector as a consultant for corporate investigations firm ChoicePoint Inc. Sources close to the commissioner were emphatic that this did not reflect any sort of personality clash with his quarrelsome boss Giuliani, as had been the case with Bratton. Safir had supervised the NYPD during a period when crime declined markedly but relations between the police and minority residents in many cases turned sour. Reverend Al Sharpton, one of Safir's sworn enemies, said the commissioner's legacy was one of tolerating violent officers and encouraging aggressive tactics, a combination that sometimes ended in tragedy.

Safir's enemies singled out the commissioner's purported complicity with Giuliani in attempting to ban the Harlem Million Youth March in September 1998. The organizers had billed the event as a show of unity and strength by young people of colour, but Giuliani denounced it as a 'hate march' led by its main organizer, the outspoken antisemite Khalid Abdul Muhammad, a prominent figure in the Nation of Islam and, later, the New Black Panther Party. The march turned out to be a storm in a teacup. In some ways, it ended up as a public relations victory for a police department heavily under fire for alleged brutality towards ethnic minorities. On the day of the march, a small group of campaigners clashed briefly with police in West 123rd Street. Three officers suffered minor injuries in the incident, while one person in the crowd was arrested on assault and other minor charges.

Safir's pro-arrest strategy went as far as having police handcuff and arrest cyclists riding without a bell or proper lights, or drivers caught without a seatbelt, and even local residents carrying open containers of alcoholic drinks at weekend basketball games. These offenders were often held in police custody for 24 hours or more, later to be hauled before a magistrate's court. The idea, it would seem, was to instil a culture of respect, if not outright fear, of the law and its enforcers. These aggressive policing tactics sparked a rash of claims of police harassment and brutality. The charges originated mostly in New York's black and Hispanic citizens – but not always.

On a sweltering August afternoon in 1999 police in the Borough Park area of Brooklyn, home to a large Hasidic population, took a 911 call from neighbours complaining about a man who had been blasting music in his flat and was now dancing in the street, clothed only in his traditional beaver hat and silk shawl. The man in question, Gidone Busch, was also reported to be menacing children with a hammer. That was when Sergeant Joseph Memoly rushed to the scene, less than ten minutes after taking the call. He immediately rang the Emergency Service Unit, standard NYPD procedure in instances involving a mentally disturbed person.

According to police reports issued after the confrontation, Busch attacked one of Memoly's partners with his hammer. By that time, several more officers were stationed in front of Busch's home, shouting at him to drop the weapon. When he continued to menace the officers, a single shot was fired, followed seconds later by a volley of twelve bullets from Memoly and two other cops. As often occurs in such heated circumstances, accounts can be murky and conflicting. The police version has Busch rushing the cops, who had formed a circle around him, with his hammer. Investigators later stated that Busch was not in physical contact with the police when he was gunned down.

The shooting sent a stream of angry Hasidic protestors into the streets. In response to the neighbourhood outcry, Safir waded into the fracas with an impressive pair of clenched fists, insisting that Busch was a mentally disturbed man who was shot while hitting a police sergeant with a hammer. The commissioner quoted seven independent witnesses who confirmed that Busch had hit one of the officers present, Sergeant Terrence O'Brien, with the hammer. Safir further called attention to the fact that only the day before the shooting, Busch had broken a man's nose with his beloved hammer. The question was never raised of why, with Broken Windows enforced to the hilt, the assailant had not been brought into custody after that attack. On this particular occasion, the NYPD got away relatively unscathed, Borough Park being a Hasidic neighbourhood Giuliani had swept with 80 per cent of the vote in the 1997 mayoral election. Three months later a Brooklyn grand jury cleared the four officers involved in Busch's death on the grounds that the victim had presented a threat to the officers and had ignored orders to drop the hammer.

Zeroing in on Crime

In Bernard Bailey Kerik, Giuliani found the ideal candidate to execute what by now had become Zero Tolerance, the tactical metamorphosis of Bratton's Broken Windows strategy. With his shaved head and chiselled features, the new commissioner looked every bit the part of the unbending law enforcer, a reflection of the years he served with the U.S. Army Military Police Corps. The mayor and his new commissioner, a man described as in possession of a 'scruffy charm', had maintained a close personal relationship since 1993, when Kerik was employed as

Giuliani's bodyguard and chauffeur during that year's mayoral race. As later events were to reveal, Kerik's fifteen-month career as commissioner marked his finest hour. Giuliani's departure from City Hall in December 2001 meant that Kerik was temporarily out of a job and would, in due course, find himself on the cusp of a slippery slope.

While the going was good, Kerik earned himself a reputation as a commander who led from the front. Shortly after taking over at One Police Plaza, he put together a handpicked 'posse' of seasoned cops to scour the city streets for criminals. Once or twice a week, the so-called 'beat-cop commissioner' would cruise New York at night with a security detail composed of officers 'who have been in shootouts, dangled from rooftops, been hit by bullets, raced into burning buildings and seen their partners die. "These are people who have put their lives on the line," Kerik said. "Every one of them is a good street cop. They have a tremendous amount of experience and know the dangers of the job."'[12] The unit was made up of nine detectives, split into three teams. Each team provided Kerik with close protection in rotating 48-hour shifts and answered to two supervisors. Kerik was chauffeured about in an unmarked black Chrysler saloon by veteran Highway Patrol cops trained in hot-pursuit driving skills.

Several nights a week Kerik would ride the subway on the lookout for offenders, while members of his detail drove along the rail route to arrest suspects apprehended by their boss. Members of the detail spoke in praise of their commissioner's old-school police tactics. 'I like it,' said Detective Craig Taylor, a fourteen-year veteran who was once in a Brooklyn shoot-out with machine-gun-toting killers and served as one of Kerik's three drivers. 'We're out there seeing whether these problems are being addressed. It so happens that we run into some bad guys when we're out there.'[13] Kerik, a karate black belt whose office walls were adorned with photos of himself wielding an M-16 rifle, can claim to have personally arrested four felons in his first six months on the job.

Kerik's primary task was to keep up Zero Tolerance pressure on criminal activities across the city. There is no doubt that this relentless course of action had been achieving the desired results. During the Bratton years between 1993 and 1996, New York saw a 23 per cent increase in arrests. Police resources were absorbed in misdemeanours such as low-level public order and minor drug offences. In the same three years, arrests in those categories rose by 40 per cent and 97 per cent, respectively.

Zero Tolerance policing is a resource-intensive policing strategy. It requires high staffing levels to achieve the necessary level of direct law enforcement in the streets. It is fair to ask whether citizens' value-for-money from the increased number of police necessary to operate a Zero Tolerance policing strategy, or whether the increase in resources actually lead to a reduction in the crime rate. The size of the NYPD increased dramatically during the first half of the 1990s. The city also experienced a forty-six percent reduction in the crime rate during the same period.[14]

The facts speak for themselves: between 1990 and 1996, the period that saw a striking decline in crime, the number of officers in the NYPD increased significantly, from around 30,000 to more than 38,000. That is roughly 3,000 more than the current number of uniformed officers.

'Broken Windows ran on autopilot through the 1990s,' says Peter Moskos, a professor at John Jay College of Criminal Justice.

After Bratton, there was not much in the way of great leadership on Broken Windows from the top, but the management structure was still there to keep it going. At the same time, crime was going down. The problems started around 2000, when murders stopped declining. That's when recorded street stops by the police started going up. Stops became a way to quantify police 'productivity'. The police department needed numbers to show they were still doing something. The means became the end. The increase in stops – and stops for the sake of stops – which didn't explode till after 2000, marked the turning point from Broken Windows to Zero Tolerance. Police weren't asking 'why?' Police were not getting information from the public as to what the Broken Windows were. Only then did 'productivity statistics' start to become the end goal. It became a way to compensate for the lack of any sustained decline in shootings in the 2000s.[15]

The crackdown also precipitated a number of court cases over claims of violations of the First Amendment of the U.S. Constitution, which guarantees basic rights like freedom of speech and assembly. CCRB complaint data shows that the issue of police misconduct is disproportionately concentrated in New York's high-crime minority neighbourhoods. A 1996 report by the American Civil Liberties Union states that three-quarters of all CCRB complaints were filed by New York's black and Latino residents. With the NYPD's unrelenting war on drugs in full swing, the issue of demographics alone was fated to provoke charges of racial profiling. This problem had been brewing for years before the launch of Broken Windows and Zero Tolerance. A survey conducted by the mayor's office as far back as the 1970s, during the Koch administration, showed that more than half of New York's black population believed police brutality was standard practice. It is instructive to take into account the other side of the coin: the same poll revealed that only 13 per cent of those interviewed had actually witnessed or been the victim of some form of police brutality.

* * *

BY THE 1990S Harlem had become the processing centre for 90 per cent of all cocaine smuggled into New York City. A number of energetic raids made it possible for the police to pinpoint the hub of this activity in a cluster of tenements in West 140th Street, between Seventh and Eighth Avenues, where eight out of 36 houses were given over to the drug trade. The NYPD's drug squad was able to shut down the Dominican-dominated drug market in this neighbourhood, but it quickly became a cat-and-mouse game in which the dealers moved to surrounding streets, which soon were branded 'Cocaine City' by the press.

The stop-and-question procedure, or stop-question-and-frisk, put into practice by drug-busting police squads had for some years been a way of life for people in Harlem and other ethnic minority neighbourhoods. The policy of random checks on bags in the streets drew severe criticism from civil rights groups, given that black people and Latinos accounted for some 85 per cent of those approached by the police. Racial profiling had started to become a contentious issue as far back as the 1960s, though it did not come to a head until the 1990s with the introduction of Zero Tolerance and the intensified war on drugs. This course of action fuelled tensions between police and minority groups throughout that decade, developing into a suppurating wound in community relations, one that even today continues to beleaguer the NYPD. The police consistently maintained that no racial calculation was involved in enforcing Zero Tolerance. They argued that cops were sent to where crime was concentrated, which happened to be in poorer neighbourhoods where the suspects, as well as the victims, were predominantly people of colour. This was one of the thornier conundrums lying in wait for Ray Kelly when, in January 2002, he returned to One Police Plaza as Kerik's replacement.

From Zero Tolerance to Ground Zero

On 17 August 2001 Kerik announced he would be stepping down as NYPD commissioner by the end of the year, when the Giuliani administration was due to leave office. Statutory limitations prevented Giuliani from seeking a third consecutive term of office. Kerik said he viewed his decision as a gesture of loyalty to Giuliani, whose management policies he cited as essential in reducing crime during the year he served as commissioner. Leaving aside the controversial tactics employed, there is no denying that crime overall, at the time of his announcement, was down 13 per cent compared with the previous year, with an 11 per cent drop in homicides. Both these markers of success had prompted several mayoral candidates to say they hoped to persuade Kerik to stay on, but he insisted this was not on the cards.

One assumes Kerik was looking forward to a seamless transition from the rigours of the NYPD to his next job, which was to keep him at the outgoing mayor's side as a senior vice president at a consulting firm set up by Giuliani. The commissioner's expectations were violently shattered on the morning of 11 September 2001. Kerik was in his office when shortly before 9 a.m., a massive blast half a mile to the west shook the building to its foundations. It was the explosion of the first of two passenger jets that crashed into the World Trade Center that morning.

When the South Tower imploded Kerik and Giuliani rushed to the scene, where they found themselves trapped inside a building at 75 Barclay Street. With telephones knocked out, Kerik's bodyguard, Detective Hector Santiago, called a 'Code Black' over the police radio frequency. This is the code for signalling a major disaster in progress. 'That's the first time I ever heard a Code Black called,' said Kerik. 'I knew it was bad, but I didn't know how bad.'[16] Kerik, along with his first deputy commissioner, the chief of department, the deputy commissioner of operations, the chief of detectives and other top brass were all in close proximity to the burning towers and were forced to dodge rubble and debris as the structures fell.

The NYPD had developed the most sophisticated antiterrorism strategies of any large police force in the country. None had devoted as much

A rescue worker reaches into a New York Police car covered with debris while New York City fire fighters spray water on smouldering ruins, following the September 11 terrorist attack on the World Trade Center, New York City.

training or had received the same amount of expert counsel on how to prepare for a terrorist catastrophe. But when those planes hijacked by terrorists crashed into the Twin Towers that Tuesday morning, the department's ability to carry out its emergency management plans found itself seriously compromised. A few minutes after the towers collapsed, all the phones went dead at police headquarters. Pager and mobile phone service was lost for nearly 24 hours, and email and other computer communications were also knocked out.

One of the most striking achievements in improvisation and commitment in this crisis was how rapidly the NYPD, often using tools no more complex than pen and paper, managed to recover. Their quick action came in response not only to the terrorist attack crisis, but to the demands of effectively policing the rest of the city. As more than 1,000 officers were dispatched to the stricken area south of 14th Street, Kerik redeployed some 10,000 others – narcotics and precinct detectives, and officers from the Organized Crime Control Bureau, the Street Crime Unit and other special units – to patrol duties. 'It's really a test for the entire department,' Kerik said, three days after the towers collapsed. 'It's a test for the managers, it's a test for the administrators and it's a test for the rank-and-file cops and the first-line supervisors. And everybody is far surpassing what I would have imagined under the circumstances. We made the best with what we had and we made it work.'[17]

Retired Captain James Dooley says the NYPD played an essential role in saving lives when the terrorists struck. 'It was mainly a rescue and recovery effort, in which hundreds of officers waded into the thick of it, protected only by masks, helmets and boots. It was, in fact, the biggest crime scene in history and it fell to the NYPD to secure it.' Dooley says the only escape route out of Manhattan on foot was across the Brooklyn or Manhattan bridges. The subway system was immediately shut down. 'We organised what became the greatest boat lift in history,' he says.

> It was bigger than the evacuation of Dunkirk, when 338,000 troops were rescued over eight days. We got some half a million people off Manhattan in nine hours. The NYPD facilitated the operation, with people queuing ten-deep at the dockside. The police coordinated with the Coast Guard, which placed the call for maritime assistance. In the end, about 90 per cent of the rescue boats were piloted by civilians.[18]

Six weeks after the clean-up ended at the World Trade Center, police officers who had been employed at the site before the attack were back on duty, patrolling the city's commuter railway stations after months of searching the wreckage at Ground Zero for human remains. These officers were members of a special force set up by the Port Authority of New York and New Jersey, the organization that owned and ran the World Trade Center. Port Authority police are responsible for patrolling New York and New Jersey's port district, which surrounds New York Harbor. The combined rescue services lost 412 workers in the 9/11 attacks. Of these, sixty were NYPD or Port Authority police. For them, the NYPD motto *Fidelis ad mortem* (Faithful Unto Death), became their epitaph. The New York Fire Department fared worse, with the loss of 343 firefighters who responded to the emergency call. Scarcely an officer called to the Twin Towers that morning has been left without a memory of personal trauma and despair. 'We spent those days raking through rubble and debris, trying to figure out whether something was organic or synthetic, what was a bone, what was plastic,' says Port Authority Police

Officer Ed McQuade. 'You know, when you think about it now, it almost seems so far away and distant.'[19]

* * *

KERIK LEFT OFFICE in January 2002 to join Giuliani Partners, a management and security consultancy. After the 2003 Gulf War, he was appointed interim interior minister of Iraq and the following year President George W. Bush nominated him to lead the Department of Homeland Security. However, Kerik withdrew his candidacy when it became known that he had employed an illegal immigrant as a nanny. That was when his career skidded into a downward trajectory. This offence might have been written off as an almost trivial misdemeanour had he been offered a position in private industry, but a senior government position was another matter. The scandal led to a grand jury investigation that eventually uncovered a number of unethical and allegedly felonious dealings, such as accepting a $250,000 interest-free 'loan' from Israeli billionaire Stef Wertheimer while Kerik was serving with the government of Iraq. In 2009 he was indicted on charges of tax fraud and making false statements about the money he had obtained from Wertheimer. Kerik pleaded guilty to eight felony tax and false statement charges and was subsequently sentenced to 48 months in federal prison. He has always maintained his innocence of criminal corruption charges. Kerik began serving his term in 2010 and was released in 2013. In 2020 former U.S. president Donald Trump granted him a presidential pardon, two years after Giuliani was taken on by Trump as one of his personal attorneys.

9

The Force Is With You

The New York City mayoral election of November 2001 ushered in a year of political surprises. The first came from billionaire businessman Michael Bloomberg, a lifelong Democrat, who decided to switch party affiliation to launch his campaign on the Republican ticket. The second surprise came as something of a shocker, when Bloomberg narrowly defeated his opponent, Mark Green, in a city in which Democrats outnumbered Republicans by a five-to-one margin. Political observers attributed Green's defeat to his unpopularity with the city's ethnic minority voters, who on this occasion turned their backs on the Democrats. This had its roots in an incident in which the candidate was associated with allegedly racist comments in the right-wing press. An investigation by the Brooklyn district attorney concluded that Green had no knowledge of these newspaper stories, but the damage had been done.

The third unexpected event came with the changeover at City Hall, when Bloomberg brought back Ray Kelly to head One Police Plaza, the first person in New York City history to serve twice as police commissioner. Kelly had experienced an action-packed career after stepping down as NYPD commissioner in 1994. He carried on as a law enforcer, first as director of an international police operation in Haiti, after which he returned to the U.S. to oversee the Secret Service for the Treasury Department. He then went on to serve as commissioner of the customs service and was later appointed an official at the international police agency Interpol. He finally took up a post as an executive at Wall Street securities firm Bear Stearns. The decision to relinquish this lucrative job in the financial services industry was not one to be taken lightly, for it threw up a difficult lifestyle choice. The $150,500 police commissioner's salary amounted to a major pay cut, but police work had always been embedded in his DNA. When he took the not-totally-unexpected call from the mayor's office, Kelly's unhesitating response was, 'Sure, it would be an honour.'

Kelly returned to his desk on the fourteenth floor of NYPD headquarters when bodies, or more accurately human remains, were still being dug up from the smouldering rubble of the World Trade Center. The drop in crime he had achieved while serving under the Dinkins administration, with his 'Safe Streets, Safe City' policy, was to continue steadily on the decline during the Giuliani years. During Kelly's previous time as commissioner, he was known as an outspoken advocate of community policing, in which neighbourhood police officers worked with local residents to fight neighbourhood crime. This approach was discarded during the Giuliani administration, which dismissed it as social work rather than a police task. On taking office, Kelly promised that a resumption of community policing, if it were to happen, would be launched in combination with an all-out war on quality-of-life offences. These could broadly be defined as anti-social misdemeanours that do not involve violence.

The 9/11 attack on the Twin Towers changed the entire panorama of policing. The priority now was to devise a strategy to shield New Yorkers from terrorism, a task that would entail a fundamental rethinking of the NYPD's role. 'We'd still have to fight street crime,' Kelly says, 'but moving forward, a large part of our responsibility – maybe the largest – would be protecting the city against another terrorist attack. No local police department had ever taken on that responsibility.'[1] Kelly's experience with Interpol made him all the more valuable at a time when the city had become the target of foreign criminals and terrorists.

At his swearing-in ceremony, Kelly spelled out the three spheres of action – his 'three Cs' – that were to guide his work as commissioner: counterterrorism, crime fighting and community relations. Four months had not yet passed since the collapse of the World Trade Center, hence Kelly made it plain that safeguarding the city from terrorism was to head his list of priorities. The spotlight fell on the Joint Terrorism Task Force (JTTF), an agency set up in 1980 under the auspices of the FBI to coordinate federal and local counterterrorism tactics. The New York agency was the first of some two hundred task forces currently operating in cities around the country. When the planes struck the Twin Towers, fewer than twenty NYPD officers had been assigned to the task force, a figure the commissioner boosted by adding more than a hundred trained counter-terrorism specialists to the unit.

The New York City public transport network was an obvious and highly vulnerable terrorist target. James Dooley was serving as transit duty captain in the aftermath of the World Trade Center attack. 'If we got a call warning us of a suspicious device at, say, Pennsylvania Station, the bomb squad could be on the scene within minutes of the alert, equipped with a robot and X-ray device,' he says. 'That was the easy part. The problematical work would be evacuating possibly thousands of commuters to safety.'[2] Dooley says there were instances when attackers conducted dry runs, by placing an inert device at a station and phoning in a bomb threat to test the police response.

Police were given special Nuclear, Biological and Radiation (NBR) training and were instructed in the National Incident Management System (NIMS). They were taught how to establish a command post at an incident site and other skills deemed essential to foil terrorist plots. 'On a citywide level we created drills with different agencies, like the NYPD, National Guard, Port Authority and the Emergency Medical Service,' says Dooley. 'It would be clever for terrorists to launch an attack in a subway tunnel, so we set up bullet-proof booths at the end of platforms that connected to tunnels leading from one borough to another. The thinking was that all tunnels going into Manhattan were particularly vulnerable. What we did was modelled after London's Ring of Steel.'[3] Fixed and moveable barriers capable of stopping a vehicle at 30 miles (50 km) per hour were set up around government buildings, and 30-foot-tall (9 m) observation points were erected in potential target areas, such as Wall Street, which was equipped with automatic licence plate readers, high-resolution cameras and facial recognition systems. Random bag checks were introduced on the overground and underground transit network, but the legal catch was that there was no requirement to open a bag. Those who refused, however, were denied access to public transport. New York Harbor was not neglected as a potential target, with every ship coming in screened for radiation by onshore detector devices.

The sheer scale of the measures introduced over such a short period of time may have struck some New Yorkers as excessive. Some constitutional rights activists interpreted the bag checks as an infringement of civil liberties, while the deployment of heavily armed officers in combat gear on subway platforms conveyed an uncomfortable sense of living

Mural in Lower Manhattan in memory of NYPD and fire brigade officers who lost their lives in the 11 September 2001 terrorist attacks.

in a city under siege. Whatever the objections, these actions served to remind people that New York was a city with terror at the forefront of its mind. This reality came to the surface a little more than a year after the World Trade Center attack, when 37 cardboard boxes were discovered affixed to the walls and girders of the Union Square subway station in Lower Manhattan. Within minutes, concern spread among commuters that they might contain bombs. The police were alerted, the station and its surrounding area were evacuated, and passing trains were barred from stopping at one of the city's busiest stations. After hours of investigation and the delicate, ultimately uneventful job of opening the boxes, the police were able to calm people's frayed nerves: the episode was a distasteful prank. At the same time, it showed that action was heavily weighted in favour of the unprecedented antiterrorism systems put in place since 9/11.

* * *

KELLY WAS CONVINCED from the outset that intelligence-gathering and counterterrorism were going to become crucial skills in policing New York City. His overriding concern was that the department lacked sufficient expertise in these operations, which were not central to the

Police Academy training syllabus. He would have to search for highly qualified experts from outside the NYPD. Kelly brought in Frank Libutti, a Marine Corps general, as deputy commissioner in charge of the newly formed NYPD Counterterrorism Bureau. This was the first police agency in the U.S. specifically tasked with protecting the civilian population against terrorist attacks. About 1,000 officers were trained in antiterrorism skills. At the same time, Kelly's personal friend David Cohen, a former CIA station chief in New York, was named head of the NYPD Intelligence Bureau. New functions and systems were introduced for compiling and analysing information globally on terrorist and international criminal activity that might be targeted at New York.

> I knew that if we were going to fight this new enemy, we couldn't rely entire on old policing methods. What might be effective against burglars in Riverdale or chain snatchers [thieves who rip gold jewellery off women] in Crown Heights was unlikely to provide much protection against a truck bomb, an improvised explosive device or an aeroplane turned into a missile . . . If we were going to protect this city against terrorists, we had to know who the terrorists were – their methods, their ideologies, their funding and their associations. We had to know everything. At this point, at least, the New York City Police Department knew hardly anything at all.[4]

Kelly created a number of new agencies to tackle this novel frontier for the NYPD. Two hundred members of the Organized Crime Control Bureau (OCCB) were given training in heavy weapons tactics as a backup to the Emergency Services Unit. This group had been formed after the Knapp Commission investigations into police corruption was set up. The city's most vulnerable targets were pinpointed, with some having escaped scrutiny after 9/11. Police filmed the lobbies of major hotels as a resource for counterterrorism officers, in the event they were called upon to respond to an attack. The Lower Manhattan Security Initiative (LMSI) was organized in 2005 to provide enhanced security to the tempting target of New York's financial district. Part and parcel of this project was the Lower Manhattan Security Coordination Center (LMSCC), staffed 24/7, which could rely on a network of hundreds of security cameras and number plate recognition scanners that fed images into a central database.

Also in 2005, Kelly announced the opening of the Real Time Crime Center (RTCC). This was hailed as a world first in policing procedures, allowing access on a 24-hour basis to an enormous store of data on people with criminal records, on a national as well as metropolitan scale. The initial team of 43 police and civilian analysts could tap into custom-built software with connectivity across multiple databases: 'Whereas CompStat analyses data after the fact, this centre provides real-time information to officers in the street. If an officer holds a suspect after a crime, critical data about that person's background can be relayed instantly.'[5] The centre was enabled to employ satellite imaging and mapping of the city, precinct by precinct. A benefit of this technology was that it freed up officers from part of their time-consuming paperwork and allowed them to focus their attention on catching criminals.

In the Nick of Time

Kelly had good reason to suspect the World Trade Center atrocity had been but a prelude to a terrorist campaign against New York, a city the jihadists despised. In their twisted thinking, this was the symbol of Zionist-dominated Western capitalism. Within a year of becoming commissioner Kelly unveiled a programme never before undertaken by a local police department. In 2003 he began to station NYPD detectives in hot spots outside the United States. Counterterrorism professionals were deployed to cities deemed to be high-risk targets, starting with Tel Aviv. The scheme steadily expanded to include Muslim cities like Abu Dhabi and Amman, European capitals Madrid, London and Paris, Canada's Montreal and Toronto, Singapore, and Santo Domingo in the Dominican Republic. The team now has more than 130 officers stationed in twelves countries across the globe. The NYPD agents' mandate is to keep a watchful eye on developments and to pick up signals of planned action that might have an impact on New York City. Team members liaise closely with local police authorities to obtain valuable intelligence on the movements of terrorist suspects.

The programme's mission broadened over time and officers are now investigating other crimes. In August 2018 the first words out of James Currie's mouth were, 'How did you get here so fast?' That was as Sergeant Edward Lee of the Intelligence Bureau walked into a room to interview him at Suvarnabhumi Airport in Bangkok. Currie, a subway cleaner from the Bronx, had left JFK airport on a flight to Abu Dhabi two days earlier. That was a day after his infant son was discovered floating lifeless in the East River. Detectives in New York had gathered evidence suggesting Currie had thrown the baby into the river, where his body was spotted by tourists. Lee had been stationed in Singapore as part of Kelly's counterterrorism programme.

'In a post-9/11 world, we wanted to learn as much as we could about terrorism,' said Thomas Galati, the department's chief of intelligence. 'As it evolved from terrorism, we started to see more and more criminal cases coming up.' Galati cited an instance in which $800,000 worth of watches were snatched in a December 2017 gunpoint heist from the A. Lange & Söhne boutique in New York's Madison Avenue. Several of the stolen watches were tracked down to a pawnshop in Amman, Jordan, by NYPD agents stationed abroad. 'The world is a small place,' he said.[6]

The team's primary role remains the detection of suspected terrorist activity that could be aimed at New York City. In this regard, the deployment of agents to strategic listening posts around the world was to pay dividends. In 2005, three years after the attack on the Twin Towers, counterterrorism agents picked up a chilling piece of intelligence which they passed on to Kelly and his staff in New York. Online chat-room messages monitored in the Middle East revealed plans to bomb the Hudson River PATH railway tunnels linking lower Manhattan and New Jersey. NYPD detectives were hastily dispatched to survey what was obviously a highly tempting and easily accessible target, with the tunnels carrying almost 250,000 passengers every weekday. Police explosives experts calculated that a relatively small blast would be capable of shattering the tunnel walls, leaving much of Lower Manhattan below 14th Street underwater. It was an apocalyptic scenario.

Kelly lost no time in activating Operation Life Raft, which put NYPD and Port Authority officers on security watch around the tunnels. Meanwhile, counterterrorism agents in other countries were busy mining data from the computer of a prime suspect, Assem Hammoud, a computer science instructor in Beirut. Hammoud's subsequent arrest and confession were kept secret, to avoid tipping off any jihadist accomplices. The police had uncovered a plot in which suicide bombers were to board PATH trains carrying rucksacks filled with explosives, which they planned to detonate under the Hudson River. The strike was set for autumn 2006. In this counterterrorism operation, the NYPD worked in close collaboration with the FBI and law enforcement agencies in six other countries.

From the standpoint of capturing terrorists, the operation was not a total triumph. Hammoud, who under Lebanese law could not be extradited, served only 26 months in prison. The real success was in detecting and preventing an attack on New York's suburban transit network. The Port Authority has since reinforced the ageing cast-iron-lined tunnels with a bomb-resistant covering. Operation Life Raft gave the police insights into the monitoring of digital forums that could be used to launch a campaign with a few short keyboard strokes.

On any given Saturday, more than 460,000 people pass through Times Square. The night of 1 May 2010 was no exception, when unnoticed by the crowds, Pakistani-born Faisal Shahzad parked his Nissan Pathfinder 4X4 in West 45th Street and Broadway, where thousands of tourists gathered to be dazzled by the display of glitzy neon adverts and brightly lit theatre entrances. Shahzad had been nursing a grudge against the capitalist system for two years, ever since the 2008 financial meltdown forced him to take out a second mortgage on his home. The year after the collapse, he travelled to his native Pakistan, where he made contact with Taliban fighters who instructed him in the art of bomb-making. Armed with his new skill, Shahzad returned to New York, where on that night in May he left his car and strolled to Grand Central Station to catch a train to his home in Connecticut.

'If you see something, say something' was the police slogan posted at critical points around the city in the wake of the Twin Towers attack. A Times Square hot-dog vendor who spotted smoke billowing from Shahzad's car did just that. He alerted mounted police officer Wayne Rhatigan, who fired off an emergency message to the NYPD Bomb Squad and then quickly went about clearing Times Square of pedestrians. Within minutes, a team from the Counterterrorism Bureau was on the spot. They ran a check on the car's interior with a remote-controlled robot. Shahzad had not perfected his skills: it was a botched job, though the device contained enough explosives to spread death and destruction across hundreds of yards of tightly packed streets. It took detectives 48 hours to trace the woman who had sold Shahzad the car. The police then found out that he was booked on a flight to Dubai that day. They swiftly raced to JFK airport, where Shahzad was bundled off a plane, brought to trial, convicted of terrorism and sentenced to life imprisonment without parole.

* * *

KELLY ACKNOWLEDGES that some of the department's activities were controversial. 'This being New York, there are always people willing to criticise and often people ready to sue,' he says. 'We got some of both on a counterterror campaign.'[7] One unexpected flashpoint was the Demographics Unit, set up as part of the Intelligence Division. The idea behind this agency was to track where people of various nationalities lived. Kelly's rationale was that if a small town in Libya produced twelve suicide bombers, for instance, it was worth knowing where their family relations lived in New York. If immigrants arrived from Moldova, it is more than likely they would be acquainted with others from their country living in the Moldovan community of the Bronx. Kelly argued that it would be foolish for the police to pretend otherwise.

This unit gathered intelligence by walking about and speaking to residents of diverse neighbourhoods. They were under instructions to identify themselves as members of the department while they recorded information about what they saw and heard. The goal was to identify locations where a would-be terrorist could blend into society. The secretive programme would routinely dispatch plainclothes detectives into mainly Muslim neighbourhoods to eavesdrop on conversations and build detailed files on where people ate, prayed and shopped. Agents searched out 'hot spots' of radicalization that might give the police an early warning about terrorist plots. Detectives were told to chat with employees at Muslim-owned businesses and gauge sentiment about America and its foreign policy. Through maps and photographs, the police noted where Albanian men played chess in the afternoon, where Egyptians watched football matches and where South Asians played cricket. The agency's name was eventually changed to the euphemistic and less inflammatory Area Assessment Unit.

It is not difficult to imagine the outcry this squad of infiltrators aroused among ethnic minorities. 'This unit created psychological warfare in our community,' said Linda Sarsour, of the Arab American Association of New York. 'Those documents, they showed where we live. That's the cafe where I eat. That's where I pray. That's where I buy my groceries. They were able to see their entire lives on those maps. And it completely messed with the psyche of the community.'[8]

NYPD mounted police providing security for a parade in Manhattan.

In 2014, under a barrage of continual pressure from civil liberties associations and ethnic minorities, mainly New York's Muslim community, the activities of the Area Assessment Unit were brought to an end. It was the first sign that the NYPD was backing away from some of the more contentious intelligence-gathering practices that had been put in place after the Twin Towers attack. Muslims had always seen the squad as a sign of the police tracking their every move. After nearly a decade spent collecting neighbourhood information, the NYPD acknowledged that the unit had failed to generate a single substantiated lead on terrorist plans.

The third key pillar of Kelly's twelve years' service in the Bloomberg administration came under the heading of community relations. As police commissioner during the Dinkins mayoralty, Kelly had overseen the birth of programmes that later were to benefit Giuliani and his successors. Foremost among these was adding several thousand new NYPD officers to the force. In Kelly's second term as commissioner, building closer ties with ordinary citizens was given a boost by a rebalancing of ethnic diversity on the force. Within four years of Kelly taking office, for the first time the hiring of racial minority officers, chiefly black and Latino, began to reflect the mix of the city as a whole. Starting in 2006, the department embarked on an assertive programme of taking on recruits who represented a myriad of ethnicities. In addition to facilitating better police ties with the community, diversity provided the department with speakers of more than fifty languages, officers who were able to help with cyber-policing and the monitoring of potential threats on the Internet.

In Pursuit of Bad Cops

Kelly had his work cut out for him on multiple fronts. Apart from building bridges to the community, dark issues of police corruption and criminal behaviour still lurked in the background. Possibly one of the most contemptible instances of the latter was the case of Louis Eppolito and Stephen Caracappa, who left the force prior to Kelly's second term as commissioner. They were NYPD detectives with a combined 44 years on the force, many of which were spent forging multi-layered links to the Mafia. The duo personified police corruption and criminality at its vilest. They were both decorated cops who exploited their links with the criminal underworld to fall in with the very people they were meant to arrest. As early as 1985, investigators suspected them of being in bed with the Lucchese and Gambino crime families. Just how deeply embedded they were with the mafiosos did not become clear until Anthony 'Gaspipe' Casso, the underboss of the Lucchese family, agreed to cooperate with the authorities in exchange for leniency under the Witness Protection Program. Casso testified that, beginning in 1985, he and his boss Vittorio Amuso had handed over to Eppolito and Caracappa $375,000 in bribes and payments for murder contracts. It became evident that the two cops had been doing the Mafia's bidding for years, providing police intelligence, protecting the gangsters' allies and using their positions of power to lure in perceived foes and deliver them to Lucchese associates.

It was one of the most shocking instances of police corruption ever to come to light in New York. The two were arrested in 2005 in Las Vegas, where they were luxuriating in gilded 'retirement'. Barrel-bodied Eppolito had also cavalierly supplemented his income by working as an actor, playing the appropriate role of 'Fat Andy' in the 1990 Martin Scorsese gangster film *Goodfellas*, as well as taking on character parts in several other Hollywood productions. The pair were charged with eight murders, two attempted murders and one murder conspiracy, along with money laundering, drug dealing and obstruction of justice. These two embodiments of the crooked cop taken to the hundredth power were convicted and sentenced in 2009, Eppolito to life plus a hundred years and Caracappa to life plus eighty years. New York City paid a total of $18.4 million to settle lawsuits with seven of the victims' families.

The CCRB report for 2005, three years after Kelly's return to office, gave an indication of the trials and tribulations the commissioner was to face in stimulating public support for the police. The report showed that complaints filed against the police had increased for the fifth straight year. The most frequently filed allegations, 4,442 in total, concerned improper use of physical force. In all, the agency received 6,796 complaints in 2005, six hundred more than the previous year. The cumulative effect of this increase is dramatic: the number of complaints filed in 2005 was 60 per cent greater than in 2001. The facile assumption was that Kelly had been thrust into the unenviable role of lion tamer, forced to crack a whip over uniformed beasts given to gratuitously dispensing rough justice. By the look of it, New York policing had retreated to the late 1920s days of Commissioner Whalen and his pronouncement, 'There is plenty of law at the end of a nightstick.' This reading of the situation was sharply at variance with reality. The underlying problem was that every reported allegation, whether serious or trivial, was transformed into a statistic.

Among the rulings on police misconduct handed down by the CCRB, a considerable number could generously be classified as open to doubt. In February 2004 a detective was reported for frisking an autistic boy sitting with his sister at a picnic table in a Queens park. Two members of the Narcotics Division suspected him of concealing cannabis under the table. The boy was told to place his hands on his head and, when he failed to comply, most probably because he did not understand the order, the cops frisked and searched him. The sister later filed a complaint at the nearby 113th Precinct. The CCRB substantiated the charge of stop-question-and-frisk without legal justification. The two officers involved were disciplined and sent off for training in department guidelines on stop-question-and-frisk procedures. This case was added to the board's tally of 1,112 improper search allegations for the year.

That same month, and likewise in the borough of Queens, an officer arrested a man who had accidentally bumped into him in the street. The plaintiff's version was that he had apologised to the cop, who turned on him with a torrent of verbal abuse. The man demanded to be treated with respect, whereupon the officer handcuffed and bundled him into his patrol car. At the precinct, the man was handed a summons for disorderly conduct, a charge later dismissed by the courts. The officer's report of the incident produced a different version of the altercation outside the pizzeria in Roosevelt Avenue. He alleged the man who bumped into him had become agitated and aggressive. He was whisked off to the precinct to run a routine check on outstanding warrants. The incident was sent to the CCRB, whose board ruled that the man had been the victim of unlawful arrest. The officer under investigation was found guilty of misconduct and forced to forfeit ten days of annual leave. The incident became one of that year's 2,978 recorded allegations against an NYPD officer in the CCRB's 'use of discourteous language' category of offences.

Not all cases brought before the CCRB could be dismissed as frivolous. Herein lay the conundrum for Kelly, as well as for his successors at One Police Plaza. It was not so much a matter of forging harmonious relations with the broader community as assuaging the grievances and mistrust that were embittering New York's two main ethnic minorities, black and Hispanic. The ratio of black victims involved in CCRB complaints has always outstripped the percentage they represent in the population. A full 57 per cent of abuse cases brought before the board in 2005 involved people of colour, who make up a quarter of New York's citizens. Latinos fared somewhat better: they account for 27 per cent of the city's residents and 20 per cent of CCRB cases.

Few white people could claim to have been subjected to the thrashing that was given to a black man, unnamed in the CCRB report, in an incident that took place in Harlem in 2003. On a May afternoon, an officer keeping watch on an East Harlem observation post spotted a known drug offender buying cocaine in the street. When he was approached by two plainclothes officers, the suspect swiftly stuffed the bag into his mouth. He subsequently declared the police had grabbed him in a stranglehold to prevent him swallowing the drugs. The two officers tackled and handcuffed the suspect – who meanwhile had managed to swallow the bag – while repeatedly delivering punches and kicks to his torso. He was taken to the 23rd Precinct in 102nd Street, and from there to hospital, where his injuries were diagnosed as muscle strain. He twice returned to the hospital on his own to seek medical attention, and after the second visit, his 'muscle strain' was revealed to be a shattered spleen and two fractured ribs. He underwent emergency surgery to have his spleen removed. The two arresting officers denied having used violent force, however the

CCRB obtained a chief medical examiner's statement confirming that the injuries were consistent with a delayed rupture of the spleen. The report stated the injury could only have been inflicted by a forceful blow.

Improper use of force, when substantiated in a court of law, does the NYPD a dishonour. It also fosters a climate of discord between the department and the civilian powers that be. Between 1994 and 1997, for instance, verified cases of police misconduct drained more than $70 million from City Hall coffers, but not directly from the NYPD budget. This in effect represents a hit on taxpayers in settlement of jury awards for claims of police misconduct, defined as anything from assault and excessive force, to false arrest and shootings by officers. One of the cases heard during this period, and which cost the city $76 million, involved two men who were brutalized by police officers in a midnight encounter in a Coney Island street. The court heard that the two plaintiffs, civic leader Gerard Papa and James Rampersant Jr, who is black, were driving along Bayview Avenue when two unmarked cars forced them to stop. Several men in plain clothes leapt out with drawn guns, opening fire without warning as Papa and Rampersant ducked under the dashboard. The agents then dragged Papa and Rampersant out of the car, kicking and punching them as they lay handcuffed on the ground. The officers argued that the incident was a case of mistaken identity.

In another incident, a young black man by the name of Carlton Brown was taken into custody by the police for allegedly driving with a suspended licence. Brown was handcuffed and taken to the 63rd Precinct in Brooklyn. In the station house, the victim later testified, the officers struck him and pushed him still handcuffed through a glass door, shattering it. Brown sustained spinal injuries and was hospitalized for more than three years. He was left permanently paralysed and was paid $16.6 million in compensation, the largest pretrial settlement by New York City in a personal injury lawsuit. After a spate of public outcries, two officers were indicted on assault charges and placed on restrictive duty. They were later acquitted by a judge.

The Kelly Controversy

Commissioner Kelly's no-holds-barred approach to preventing terrorism and ridding the streets of criminals was applauded by most New Yorkers, albeit with concern voiced from some quarters, specifically ethnic minority communities, over the alleged erosion of civil liberties his controversial tactics brought with them.

'Having watched 9/11 from my office window, I, for one, am not unhappy to see how Kelly foiled numerous follow-up terrorist attacks,' says Rita Jakubowski, who sits on the board of the West 44th Street Better Block Association, a group that acts as a liaison between the local authorities and the community. 'I certainly found peace of mind in the fact that I could safely ride public transportation and walk alone in Hell's Kitchen late at night in the ensuing years, as opposed to the opposite experience of the 1980s. But I also cringed to watch the dreadful and often excessive measures taken to control crime during the Kelly years.' The commissioner, whose policing philosophy proved effective in many ways, was also an avid proponent of stop-question-and-frisk in New York City, which peaked at almost 700,000 detentions in 2011. Of these, 75 per cent were black people and Latinos. So the answer really depends on whether you are black or white, rich or poor, and also upon your view of what is necessary to achieve and maintain quality of life or what defines a successful administration. This became Kelly's signature legacy, and Bloomberg's as well.' To put the 2011 figure into perspective, the number of reported stop-and-frisk incidents in 2002, when Kelly became commissioner, came to about 100,000 for the year. It should be kept in mind that the stop-and-frisk policy was not a Kelly exclusive. It came in with Bratton, continued under Kerik, and was followed up with increased vigour by Kelly.

The expression 'stop-and-frisk' has a nasty ring to it. Former head of the IAB Charles Campisi maintains that the term 'stop-question-and-frisk' would more accurately describe the procedure employed.

The media jumped on the name 'stop-and-frisk', which is very misleading. When suspects were stopped and questioned about possible criminal conduct, they were not necessarily frisked. A frisk follows a stop only when there is reason to believe that a person may possess a weapon. Stop-question-and-frisk is a U.S. Supreme Court recognized exception to the search warrant requirement and is codified in the New York State Criminal Procedure Law. When I first joined the NYPD [in 1973] the Stop-and-question Report was only prepared when an officer used force to stop or frisked someone, or the stop resulted in an arrest. If an officer stopped four or five kids hanging out on a corner and after talking with them, just sent them on their way, no report was prepared. The number of people stopped was also somewhat exaggerated. We had cases where police officers submitted a Stop-and-question Report as a means to inflate their monthly activity statistics, when in fact they did not stop anyone. The form was filled out very vaguely with no name or addresses, in an effort to make it appear they were working. These were documented cases and disciplinary procedures followed.[10]

Did stop-question-and-frisk work? There are arguments to suit all persuasions regarding the part this procedure played in cutting New York's crime rate. The police carried out about 5 million street stops during Kelley's term in office. During this period, the number of murders in New York dropped by half, with a 45 per cent cut in other major crimes. On the face of it, there would appear to be a persuasive argument for linking this reduction in crime to an intensification of stop-question-and-frisk. Yet nearly 90 per cent of those stopped during Kelly's stint as commissioner were innocent, and only about 1.5 per cent of those searched were found to be carrying a concealed weapon. A study by the Department of Criminology at the University of Pennsylvania claimed that the difference stop-question-and-frisk made to crime reduction was negligible. It cited instead as a major factor an increased police presence in high crime neighbourhoods.

The NYPD's deployment of extra police to high crime neighborhoods contributed far more to the crime reduction than the use of stop, question, and frisk. Research on the NYPD's program of Operation Impact found that extra police deployed to high crime areas in New York was a major factor in the crime decline. The additional use of stop, question, and frisk made almost no difference. The stops only had a detectable impact on crime when they were based on probable cause, and these kinds of stops were very rare ... Saturating high crime neighborhoods with extra police helped reduce crime in New York, but the bulk of investigative stops did not play a meaningful role in crime reduction.[11]

Killings by police had been on the wane for more than four decades. By the time Kelly made his departure from the NYPD, the number of fatalities from police shootings or use of excessive force had dropped

NYPD officers on night patrol in Times Square.

from 93 in 1971 to eight by the end of 2013. There were times, however, when stop-question-and-frisk could go badly wrong. In these instances, it did not take much to unleash a torrent of anti-police fury. On 17 July 2014, NYPD officer Daniel Pantaleo was on patrol on Staten Island when he spotted a 43-year-old black man, Eric Garner, selling untaxed cigarettes not far from the nearby Staten Island Ferry Terminal. By anyone's definition it ranked as a petty misdemeanour. Garner was not unknown to the local police; for years he had played a cat-and-mouse game with officers who came to arrest him. When Pantaleo and several other officers approached him that day, Garner allegedly complained that he was fed up being harassed by the police. He was placed under arrest, but fought back and was wrestled to the ground, where Pantaleo grabbed him in a chokehold. For several minutes Garner repeatedly cried, 'I can't breathe.' When he lost consciousness, the police called for an ambulance. One hour later, he was pronounced dead in hospital.

A month after Garner's death, narcotics officers arrested Ramsey Orta, the person whose visceral mobile phone images of Garner's deadly arrest helped set off a citywide debate over police practices. In a highly controversial action, Orta, a member of Copwatch (a system of monitoring and documenting police interaction with the public) was charged with two counts of criminal possession of a semi-automatic handgun, which police said he tried to pass to a teenager in a drug-prone street near the spot where officers had the fatal confrontation with Garner.[12]

Garner's death was the start of a succession of killings by police elsewhere that captured national attention and ignited a debate over race and law enforcement. After shootings in Missouri, South Carolina and Maryland, the deaths of black men at the hands of local police were confronted with a level of scrutiny that would have been almost unthinkable only a short time before the Garner affair. In 2019 the U.S. Department of Justice declined to bring criminal charges against Pantaleo. Later that year, an administrative judge recommended that Pantaleo's employment be terminated. Shortly afterwards, he was dismissed from the department and stripped of his pension benefits. This brought to an end a bitter battle that had cast a shadow over the NYPD and helped to galvanize the Black Lives Matter protests, which led to changes in policing practices in New York City and around the country.

The Return of Broken Windows Man

On 1 January 2014 Ray Kelly stepped down as commissioner, simultaneous with the departure from City Hall of Michael Bloomberg, who had served his maximum three terms as mayor. Bloomberg handed over to the Democratic winner of the mayoralty race, the long-serving councilman and champion of the underdog Bill de Blasio. It fell to de Blasio's newly appointed NYPD commissioner to deal with the Garner case and a tide of anti-police-racism protests. That man was William Bratton, whom de Blasio brought in from California where he had been working as a consultant for the city of Oakland.

Bratton had already acquired an international reputation when de Blasio offered him the job of NYPD commissioner. In 2009 UK ambassador to the United States Sir Nigel Sheinwald bestowed upon Bratton, who at the time was serving as Los Angeles police chief, the honorary title of Commander of the Most Excellent Order of the British Empire (CBE) at a ceremony in the British ambassador's residence. The award was in recognition of his work to promote cooperation between U.S. and British police forces throughout his career. Two years later, in the summer of 2011 when serious rioting and looting convulsed London and several other UK cities, the police had struggled to contain the mobs. Prime Minister David Cameron called Bratton to discuss working as a consultant, to work on a policing strategy to devise an appropriate response to such outbreaks of violence. Bratton later voiced his disappointment at not getting the chance to run London's Metropolitan Police, an appointment that was vetoed by Theresa May, who was serving as home secretary, on the grounds that the post needed to be held by a UK citizen.

On the morning of 2 January 2014 Bratton delivered a conciliatory message to New Yorkers. His remarks were addressed in particular at those ethnic minorities who were nursing anger at the aggressive tactics of Kelly's signature programme, Operation Impact. Once the wail of the bagpipes had faded at his swearing-in ceremony, the commissioner signalled his intention to shift the NYPD away from the belligerent style of patrolling that had alienated many minority groups. Bratton said the strides the department had made in reducing crime should long ago have given way to fewer confrontational encounters between the police and the public. 'Crime is down to such extraordinarily low levels in this city versus where it was that there is an expectation – or there should be an expectation – that the intrusion of police into citizens' lives should also diminish,' he said. 'But we had the reverse happening.' Bratton pledged a new era of policing that would be 'a collaboration unlike any that we have ever seen. That's why I came back.'[13]

Bratton set himself the task of changing how minor criminal offences were handled, exploring ways to make the outcomes less punitive and mulling a new form of warnings in lieu of arrest or summonses. He created a new centralized unit, the Force Investigation Division (FID), to probe fatal police encounters. The bureau was set up to centralize and standardize how each incident of police firing their guns and using other types of force was reported and investigated. Bratton said the unit 'was not a direct result of the Garner incident but rather something that I recognized a need for on a more general basis'. He said the notion of retraining the police pre-dated Garner's death, but added, 'There is no question that the Garner incident added new dimensions and certainly new immediacy.'[14]

The trouble was that the Garner killing, instead of fading away, became a catalyst for more violence and hostility between the police department and the City Hall powers that be. On 20 December 2014 Ismaaiyl Abdullah Brinsley, a black supremacist with an arrest record for robbery and illegal possession of weapons, gunned down two officers in the Bedford–Stuyvesant area of Brooklyn, ostensibly in revenge for the death of Eric Garner. That night, Brinsley approached officers Rafael Ramos and Wenjian Liu as they sat in their patrol car. He shot the officers at point-blank range before turning the gun on himself. The murder became the accelerant of an ugly confrontation between the biggest NYPD union, the Police Benevolent Association, and Mayor de Blasio. Two days after the officers' killing, Patrick Lynch, president of the PBA, openly blamed the mayor for the tragedy. 'There's blood on many hands tonight,' he said. 'That blood on the hands starts at the steps of City Hall in the office of the mayor.'[5]

There was more to follow. In April 2016 two NYPD detectives were charged with having assaulted a uniformed Postal Service employee in Queens in October of the previous year. Karim Baker said the police had been harassing him since 2014 for having given street directions to a stranger on the fateful night of 20 December. The stranger in question was Ismaaiyl Abdullah Brinsley, who was seeking the Marcy Houses apartment complex where he believed a patrol car would be parked. The indictment was handed down by a grand jury that watched surveillance video of the incident and heard a 911 call that appeared to contradict the detectives' account. The video showed them kicking and dragging Baker along the street. Baker's lawyer, Eric Subin, argued that the stop was part of a campaign of harassment by the police. He claimed this had started when Baker told Ismaaiyl Brinsley how to get to the street he was seeking on the night of the murder. Detectives Angelo Pampena and Robert Carbone were charged with felony and misdemeanour assault, in an indictment announced by the Queens district attorney, Richard Brown, and Bratton himself. In March 2017, the year after Bratton stepped down, Queens Supreme Court Judge Michael Aloise found the detectives not guilty of all charges in a five-count indictment that included second- and third-degree assault. The men chose to be tried by judge rather than jury. The courtroom had been packed by fellow officers in a show of support during most of the six-day proceedings. Civil liberty groups were a good deal less happy with the verdict.

In Bratton's report on quality-of-life policing, the system that had been successfully implemented on the subway between 1990 and 1993, he stated that his mission as de Blasio's commissioner would be to reinforce discretion in the department. 'I want the police to be problem solvers, not merely crime fighters. I want to make it clear that results matter, not numbers. I have said the same to thousands of cops at training sessions and roll calls and via internal messages and videos. We're not just telling our officers, however.'

The department began actively exploring ways to divert people from the criminal justice system or, once they were in, to minimize their exposure to it. In conjunction with the Metropolitan Transport Authority (MTA). the Department of Homeless Services and the Bowery Residents' Committee, Bratton introduced an innovative programme in which officers and social workers conducted joint patrols in the subway. During the programme's first months in 2014, the outreach teams placed 388 individuals in shelters, compared with 63 during the same period in 2013.[16]

On 16 September 2016 Bratton marked his final day as police commissioner by strolling through a receiving line of hundreds of officers. There was a joyful smile on his face as he exited police headquarters to the strains of the bagpipes that had accompanied him into office nearly three years previously. Bratton left the job to start a risk management operation at Teneo Holdings. He had been making up to $1.9 million as a consultant in 2013, before he accepted de Blasio's call to return to the force. His last salary in the private sector marked a considerable step up from the $208,000 he was earning as commissioner.

Damned if You Do, Damned if You Don't

De Blasio's choice of commissioner to replace Bratton was Chief of Department James Patrick O'Neill, a burly Irish American with an engaging smile, and the highest-ranking uniformed member of the force, with 33 years of experience under his belt. O'Neill was a respected commander, credited with having devised the strategy of neighbourhood policing, a linchpin in mending the department's frayed relationships with the city's communities of colour. O'Neill said the department's success would be shaped by its ability to work with people of these communities. 'With the help of every New Yorker we will continue to facilitate all the good that is done daily by law abiding residents in our neighbourhoods,' he said at his swearing-in ceremony.

Confronted by sudden spikes in shootings in 2014 and 2015, de Blasio had O'Neill develop strategies to curb gun crime. One new piece of technology employed was ShotSpotter, a detection device that pinpoints the location of gunfire. The system works by installing sensors around an area to pick up sounds from the street that might be gunfire. It uses sensors to locate where the shots were fired from and then sends the information to nearby police precincts.

O'Neill could count on more than 1,300 new police officers under his command. These were the cops Bratton had persuaded de Blasio to hire during his commissionership. This intake of recruits took the department's strength close to its current level of about 36,000 officers and 19,000 civilian employees, the largest police force in the United States. Many of these recruits were deployed to new counterterrorism units. One was the new heavily armed Critical Response Command, equipped and ready to respond to terrorist and active-shooter attacks. Another was the Strategic Response Group, also set up in 2015 as a rapid reaction force tasked with immediate intervention during periods of civil unrest, terrorist incidents or other citywide emergencies.

The commissioner needed to juggle the tasks of keeping the NYPD on track in its move away from aggressive policing, as embodied in the stop-question-and-frisk practice, while simultaneously ensuring that crime rates remained at their lowest levels since the 1950s. At the same time, it was imperative to maintain a sharp vigilance in meeting the threat of future terrorist strikes. O'Neill's baptism by fire came on the very day of his inauguration as commissioner. On 17 September 2016 Lower Manhattan's fashionable Chelsea district was rocked by an explosion that left 29 people with injuries of varying severity. The blast was caused by a pressure-cooker bomb packed with shrapnel. Police counterterrorism training yielded quick results. No sooner had O'Neill taken the commissioner's oath of office than a detective approached to relay the news: 'We got him.' A second device was found four streets away and deactivated by Bomb Squad specialists. Two days later, police arrested an Afghan-American, Ahmad Khan Rahimi, as the sole suspect. Rahimi was not an active member of a terrorist group but was known to be a devoted follower of Al-Qaeda and its extremist ideology. Later that year, Rahimi was convicted of eight federal crimes and handed a mandatory sentence of life imprisonment without parole.

As later events were to show, O'Neill's counterterrorism officers could not afford to let their guard down. Only one year and a few weeks after the pressure-cooker bomb incident, New York was rocked by the 2017 Halloween Massacre. This was the first jihadist assault in sixteen years that left a trail of death in the city. On 31 October, a van racing seemingly out of control along West Street in Lower Manhattan slammed into cyclists and joggers in its erratic path. This turned into a near mile-long rampage that left eight people dead and a dozen injured. When the speeding van crashed into a parked school bus, the driver clambered out and began to make a run for it, while menacing bystanders with two guns. It was quick action by Officer Ryan Nash, patrolling along Chambers Street, that prevented even worse carnage. Ryan gave chase, firing nine shots at the suspect. He was brought down with a bullet to the abdomen. The assailant was identified as Sayfullo Saipov, an Uzbek terrorist. Police searching the van found an ISIS flag and jihadist propaganda inside. Saipov was put on trial and found guilty of eight federal offences. He was sentenced to life imprisonment without parole. When the verdict was read out, Saipov leapt to his feet and shouted that the matter was of no interest to him. It was not 'Allah's judgement'.

One of O'Neill's more innovative counterterrorism initiatives was the use of an elite team of 'vapour wake' canines in large gatherings and at transit hubs. Fourteen of these Labradors, who completed an eighteen-month training programme, were brought in to police the Macy's Thanksgiving Day Parade in 2017, where they were deployed to track an explosive trail to bombs or suicide bombers. Unlike normal bomb-sniffing

NYPD transit bureau K-9 police officer and K-9 German Shepherd providing security on Broadway during the 2014 Super Bowl week in Manhattan.

dogs, which are adept at identifying explosives in stationary objects such as rubbish bins, 'vapour wake' dogs keep their noses up and look for mobile threats. The dogs are sensitive to so-called thermal plumes left behind in a person's wake. They are trained to avoid the distractions of large crowds and loud noises typical of large events, and they can sense explosive particles and even firearm residue in this wake.

* * *

O'NEILL'S SELF-IMPOSED mission was to heal relations between the department and New York's minority groups. The programme he sought to implement was aimed at fostering local residents' trust in the police. O'Neill had two key allies under his command, both of whom were instrumental in putting his plan into effect. Carlos Gómez, who occupied O'Neill's previous role as chief of department, and the chief of patrol Terence Monahan, worked with the commissioner to create a new policing model. The aim was to re-sector a number of precincts to form natural neighbourhoods and place the same cops in the same sectors every day. They also set up a position called the neighbourhood coordination officer (NCO), who was to serve as a conduit between the community and local police.

O'Neill was starting from a logical premise. The more personal contact officers have among the communities they serve, the more people will learn to trust and respect members of the force. The commissioner was always a believer in the NYPD's willingness and ability to create positive relationships with the citizenry, provided they are given the chance and the tools to do so. 'What I saw made me the person I am today,' he said, reflecting on his previous position as chief of department.

> Even back then, everybody said police officers have to get closer to the community, but if you look at the way that we did business, we really didn't have an opportunity to do that. If you're doing twenty to twenty-five radio runs and 911 runs in an eight-hour period, there's no chance to make a connection. And you might be working in a different sector every day. It was effective for fighting crime but it wasn't effective for community relations.[17]

Cop vs Mayor

Despite O'Neill's best efforts, an attitude of anger and mistrust continued to prevail on both sides. De Blasio came to office on a policy that many in the NYPD interpreted as an attempt to emasculate police effectiveness in keeping crime under control. The highlights of his electoral platform included de-escalation training for officers, reduced prosecutions for cannabis possession, implementation of police body cameras and an end to the post-9/11 programme of surveillance on Muslim residents. In essence, his aim was to support socially liberal and progressive policies in the city's economy, urban planning, public education, privatization and police relations with local communities. Safir, Kerick and Kelly continued to direct their energies toward crime control. De Blasio, on the other hand, believed the police needed a change of focus. It goes almost without saying that this softly, softly approach was destined to raise hackles among a large number of the department's rank and file. As a high-ranking police official who wished to remain anonymous commented:

> De Blasio ran his election campaign on an anti-police agenda. He played off the idea that the police were oppressive to minority communities. He debased the police whenever he could. He blamed them for all the ills of the city and promised major reform. His rhetoric was blamed for inciting the violence perpetrated against police officers, who were being assassinated because of the hatred de Blasio spewed. He encouraged the City Council to pass anti-police legislation that allowed people who had negative contact with the police to sue if they believed that the contact was racially motivated. The burden of proof shifted to the individual officer to prove he or she acted appropriately. The result was that officers second-guessed themselves and withdrew from the proactive policing that had been so effective in the past.[18]

On 4 November 2019 O'Neill went to City Hall to tender his resignation to de Blasio. After more than three years on the job, the commissioner had been forced to contend with a range of pressures, from deadly jihadist terrorism to allegations of racism from civil liberty groups, along with a wave of anger from his own officers. By all accounts, O'Neill was doing a good job with the tools he had to hand, but there was an unspoken consensus that it was always going to be a frustrating one. O'Neill went on the offensive to point out that, during his years as commissioner, murder rates in New York had fallen to levels not seen for decades.

Rumours had been circulating for some time that O'Neill was intending to take up a high-paying job in the private sector. There was strong speculation that his decision was motivated at least in part by the flak he took after his sacking of Daniel Pantaleo, the officer who had placed Eric Garner in a lethal chokehold five years previously. O'Neill came under fire from NYPD unions for what they saw as a failure to defend the police from de Blasio's liberal and, in their view, anti-police agenda. No sooner had O'Neill stepped down, Ed Mullins, president of the Sergeants Benevolent Association (SBA), labelled him 'a puppet of de Blasio's incompetent and dishonest mayoral administration.' To this broadside, he added that O'Neill had been 'the catalyst for New York City's hands-off policing and ongoing descent of overall quality of life and violent street crimes, of which we are seeing an increase'.[19] On the other side, O'Neill earned the ire of some ethnic minority leaders for delays in disciplining police officers who were accused of misconduct.

NYPD counter-terrorism officer providing security at the New York 2018
U.S. Tennis Open.

O'Neill passed over the malicious gossip at his farewell address, when he noted he was 'not getting any younger and wanted to spend more time with his family'. O'Neill's next job was head of security for Visa. In April 2020 he returned to public office to serve as de Blasio's senior advisor on the coronavirus pandemic, tasked with monitoring the city's medical supply line to public hospitals.

De Blasio's next appointment was Chief of Detectives Dermot F. Shea – like many of his predecessors, a descendant of Irish immigrants – who in his prior role at the NYPD had been in charge of the use of data-driven analysis to develop policing strategies. Shea began his police career in an era when New York was a much more violent city than it is today. In 1991, the year he joined the department as an officer in the 46th Precinct in the Bronx, New York recorded more than 2,000 murders. In less than three decades, that figure had been cut to fewer than three hundred. Patrick Lynch, president of the PBA, welcomed Shea's appointment, describing it as a hopeful sign for rank-and-file officers. He said the police were in need of support from the top. He looked forward to the opportunity of working with the new commissioner to 'combat the current anti-police atmosphere', throwing a guarded barb at O'Neill as well as de Blasio.

Shea hinted at an attempt to repair bridges when he pledged to build on the work of his predecessor O'Neill while prioritizing a crackdown on gangs and getting guns off the streets. Though overall crime in New York had reached a record low the year Shea took over, the numbers began ticking up again in early 2020. Another issue he will have to face is New York State's bail reforms, roundly hated by the police, which were enacted in January 2020. Shea, along with his NYPD colleagues, feel rising crime is linked to this piece of legislation. 'It's affecting it significantly,' he said. The reforms did away with the requirement for cash bail bonds, allowing a number of those arrested for crimes to immediately return to the streets.

> I'm optimistic we will have some movement on reforming the reform with the legislators. What that looks like will be the key test. I think the reform was well-intended and probably you could argue should have been done earlier in terms of levelling the playing field. But there is growing recognition that some changes have to be made because you cannot forget about public safety, and you cannot forget about victims.[20]

The coronavirus pandemic that hit New York like a force of nature in March 2020 also brought on a severe stress test between the NYPD and Mayor de Blasio. Policing the city, which had taken a heavy toll from the disease, became an immensely strenuous task under lockdown. The enforcement of social distancing and crowd control placed the police under even greater pressure after the killing of George Floyd, an unarmed black man who was choked to death by a policeman in Minneapolis on 25 May. In New York, Floyd's death sparked three days and nights of protests, in which the police were accused of employing disproportionate force against demonstrators.

As always, it is possible to trace a grey line between what appears to be gratuitous police violence and deliberate crowd provocation. The NYPD found itself hard-pressed to justify tactics like driving a police car into the crowds in response to missiles hurled at the vehicle. In another incident that exploded on social media, police were shown swinging their batons at unarmed marchers and using pepper spray on those who 'took the knee' in solidarity with the Black Lives Matter movement. De Blasio found himself trapped between the proverbial rock and a hard place. The mayor's initial response was to stand behind Commissioner Shea in defence of police action, pinning the blame on provocateurs among the demonstrators. With the unabated explosion of outrage by anti-racism protestors, the mayor began to backtrack on his unqualified support for the NYPD.

Mayor Bill de Blasio leads a parade in Manhattan flanked by NYPD officers.

Hundreds took to the streets of Manhattan to protest the 2020 death of George Floyd at the hands of Minneapolis police.

This poisonous and semi-anarchical atmosphere touched off an escalation of gun crime in the city, in which shootings for June 2020 alone recorded a 130 per cent increase over the same month the previous year. The 4th July holiday weekend was marked by 44 firearms incidents involving 63 victims. The situation looked to be cascading out of control, at which point de Blasio attempted to contain the turmoil with a promise of legal reforms. The first step was the repeal of New York Civil Rights Law Section 50-A, a statute enacted in 1973 under pressure from police unions. The thinking behind this law was to put an end to the alleged practice of discrediting arresting officers in court by revealing their disciplinary record. The regulation was later extended to bar the public and press from obtaining information the police considered prejudicial to a fair trial. Subsequent to the George Floyd killing and 50-A repeal, several agencies pledged to examine NYPD misconduct cases. This reflected de Blasio's demand in May for an independent review of charges brought against the police.

It looked like de Blasio and Shea had come to an agreement on the need for reform when, on 15 June, the commissioner announced the disbanding of the department's anti-crime units. These were staffed by plainclothes teams that had been the protagonists of some of the city's most notorious police shootings. Shea explained that, in his estimation, these units were based on an outdated policing model harking back to the 'stop-and-question' era. 'This is twenty-first-century policing,' he said. 'The key difference is that we must do it in a manner that builds trust between the officers and the community they serve.'[21]

The gloves were off once again when, on 29 June, de Blasio dropped a bombshell. Under intense pressure from activists and City Council members, the mayor agreed a $1 billion cut in the NYPD's $6 billion annual budget. De Blasio said the funds would be redirected to moving school-safety agents, who are unarmed but wear police uniforms, into the Department of Education, cancelling a July class of roughly 1,100 police recruits and shifting certain homeless outreach operations away from police control. In addition to the $1 billion reduction in operating expenses, more than $500 million would be cut from the NYPD's capital budget, with the money used to build youth recreation centres and for public housing developments. The announcement appeared to boost de Blasio's standing in the public eye. A citywide poll following the announcement found that 55 per cent of New Yorkers supported defunding the NYPD and redirecting that money to other local services, while 34 per cent opposed the move and 10 per cent of respondents were unsure.[22]

It took Shea all of one week to launch his counter-attack. Speaking on the unprecedented surge in gun violence over the 4 July weekend, the commissioner pointed the finger at his particular bête noire, the bail reforms which had been enacted in January 2020. The purpose of these reforms was to reduce the number of people jailed while awaiting trial simply because they could not afford to put up bail. Shea pointed to the low number of inmates incarcerated in Rikers Island jail, saying 'bad people' were not being held properly accountable. 'We can fix this,' he said. 'We don't need a lot of new things. What we need is support and that's in short supply. We need tools – we need laws that makes sense – and then we need resources.'[23]

In the light of conflicts that often arise between the NYPD commissioner and the mayor, on 8 July New York State Attorney General Letitia James announced a proposal of far-reaching political implications. James said an independent panel should oversee the NYPD and hire the commissioner. She said the wave of protests over the summer had shaken New Yorkers' belief in the police and recommended that an independent panel, exclusive of the mayor, take responsibility to appoint the police commissioner and oversee the hiring and firing of officers. 'It is impossible to deny that many New Yorkers have lost faith in law enforcement,' James said. 'I believe we need to bridge the undeniable divide between police and the public.'[24] The creation of an independent commission to oversee the city's police force would signal a landmark event for New York City, given that the police commissioner has served at the mayor's pleasure since the nineteenth century. Whether the idea put forward by the attorney general finds favour with legislators is likely to be the work of many months. It would undoubtedly stand as a game-changer in New York's history of policing.

* * *

THE TERM 'POLICE', as used to describe a body charged with enforcing the law and maintaining order, derives from the Latin *politia*, which in turn is the Latinization of the Greek *politeia*, signifying 'citizenship' or 'civil polity'. The modern dictionary definition of 'police' refers to a civil force responsible for the detection and prevention of crime and the maintenance of public order.

Officer Andrew Beirne, of the fabled 9th Precinct in the East Village, points out that ordinary citizens often fail to understand this role and the officers who are there to see that it is carried out. 'People don't realize that we come from this society,' he says. 'We are of the people we police and we're following orders of the people we all elected to office. We don't do our job with a chip on our shoulder. We go where the citizens of New York need us.'[25]

No matter who occupies the seat behind Teddy Roosevelt's desk on the top floor of One Police Plaza, the mission of the NYPD, as enshrined in the department's code of ethics, remains unchanged: to enhance the quality of life in New York City by working in partnership with the community to enforce the law, preserve peace, protect the people, reduce fear and maintain order. If ever there was a damned if you do, damned if you don't job, it is that of the NYPD officer. It is a tough message to convey to New Yorkers, for there are those who perceive the police as an oppressor and a target for their grievances, while there are moments when the cop on the beat is welcomed as their salvation.

* * *

IT IS WORTH CONCLUDING with this account by Officer Andrew Beirne of a single arrest that was quite common in the 9th Precinct during the summer months, due to the large number of bars in the East Village and the neighbourhood's reputation as a nightlife destination.

Coda

On 3 March 2013, I was working overnight with my partner Joseph Gavin in sector Charlie, meaning we were driving around in a marked police car in uniform. This meant we were responsible for any jobs that occurred west of Avenue C, east of First Avenue, south of 7th Street and north of East Houston Street. So we were covering a fifth of the area of the Ninth while other teams covered the rest.

At midnight 48, or 48 minutes after midnight, we received a call of "10-34 assault in progress in front of 81 Avenue A." We arrived to see a large crowd in front of the Sing Sing Karaoke Bar. Working our way to the middle of it we found two bouncers holding a 5 ft 6 in. 29-year-old black male by the name of Joel Jameson to the floor.

We picked him up as one bouncer explained that Mr Jameson had attacked him with a broken bottle and had given him a few scratches on his shoulder. Mr Jameson chose to remain silent, but we had enough evidence in front of us to affect a felony arrest. I took M. Jameson to Bellevue Hospital because his hands were cut up during the attack and Joe stayed to gather witness statements.

What we put together was this: Mr Jameson was out socializing and had a few too many. He got into an argument with the one of the lady bartenders and was escorted out of the bar. He was observed (by us later, on security footage from the bar and bodega) going next door to a bodega and buying a single bottle of Guinness. He quickly downed it, spent several moments tapping the empty bottle on the curb until he had fashioned a weapon and went back into the bar. Note to the drinking public – today's bars/pubs are wired for video like a Las Vegas casino for *exactly* this sort of thing.

In full high-definition color, we (and the prosecuting attorney) watched him charge through the door and try to bury his improvised shiv into the doorman's throat. The bouncer at the door was looking down at another patron's ID when he somehow sensed the attack coming from the side and flinched, bringing his shoulder up and getting a few scratches instead of a mortal wound. With remarkably little violence Mr Miguel Correa, a strapping 32-year-old from the Bronx, scooped up his attacker, who had lost his weapon during his lunge and carried him out of the bar and pinned him to the sidewalk to wait for our arrival.

Mr Jameson was charged with assault in the second degree, which is a felony. He was bailed out by his wife who was not out with him on the night in question. As was the practice in New York City in 2013, he was offered a plea deal which he vehemently refused. This led to an odd encounter. Mr Jameson was running out the clock on his plea deal offer and the assistant district attorney handling the case wanted to start the trial the moment she got the final refusal. As such, Joe Gavin and myself found ourselves doing a day tour for overtime to be on standby in case the trial started.

When officers are called to a trial, they are sequestered in a room to wait so the testimony of others does not color their own account of the facts. However, we were not yet technically there for a trial, so we just had to make do sitting in the hall out in front of the court room. There we witnessed Mr Jameson arrive, furiously arguing with his public defender. Mr Jameson wanted to go to trial because the staff at the karaoke bar had been disrespectful to him and they must learn!

His attorney was begging him to take the deal. She was explaining if anyone saw the footage, they would think he was a horrible person and lock him up for much longer. This went back and forth for thirty minutes until, perhaps because he saw the smiles on our faces as we imagined the prospect of a trial, he ultimately took the deal to go to jail for three years. They cut a few months off for good behavior and he was promptly rearrested in the summer of 2016 for a similar incident.

This sort of thing happened every weekend, with someone picking up an object to strike someone, thus turning a name-calling dispute into a felony arrest for us. So please take two things from this narrative:

1. Hit people with your fists in New York City. It is usually a violation and at worst a misdemeanor.

2. Broken bottles make very poor weapons and almost always cut up the perpetrator as well as the victim, leaving us with plenty of evidence.

References

Introduction

1 Herman Melville, *Moby Dick* (London, 1851).
2 The corner of West 54th Street and Broadway, where Fitzgerald lived, has been officially designated 'Big Apple Corner'.
3 Gotham was first used as a nickname for New York City by Washington Irving in *The Salmagundi Papers*. It was a satirical reference to the Nottinghamshire town of Gotham, England, whose inhabitants acquired a reputation for doing ridiculous things, like trying to drown an eel. There was, however, method in their apparent madness. The story goes that King John intended to travel through the district. At that time, any road the king travelled on had to be made a public highway, something the people of Gotham opposed. When the royal messengers arrived, they put on a show of lunacy, which in the twelfth century was believed to be contagious.

1: The Green Light

1 *The New Yorker* (19 July 2020), p. 54.
2 *The New York Genealogical and Biographical Record*, New York Historical Society (April 1930), vol. LXI, no. 2, pp. 176–7.
3 From 1898, when New York consolidated into its present form, until 1929, the numbers of the combined precincts shifted quite a bit. The basic allocation of numbers was Manhattan 1 to 39, the Bronx 40 to 59, Brooklyn 60 to 99, Queens 100 to 119 and Staten Island 120 and above. Not all precinct numbers were used in each borough, in order to leave room for new precincts. Although precincts have been added over the years, many have been abolished and merged with neighbouring ones. Not all precincts have numbers: the 22nd Precinct is now the Central Park Precinct, the 14th Precinct is now Midtown South and the 18th Precinct is Midtown North.
4 *The Independent Reflector* (New York, 5 March 1753), p. 89.
5 New York State Archives, Document NYSA_A1809-78_V06_0043.
6 Arthur Peterson, *New York as an Eighteenth-century Municipality* (New York, 1917), vol. I, p. 160.

7 Carl Brindenbaugh, *Cities in the Wilderness* (New York, 1938), p. 79.

8 The NYPD uniform shoulder patch depicts a windmill representing the Dutch, the city's first colonists. The image is supported by Dexter, a sailor representative of the shipping trade, and on the other side a Native American of Manhattan, symbolic of the island's original inhabitants. An American eagle spreads its wings atop the shield, and above that are the five stars of the city's boroughs, aligned under the Scales of Justice.

9 John Holt worked variously as newspaper publisher, printer and postmaster. He became 'public printer' for the colony and was the first person in New York to recommend a news dealers' system for the delivery of newspapers instead of using post riders, which was a dangerous undertaking.

10 Edwin G. Burrows and Mike Wallace, *Gotham* (New York, 1999), p. 250.

11 James F. Richardson, *The New York Police* (New York, 1970), p. 12.

12 Burrows and Wallace, *Gotham*, p. 267.

13 *New York Times* (13 October 1985), p. 159.

14 Douglas Muzzio, *City Journal* [New York] (Autumn 2018), p. 34.

15 James Lardner and Thomas Reppetto, *NYPD: A City and Its Police* (New York, 2000), p. 5.

16 *Old Hays and His Descendants*, *NYPD News* (17 May 2019).

17 Lardner and Reppetto, *NYPD: A City and Its Police*, p. 5.

18 *Brooklyn Daily Eagle* (22 June 1850), p. 2.

19 'An Eyewitness Account of the Flour Riot in New York', *Niles' Weekly Register*, 1/26 (25 February 1837), series V, pp. 433–44.

20 After the NYPD came into being, the department issued an order directing the 7,500 members of the force to wear a new style uniform button, the cost of which came out of the officers' own pockets. The old brass version, known as the 'consolidation button', was replaced with a gold-plated one carrying the Seal of the City of New York and the words 'New York City Police'. Having to pay for their uniform buttons understandably caused a good deal of resentment among the officers, mainly because of the comparatively exorbitant cost of 15 cents per button, compared with 7 cents for the old variety. Moreover, many complained that the front and back pieces of the two-part button came apart easily and that a sharp shank on the rear damaged the uniform's cloth. Police Commissioner Colonel Michael C. Murphy's rationale for introducing the change was that, when wearing the old buttons, police officers could be mistaken for tram conductors, though there is no documented evidence to support this fanciful theory. This gave rise to allegations that Murphy was taking a cut from the manufacturer of the buttons purchased. In 1902 Murphy's successor, John C. Partridge, issued a counter-order dispensing with what had come to be known as the 'Murphy Button', and re-authorized the wearing of the Consolidation button.

2: Turn of the Century Blue

1 Christopher Thale, 'The Informal World of Police Patrol', *Journal of Urban History*, XXXIII/2 (2007), p. 185.

2 J. W. Gerard, *London and New York: Their Crime and Police* (New York, 1853), p. 19.

3 James F. Richardson, *The New York Police* (New York, 1970), p. 29.
4 Thomas J. Belvin, *Contemporary Account of the Terrific and Fatal Riot at the New York Astor Place Opera House* (New York 1849), p. 24.
5 The Native American Party, renamed the American Party in 1855 and commonly known as the Know Nothing movement, was an American nativist political party active in the mid-nineteenth century. Starting originally as a secret society, it was primarily anti-Catholic, xenophobic and hostile to immigration.
6 *New York Times* (13 July 1871), p. 1.
7 The Dead Rabbits Riot was featured in the History Channel documentary television series History's Mysteries in 1998. The story of the New York Dead Rabbits is told, in fictionalized form, in Martin Scorsese's 2002 film *Gangs of New York*.
8 Major General Charles W. Sandford, Report in New York State National Guards archive (December 1863), series I, vol. XXVIII, p. 1.
9 Edwin G. Burrows and Mike Wallace, *Gotham* (New York, 1999), p. 893.
10 It is worth noting that Tammany Hall boss Mayor Fernando Wood, whose second term of office ended a year before the riots, was nevertheless a guiding spirit of the insurrection. Wood argued that New York should side with the Confederacy in the Civil War, since the city profited from the cotton trade with the South.
11 James Lardner and Thomas Reppetto, *NYPD: A City and Its Police* (New York, 2000), p. 40.
12 *New York Times* (19 July 1857) p. 1.
13 Leslie Charteris, *The Saint in New York* (London, 1935), p. 50.
14 Burrows and Wallace, *Gotham*, p. 1,167.
15 *New York Times* (12 September 1894), p. 4.
16 Lardner and Reppetto, *NYPD: A City and Its Police*, p. 110.
17 The rank of roundsman dates back to the New York State Metropolitan Police after they took control of the city from the Municipal Police in 1857. In the late 1850s, the rank of roundsman signified an acting supervisor rank below sergeant and was not common within the department until the early 1860s, when it became an actual rank. Roundsmen wore two large inverted blue chevrons and a numbered helmet device under a 'Roundsman' rocker.
18 *New York Times* (1 December 1895), p. 1.
19 *New York Times* (31 May 1903), p. 12.
20 Although Battle was the first person of colour to join the NYPD, two black patrolmen had previously served with the Brooklyn police. Wiley T. Overton and Moses Cobb were appointed Brooklyn patrolmen in 1891 and 1892, respectively. Cobb was born into slavery in 1856 in Kinston, North Carolina. As a young man, he walked from his home to Brooklyn on foot in search of a better life. While working on the wharves, he scored second-highest on the civil service exam and was sworn into the Brooklyn Police Department. Cobb was also Battle's brother-in-law and mentor.
21 *Greater New York Charter*, p. 151.

3: The Slippery Slope

1 *Bemidji Daily Pioneer* (Minnesota, 19 October 1905), p. 1.
2 *New York Times* (16 April 1903), p. 1.
3 *New York Times* (19 April 1903), p. 1.
4 In the 1890s Giuseppe Morello founded a gang known as the 107th Street Mob, which would later evolve into the Morello mobster family. Today the Morellos are known as the Genovese, the oldest of New York's five ruling Mafia families.
5 *Brooklyn Daily Eagle* (21 April 1903), p. 4.
6 Ibid.
7 In 2014 a 28-year-old man, Domenico Palazzotto, was heard on an Italian police wiretap bragging to an associate that his great-uncle, Paolo Palazzotto, had carried out the killing on behalf of a local Mafia leader, Don Vito Cascio Ferro. The claim, reported by the Italian news agency ANSA, was not included among the charges against the younger Palazzotto, who was one of some ninety suspected members of the Mafia arrested that year in Palermo. Nor did it amount to proof of his elder's responsibility.
8 In a barrel murder, the corpse was deposited in a barrel and abandoned. The barrel was deposited in the sea if the body was not meant to be found, or sometimes shipped by rail to a distant city and a non-existent address. In other cases, the barrel was simply left in a field or even on a street corner. This particularly grotesque style of Mafia rub-out came into vogue in New York with the first waves of Italian immigrants who turned to a life of crime.
9 James Lardner and Thomas Reppetto, *NYPD: A City and Its Police* (New York, 2000), p. 150.
10 Ibid.
11 *New York Times* (30 October 1910), p. 46.
12 Bernard Whalen and Jon Whalen, *The NYPD's First Fifty Years* (Lincoln, NE, 2014), p. 70.
13 Ibid., 6.
14 Peter Moskos, *Cop in the Hood* (Princeton, NJ, 2008), p. 93.
15 *New York Times* (3 March 1912), p. 55.
16 Ibid., p. 87.
17 Elizabeth Evens, 'Sherlock Holmes in Skirts', *BBC History Magazine* (November 2020), p. 43.
18 *Evening World* (13 December 1920), p. 1.
19 Henry Louis Mencken, *New Yorker* (20 September 1941), p. 27.
20 Ibid.

4: 'Don't Be Afraid to Muss 'Em Up'

1 Donald L. Miller, *Supreme City* (New York, 2014), p. 30.
2 Grover Aloysius Whalen, *Mr. New York* (New York, 1955), p. 141.
3 *New York Times* (22 March 1934), p. 3.
4 Lewis J. Valentine, *Night Stick* (New York, 1947), p. 120.
5 Cecil Beaton, *Portrait of New York* (London, 1948), pp. 58–9.
6 Bernard Whalen and Jon Whalen, *The NYPD's First Fifty Years* (Lincoln, NE, 2014), p. 201.

7 Reproduced in an article in the *New York Daily News* (29 March 1999).

5: A Valentine for the Mob

1 *New York Times* (3 July 1931), p. 3.
2 *New York Times* (1 February 1946), p. 22.
3 Philip Messing, Robert Mladinich and Bernard Whalen, *Case Files of the NYPD* (New York, 2018), p. 143.
4 Willie Sutton and Edward Linn, *Where the Money Was: The Memoirs of a Bank Robber* (New York, 1976), p. 160.
5 Peter Maas, *Serpico* (New York, 1973), p. 48.
6 The numbers racket consisted of placing a small bet on which three numbers would appear on some agreed-upon standardized daily tabulation. The chances of success were 999 to one. The winning pay-off, however, was 600 to one. 'Originally the numbers came from the New York Clearing House. But in 1931, it was discovered that its figures were being used in policy and discontinued reporting the exact numbers. Policy entrepreneurs quickly turned to the New York Stock Exchange's daily quotation of stocks traded. But this new source lasted only a month until the Exchange also caught on and began publishing only approximate and rounded numbers such as 1,500,000. Within a short while, in 1931 policy gamblers came up with an exceptionally complex system based on the results of pari-mutuel wagering at certain racetracks.' Alan Block, *East Side, West Side* (Cardiff, 1980), p. 150.
7 *New York Times* (25 April 1970), p. 18.
8 Maas, *Serpico*, p. 12.
9 Leonard Levitt, *NYPD Confidential* (New York, 2009), p. 8.
10 Charles Campisi, *Blue on Blue* (New York, 2017), p. 20.
11 Frank Serpico, in conversation with the author, February 2020.

6: Fear City

1 *New York Daily News* (30 October 1975), p. 1.
2 See *New York Times* (27 March 1964): '37 Who Saw Murder Didn't Call the Police'.
3 Elizabeth Evens, 'Sherlock Holmes in Skirts', *BBC History Magazine* (November 2020), p. 43.
4 The first steps toward the creation of the Civilian Complaint Review Board (CCRB) were taken in 1950, when a coalition of eighteen organizations formed what was called the Permanent Coordination Committee on Police and Minority Groups, set up to lobby officialdom to investigate police misconduct in general, and 'police misconduct in their relations with Puerto Ricans and Negros specifically'. In response to these demands, the NYPD established the Civilian Complaint Review Board in 1953 as an investigative committee of three deputy police commissioners. While the board was granted wider authority under Mayor Robert Wagner in 1955, it remained an organization within the police department – police officers conducted the investigations and the decision on whether or not

to recommend discipline was made by the deputy commissioners. The CCRB exists today as a fully independent civil department, staffed with 142 civilian investigators and about a dozen miscellaneous employees. Additionally, three officers from the NYPD's Monitoring and Analysis Section of the Department Advocate's Office work with the CCRB at their office in Lower Manhattan. Their role is to provide the investigators with access to certain restricted NYPD documentation.

5 Charles Campisi, in conversation with the author, September 2020.
6 *New York Times* (10 September 2012), p. 3.
7 Kevin Baker, *The Guardian* (18 May 2015), p. 22.
8 Philip Messing, Robert Mladinich and Bernard Whalen, *Case Files of the NYPD* (New York, 2018), p. 207.
9 *New York Times* (14 July 1977), p. 21.
10 *New York Magazine* (5 March 1979), p. 40.

7: Get Those Broken Windows Fixed

1 *The Guardian* (12 June 2002), p. 16.
2 *New York Times* (11 June 2002), p. 27.
3 The NYPD currently operates a fleet of nearly 10,000 vehicles. They range from the standard patrol car to pursuit cars, sport utility vehicles (SUVs), Dog Squad transport vehicles, high-visibility decoy cars, unmarked cars and riot-control vehicles.
4 Leonard Levitt, *NYPD Confidential* (New York, 2009), p. 53.
5 James Lardner and Thomas Reppetto, *NYPD: A City and Its Police* (New York, 2000), p. 296.
6 *New York Times* (31 March 1990), p. 27.
7 *Tampa Bay Times* (7 September 2016), p. 13.
8 *Mollen Commission Report*, John Jay College of Criminal Justice, p. 1.
9 Lardner and Reppetto, *NYPD: A City and Its Police*, pp. 306–7.
10 Ray Kelly, *Vigilance* (New York, 2016), p. 89.
11 Ibid., p. 95.
12 William J. Bratton, *Broken Windows and Quality-of-life Policing in New York City*, NYPD report (2015), pp. 2–3.
13 Jeffrey Kroessler, in conversation with the author, 12 November 2019.
14 William Bratton, *Turnaround* (New York, 1998), p. 140.
15 Ibid., p. 152.
16 Ibid., p. 155
17 Christopher Dickey, *Securing the City* (New York, 2009), p. 102.
18 Jack Maple, *The Crime Fighter* (New York, 1999), p. 65.
19 Ibid., p. 93.
20 *New York Times* (11 June 1999), p. 3.

8: Zero Means Zero

1 Index crimes are the eight types of offences the FBI combines to produce its annual crime index. These include wilful homicide, forcible rape, robbery,

burglary, aggravated assault, larceny over $50, motor vehicle theft and arson.

2 John Buntin, *Assertive Policing, Plummeting Crime: The NYPD Takes on Crime in New York City* (Cambridge, MA, 1999), p. 22.

3 *Time* (15 January 1996), p. 14.

4 Leonard Levitt, *NYPD Confidential* (New York, 2009), p. 100.

5 The United States Marshals Service is the nation's first federal law enforcement agency. It was created within the Department of Justice by the Judiciary Act of 1789, during the presidency of George Washington, as the Office of the United States Marshal. It occupies a uniquely central position in the federal justice system as the enforcement arm of the federal courts and is involved in virtually every federal law enforcement initiative.

6 The film features the song 'This Is Not America', written and performed by David Bowie and the Pat Metheny Group.

7 Charles Campisi, in conversation with the author, September 2020.

8 Levitt, *NYPD Confidential*, p. 178.

9 Charles Campisi, in conversation with the author, September 2020.

10 The serial rapist being hunted by the police was eventually caught and sentenced to 155 years in prison. Justice Joseph Fisch, the presiding judge at Isaac Jones's trial, said the defendant's crime spree might have contributed to the fatal police shooting of Diallo. Jones was a career criminal accused of raping, sexually abusing or robbing 29 women over five years in different parts of the city, including the neighbourhood of the Bronx where Diallo was gunned down.

11 Elias B. Silverman, *NYPD Battles Crime* (Boston, MA, 1999), p. 149.

12 *New York Post* (5 March 2001), p. 15.

13 Ibid.

14 Chris Cunneen, 'Racism, Discrimination and the Over-representation of Indigenous People in the Criminal Justice System', *Current Issues in Criminal Justice*, x/3 (March 1999), p. 31.

15 Peter Moskos, in conversation with the author, 15 November 2019.

16 *New York Daily News* (27 September 2001), p. 1.

17 *New York Times* (17 September 2001), p. 1.

18 James Dooley, in conversation with the author, 14 November 2019.

19 Retrieved from www.cnn.com/us, 21 July 2002.

9: The Force Is With You

1 Ray Kelly, *Vigilance* (New York, 2016), p. 166.

2 James Dooley, in conversation with the author, 14 November 2019.

3 Ibid. The Traffic and Environmental Zone, commonly known as the 'Ring of Steel', is the security and surveillance cordon consisting of road barriers, checkpoints and several hundred CCTV cameras surrounding the City of London, the financial district at the heart of Greater London. The measures have been used since the 1990s to deter terrorism and other threats.

4 Kelly, *Vigilance*, p. 174.

5 Colin Evans, *New York Police Department* (New York, 2011), p. 90.

6 *New York Times* (21 August 2018), p. 4.
7 Kelly, *Vigilance*, p. 205.
8 *New York Times* (15 April 2014), p. 9.
9 Rita Jakubowski, in conversation with the author, 11 February 2020.
10 Charles Campisi, in conversation with the author, September 2020.
11 John MacDonald, *Does Stop-and-frisk Reduce Crime?*, University of Pennsylvania, Department of Criminology Report (Philadelphia, PA, 2016).
12 Copwatch was set up in 1990 as a network of volunteers, effectively vigilantes, who monitor police activity. The so-called 'Copwatchers' go out on foot or driving patrols in their communities and record interactions between the police, suspects and civilians. The organization's aim is to act as a deterrent against police misconduct. Two years after Garner's death, the BBC documentary *NYPD: Biggest Gang in New York?* Was shown on BBC One, focusing on the activities of Copwatchers in New York, including Ramsey Orta.
13 *New York Times* (2 January 2014), p. 1.
14 *New York Times* (13 June 2015), p. 10.
15 *Time* (22 December 2014), p. 14
16 William J. Bratton, *Broken Windows and Quality-of-life Policing in New York City*, NYPD Report (2015), p. 4
17 *New York Times* (31 October 2017), p. 3.
18 Anonymous source, in conversation with the author, November 2019.
19 *The Guardian* (4 November 2019), p. 3.
20 *Irish Central* on irishcentral.com (13 March 2020).
21 *New York Times* (15 June 2020), p. 3.
22 *The Marist Institute for Public Opinion* (MIPO), www.maristpoll.marist.edu, accessed 10 July 2020.
23 Quoted in an online interview with Spectrum News, www.spectrumlocalnews.com/splash, accessed 6 July 2020.
24 *New York Times*, 8 July 2020, p. 3
25 Andrew Beirne, in conversation with the author, September 2019.

Bibliography

Allen, Oliver E., *The Tiger: The Rise and Fall of Tammany Hall* (New York, 1993)
Asbury, Herbert, *The Gangs of New York* (London, 2002)
Beaton, Cecil, *Portrait of New York* (London, 1948)
Belvin, Thomas J., *Contemporary Account of the Terrific and Fatal Riot at the New York Astor Place Opera House* (New York, 1849)
Block, Alan, *East Side, West Side* (Cardiff, 1980)
Board of Aldermen, *Police in New York: An Investigation* (New York, 1971)
Bratton, William J., *Broken Windows and Quality-of-life Policing in New York City*, NYPD Report (2015)
——, *Turnaround* (New York, 1998)
——, and Rudolph W. Giuliani, *Getting Guns off the Streets of New York*, Police Strategy Report No. 1 (New York, 1994)
Brindenbaugh, Carl, *Cities in the Wilderness* (New York, 1938)
——, *Cities in Revolt* (New York, 1955)
Buntin, John, *Assertive Policing, Plummeting Crime: The NYPD Takes on Crime in New York City*, Harvard Kennedy School of Government (Cambridge, MA, 9 August 1999)
Burrows, Edwin G., Wallace, Mike, *Gotham* (New York, 1999)
Campisi, Charles, *Blue on Blue* (New York, 2017)
Charteris, Leslie, *The Saint in New York* (London, 1935)
Chepesiuk, Ron, *American Gangster* (Lancaster, 2007)
Conlon, Edward, *Blue Blood* (New York, 2004)
Costello, Augustine, E., *Our Police Protectors* (Princeton, NJ 1972)
Cronin, Michael and Ruff, Joshua, *New York City Police* (Charleston, SC, 2012)
Cunneen, Chris, *Current Issues in Criminal Justice*, x/3 (1999)
Dash, Mike, *Satan's Circus* (London, 2008)
Dennis, Norman, George Erdos and David Robinson, *The Failure of Britain's Police: London and New York Compared* (London, 2003)
Dickey, Christopher, *Securing the City* (New York, 2009)
Evans, Colin, *New York Police Department* (New York, 2011)
Gerard, James W., *London and New York: Their Crime and Police* (New York, 1853)
Greater New York Charter (Albany, 1897)
Greene, Jack R., ed., *The Encyclopedia of Police Science*, 2 vols (New York, 2007)

Headley, Joel Tyler, *The Great Riots of New York, 1712–1873* (New York, 1971)

Jackson, Kenneth T., ed., *The Encyclopedia of New York City*, (New York, 1995)

Jeffers, H. Paul, *Commissioner Roosevelt* (New York, 1994)

——, *The Napoleon of New York* (New York, 2002)

Johnson, David, *American Law Enforcement: A History* (New York, 1981)

Johnson, Marilynn S., *Street Justice* (Boston, MA, 2003)

Karmen, Andrew, *New York Murder Mystery* (New York, 2000)

Kelling, G. L., and W. J. Bratton, 'Declining Crime Rates: Insiders' Views of the New York City Story', *Journal of Criminal Law and Criminology*, LXXXVIII/4 (1998), pp. 1217–31

Kelly, Ray, *Vigilance* (New York, 2016)

Kroessler, Jeffrey A., *New York, Year by Year: A Chronology of the Great Metropolis* (New York, 2002)

Lankevich, George, J., *American Metropolis* (New York, 1998)

Lardner, James, and Thomas Reppetto, *NYPD: A City and Its Police* (New York, 2000)

Levitt, Leonard, *NYPD Confidential* (New York, 2009)

Maas, Peter, *Serpico* (New York, 1973)

Mandelbaum, Seymour, J., *Boss Tweed's New York* (New York, 1965)

Maple, Jack, *The Crime Fighter* (New York, 1999)

Melville, Herman, *Moby Dick* (London, 1851)

Messing, Philip, Robert Mladinich and Bernard J. Whalen, *Case Files of the NYPD* (New York, 2018)

Miller, Donald L., *Supreme City* (New York, 2014)

Mollen Commission Report, John Jay College of Criminal Justice (July 1994, archived 21 July 2011)

Moskos, Peter, *In Defense of Flogging* (New York, 2011)

——, *Cop in the Hood* (Princeton, NJ, 2008)

Myers, Gustavus, *The History of Tammany Hall* (New York, 1901, 1968)

Nevius, James, and Michelle Nevius, *A Streetwise History of New York City* (New York, 2009)

Patterson, James, *NYPD Red 3* (London, 2015)

Peterson, Arthur, *New York as an Eighteenth-century Municipality*, 2 vols (New York, 1917)

Punch, Murice, *Zero Tolerance Policing* (University of Bristol, 2007)

Richardson, James F., *The New York Police* (New York, 1970)

Sante, Luc, *Low Life: Lures and Snares of Old New York* (New York, 1991)

Silverman, Elias B., *NYPD Battles Crime* (Boston, MA, 1999)

Stoddard, Lothrop, *Master of Manhattan: The Life of Richard Croker* (New York, 1931)

Sutton, Willie, and Edward Linn, *Where the Money Was: The Memoirs of a Bank Robber* (New York, 1976)

Thale, Christopher, 'The Informal World of Police Patrol', *Journal of Urban History*, XIII/2 (2007), pp. 183–216

Valentine, Lewis J., *Night Stick* (New York, 1947)

Viteritti, Joseph P., Police, *Politics and Pluralism in New York City* (London, 1973)

Waters, Luke, *NYPD Green* (Dublin, 2015)

Whalen, Bernard, and Jon Whalen, *The NYPD's First Fifty Years* (Lincoln, NE, 2014)
Whalen, Grover Aloysius, *Mr. New York* (New York, 1955)
Willis, Clint, ed., *NYPD* (New York, 2002)

Acknowledgements

As has been the case with each of my previous books, Helen Crisp has taken time out from a hectic work schedule to cast a critical eye over the manuscript. Her comments and suggestions have always proved invaluable – and have saved me not a little potential embarrassment. My agent, Duncan McAra, has been a steadfast ally in my latest undertaking and, indeed, he has successfully fought my corner for more than fifteen years. I am grateful to commissioning editor Vivian Constantinopoulos at Reaktion Books and project editor Phoebe Colley, for their support in seeing the book through to publication. Thanks are also due to the rest of the Reaktion team. New York is a superb place to conduct research, for the vast array of material available to the writer as well as the helpfulness of library and archive staff. My gratitude goes to Special Collections Librarian Ellen Belcher and Public Relations Coordinator Jan Benjamin at the John Jay College of Criminal Justice. Mention must be made of the help and enlightenment offered by three JJCCJ faculty members, each a font of knowledge on NYPD matters: professors Jim Dooley, Peter Moskos and Jeffrey Kroessler. The New-York Historical Society is a wonderful source of information, as is The Gothamist Daily (www.gothamist. com), for the insight of its collection into NYPD affairs and the New York news scene in general. The *New York Times* historical archive is a treasure trove of day-by-day reporting on police matters. I am greatly indebted to the work of the paper's veteran investigative journalists Sam Roberts and David Burnham. It has been a privilege to speak with several distinguished retired NYPD officers, most notably Andrew Beirne of the celebrated 9th Precinct and former head of the Internal Affairs Bureau Charles Campisi. Heartfelt thanks go to a cop who hardly needs an introduction, Frank Serpico. I am very grateful to Frank for taking on the role of unofficial fact-checker. His expert knowledge has undoubtedly brought the work up to a satisfactory level of accuracy.

Ernest Hemingway once stated that the most important part of writing a book is to have something to say. He also made the point that environment and a comfortable routine in the author's working day are essential factors in a day's work. I hope this book lives up to that first prerequisite. As for the rest, the view of New York Harbour from my room at the Wagner Hotel could not fail to inspire. A caffeine boost to kickstart the day was fulfilled by the morning pilgrimage to Gregorys Coffee shop. It may seem a bit louche for an author to offer his thanks to a tavern, but equally it would be remiss not to include McSorley's Old Ale House in the acknowledgements. If ever there was a place to inspire a story about New York City cops, that is McSorley's, which has been joined at the hip with the department, in its various guises, since the bar was founded in 1854. The great saloon, with its sawdust-covered floor and mahogany tabletops, from the day it opened its glass-fronted doors has hosted a police presence. In the late 1890s, Police Commissioner

Theodore Roosevelt would frequently go undercover in McSorley's, on the lookout for cops drinking on the job. In 1934, the McSorley family sold the bar to retired NYPD Detective Dan O'Connell, who drank at the bar his entire adult life. On his first day as new owner, O'Connell locked his NYPD handcuffs to the foot railing, where they remain to this day. Finally, at the risk of my being held up to derision as an antediluvian reptile, the collection of Palomino Blackwing pencils arrayed on my writing table enabled me to scribble my way through a stack of notebooks, to produce what I hope the reader will deem a worthy undertaking.

Photo Acknowledgements

The author and publishers wish to express their thanks to the below sources of illustrative material and/or permission to reproduce it. Every effort has been made to contact copyright holders; should there be any we have been unable to reach or to whom inaccurate acknowledgements have been made please contact the publishers, and full adjustments will be made to any subsequent printings.

Getty Images: pp. 128 (Jim Garrett/NY Daily News), 158 (Mel Finkelstein/NY Daily News Archive); from John Hardy, *Manual of the Corporation of the City of New York* (New York, 1871): p. 44; from *Harper's New Monthly Magazine*, LXXIV/442 (March 1887): p. 52; Library of Congress, Prints and Photographs Division, Washington, DC: pp. 32, 49, 57, 62, 67, 75, 78, 84, 85, 87, 89, 103, 115, 137, 140, 198; Shutterstock: pp. 34 (Christopher Penler), 204 (Leonard Zhukovsky), 210 (Stuart Monk), 217 (Wangkun Jia), 223 (Leonard Zhukovsky), 226 (Leonard Zhukovsky), 228 (Aleksandr Dyskin), 229 (Steve Sanchez Photos).

INDEX

Page numbers in *italics* indicate illustrations